Mechanics 2

Douglas Quadling

Series editor Hugh Neill

CAMBRIDGE UNIVERSITY PRESS
Cambridge, New York, Melbourne, Madrid, Cape Town, Singapore,
São Paulo, Delhi, Dubai, Tokyo, Mexico City

Cambridge University Press
The Edinburgh Building, Cambridge CB2 8RU, UK

www.cambridge.org
Information on this title: www.cambridge.org/9780521549011

© Cambridge University Press 2001, 2004

First published 2001
Second edition 2004
Reprinted 2010, 2011

Printed in India by Replika Press Pvt. Ltd

A catalogue record for this publication is available from the British Library

ISBN 978-0-521-54901-1 Paperback

Cover image © Digital Vision

Contents

Introduction

Cambridge Advanced Mathematics has been written especially for the OCR modular examination. It consists of one book or half-book corresponding to each module. This book is the second Mechanics module, M2.

The books are divided into chapters roughly corresponding to syllabus headings. Occasionally a section includes an important result that is difficult to prove or outside the syllabus. These sections are marked with an asterisk (*) in the section heading, and there is usually a sentence early on explaining precisely what it is that the student needs to know. The final chapter, which reviews ideas introduced earlier from a more mature standpoint, is primarily for students aiming at higher grades, and contains some more challenging examples and exercises.

Occasionally within the text paragraphs appear in a grey box. These paragraphs are usually outside the main stream of the mathematical argument, but may help to give insight, or suggest extra work or different approaches.

Numerical work is presented in a form intended to discourage premature approximation. In ongoing calculations inexact numbers appear in decimal form like 3.456... , signifying that the number is held in a calculator to more places than are given. Numbers are not rounded at this stage; the full display could be, for example, 3.456 123 or 3.456 789. Final answers are then stated with some indication that they are approximate, for example '3.46 correct to 3 significant figures'.

The value of g is taken as $9.8 \, \text{m s}^{-2}$.

Some chapters contain practical experiments, which are intended to reinforce the theory. There are plenty of exercises, and each chapter contains a Miscellaneous exercise which includes some questions of examination standard. Questions which go beyond examination requirements are marked by an asterisk. In the middle and at the end of the book there is a set of Revision exercises and there are two practice examination papers. The author thanks Richard Davies and David A. Lee, the OCR examiners who contributed to these exercises, and also Steve Green and Peter Thomas, who read the books very carefully and made many extremely useful and constructive comments.

The author thanks OCR and Cambridge University Press for their help in producing this book. However, the responsibility for the text, and for any errors, remains with the author.

1 The motion of projectiles

In this chapter the model of free motion under gravity is extended to objects projected at an angle. When you have completed it, you should

- understand displacement, velocity and acceleration as vector quantities
- be able to interpret the motion as a combination of the effects of the initial velocity and of gravity
- know that this implies the independence of horizontal and vertical motion
- be able to use equations of horizontal and vertical motion in calculations about the trajectory of a projectile
- know and be able to obtain general formulae for the greatest height, time of flight, range on horizontal ground and the equation of the trajectory
- be able to use your knowledge of trigonometry in solving problems.

Any object moving through the air will experience air resistance, and this is usually significant for objects moving at high speeds through large distances. The answers obtained in this chapter, which assume that air resistance is small and can be neglected, are therefore only approximate.

1.1 Velocity as a vector

When an object is thrown vertically upwards with initial velocity u, its displacement s after time t is given by the equation

$$s = ut - \tfrac{1}{2}gt^2,$$

where g is the acceleration due to gravity.

One way to interpret this equation is to look at the two terms on the right separately. The first term, ut, would be the displacement if the object moved with constant velocity u, that is if there were no gravity. To this is added a term $\tfrac{1}{2}(-g)t^2$, which would be the displacement of the object in time t if it were released from rest under gravity.

You can look at the equation

$$v = u - gt$$

in a similar way. Without gravity, the velocity would continue to have the constant value u indefinitely. To this is added a term $(-g)\,t$, which is the velocity that the object would acquire in time t if it were released from rest.

Now suppose that the object is thrown at an angle, so that it follows a curved path through the air. To describe this you can use the vector notation which you have already used for force. The symbol **u** written in bold stands for the velocity with which the object is thrown, that is a speed of magnitude u in a given direction. If there were no gravity, then in time t the object would have a displacement of magnitude ut in that direction. It is natural to denote this by $\mathbf{u}t$, which is a vector displacement.

To this is added a vertical displacement of magnitude $\frac{1}{2}gt^2$ vertically downwards. In vector notation this can be written as $\frac{1}{2}\mathbf{g}t^2$, where the symbol $\mathbf{g}$ stands for an acceleration of magnitude g in a direction vertically downwards.

To make an equation for this, let $\mathbf{r}$ denote the displacement of the object from its initial position at time $t = 0$. Then, assuming that air resistance can be neglected,

$$\mathbf{r} = \mathbf{u}t + \tfrac{1}{2}\mathbf{g}t^2.$$

In this equation the symbol $+$ stands for vector addition, which is carried out by the triangle rule, the same rule that you use to add forces. This is illustrated in Fig. 1.1.

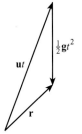

Fig. 1.1

Example 1.1.1
A ball is thrown in the air with speed $12\,\mathrm{m\,s^{-1}}$ at an angle of $70°$ to the horizontal. Draw a diagram to show where it is 1.5 seconds later.

If there were no gravity, in 1.5 seconds the ball would have a displacement of magnitude $12 \times 1.5\,\mathrm{m}$, that is $18\,\mathrm{m}$, at $70°$ to the horizontal. This is represented by the arrow $\overrightarrow{OA}$ in Fig. 1.2, on a scale of 1 cm to 5 m. To this must be added a displacement of magnitude $\frac{1}{2} \times 9.8 \times 1.5^2\,\mathrm{m}$, that is $11.0\,\mathrm{m}$, vertically downwards, represented by the arrow $\overrightarrow{AB}$. The sum of these is the displacement $\overrightarrow{OB}$.

So after 1.5 seconds the ball is at B. You could if you wish calculate the coordinates of B, or the distance OB, but in this example these are not asked for.

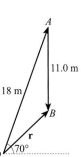

Fig. 1.2

Example 1.1.2
A stone is thrown from the edge of a cliff with speed $18\,\mathrm{m\,s^{-1}}$. Draw diagrams to show the path of the stone in the next 4 seconds if it is thrown

(a) horizontally,   (b) at $30°$ to the horizontal.

These diagrams were produced by superimposing several diagrams like Fig. 1.2. In Figs. 1.3 and 1.4 (for parts (a) and (b) respectively) this has been done at intervals of 0.5 s, that is for $t = 0.5, 1, 1.5, \ldots, 4$ The displacements $\mathbf{u}t$ in these times have magnitudes $9\,\mathrm{m}, 18\,\mathrm{m}, \ldots, 72\,\mathrm{m}$. The vertical displacements have magnitudes $1.2\,\mathrm{m}, 4.9\,\mathrm{m}, 11.0\,\mathrm{m}, \ldots, 78.4\,\mathrm{m}$. The points corresponding to A and B at time t are denoted by A_t and B_t.

You can now show the paths by drawing smooth curves through the points $O, B_{0.5}, B_1, \ldots, B_4$ for the two initial velocities.

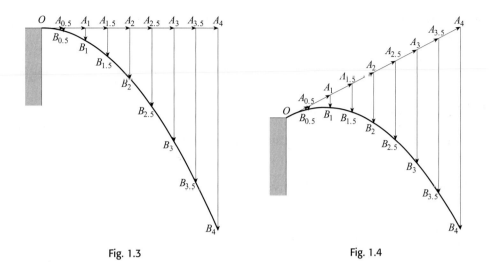

Fig. 1.3   Fig. 1.4

The word **projectile** is often used to describe objects thrown in this way. The path of a projectile is called its **trajectory**.

A vector triangle can also be used to find the velocity of a projectile at a given time. If there were no gravity the velocity would have the constant value **u** indefinitely. The effect of gravity is to add to this a velocity of magnitude gt vertically downwards, which can be written as the vector $\mathbf{g}t$. This gives the equation

$$\mathbf{v} = \mathbf{u} + \mathbf{g}t,$$

assuming that air resistance can be neglected. This is illustrated in Fig. 1.5.

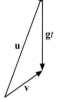

Fig. 1.5

Example 1.1.3
For the ball in Example 1.1.1, find the velocity after 1.5 seconds.

The vector **u** has magnitude $12 \, \text{m s}^{-1}$ at 70° to the horizontal. The vector $\mathbf{g}t$ has magnitude $9.8 \times 1.5 \, \text{m s}^{-1}$, that is $14.7 \, \text{m s}^{-1}$, directed vertically downwards.

To draw a vector triangle you need to choose a scale in which velocities are represented by displacements. Fig. 1.6 is drawn on a scale of 1 cm to $5 \, \text{m s}^{-1}$. You can verify by measurement that the magnitude of **v** is about $5.3 \, \text{m s}^{-1}$, and it is directed at about 40° below the horizontal.

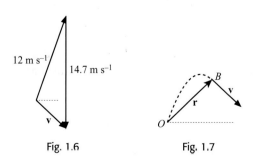

Fig. 1.6   Fig. 1.7

Fig. 1.7 combines the results of Examples 1.1.1 and 1.1.3, showing both the position of the ball after 1.5 seconds and the direction in which it is moving.

Exercise 1A

1 A stone is thrown horizontally with speed $15 \, \text{m s}^{-1}$ from the top of a cliff 30 metres high. Construct a diagram showing the positions of the particle at 0.5 second intervals. Estimate the distance of the stone from the thrower when it is level with the foot of the cliff, and the time that it takes to fall.

2 A gargoyle discharges water from the roof of a cathedral, at a height of 60 metres above the ground. Initially the water moves with speed $1 \, \text{m s}^{-1}$, in a horizontal direction. Construct a diagram using intervals of 0.5 seconds to find the distance from the cathedral wall at which the water strikes the ground.

3 A particle is projected with speed $10 \, \text{m s}^{-1}$ at an angle of elevation of 40°. Construct a diagram showing the position of the particle at intervals of 0.25 seconds for the first 1.5 seconds of its motion. Hence estimate the period of time for which the particle is higher than the point of projection.

4 A ball is thrown with speed $14 \, \text{m s}^{-1}$ at 35° above the horizontal. Draw diagrams to find the position and velocity of the ball 3 seconds later.

5 Two particles A and B are simultaneously projected from the same point on a horizontal plane. The initial velocity of A is $15 \, \text{m s}^{-1}$ at 25° to the horizontal, and the initial velocity of B is $15 \, \text{m s}^{-1}$ at 65° to the horizontal.

   (a) Construct a diagram showing the paths of both particles until they strike the horizontal plane.

   (b) From your diagram estimate the time that each particle is in the air.

1.2 Coordinate methods

For the purposes of calculation it often helps to use coordinates, with column vectors representing displacements, velocities and accelerations, just as was done for forces in M1 Chapter 9. It is usual to take the x-axis horizontal and the y-axis vertical.

For instance, in Example 1.1.2(a), the initial velocity $\mathbf{u}$ of the stone was $18 \, \text{m s}^{-1}$ horizontally, which could be represented by the column vector $\begin{pmatrix} 18 \\ 0 \end{pmatrix}$. Since the units are metres and seconds, $\mathbf{g}$ is $9.8 \, \text{m s}^{-2}$ vertically downwards, represented by $\begin{pmatrix} 0 \\ -9.8 \end{pmatrix}$. Denoting the displacement $\mathbf{r}$ by $\begin{pmatrix} x \\ y \end{pmatrix}$, the equation $\mathbf{r} = \mathbf{u}t + \frac{1}{2}\mathbf{g}t^2$ becomes

$$\begin{pmatrix} x \\ y \end{pmatrix} = \begin{pmatrix} 18 \\ 0 \end{pmatrix}t + \frac{1}{2}\begin{pmatrix} 0 \\ -9.8 \end{pmatrix}t^2, \quad \text{or more simply}$$

$$\begin{pmatrix} x \\ y \end{pmatrix} = \begin{pmatrix} 18t \\ 0 \end{pmatrix} + \begin{pmatrix} 0 \\ -4.9t^2 \end{pmatrix} = \begin{pmatrix} 18t \\ -4.9t^2 \end{pmatrix}.$$

You can then read along each line to get the pair of equations

$$x = 18t \quad \text{and} \quad y = -4.9t^2.$$

From these you can calculate the coordinates of the stone after any time t.

You can turn the first equation round as $t = \frac{1}{18}x$ and then substitute this in the second equation to get $y = -4.9\left(\frac{1}{18}x\right)^2$, or (approximately) $y = -0.015x^2$. This is the equation of the trajectory. You will recognise this as a parabola with its vertex at O, shown in Fig. 1.8.

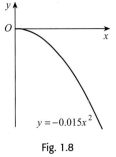

$y = -0.015x^2$

Fig. 1.8

You can do the same thing with the velocity equation $\mathbf{v} = \mathbf{u} + \mathbf{g}t$, which becomes

$$\mathbf{v} = \begin{pmatrix} 18 \\ 0 \end{pmatrix} + \begin{pmatrix} 0 \\ -9.8 \end{pmatrix} t = \begin{pmatrix} 18 \\ 0 \end{pmatrix} + \begin{pmatrix} 0 \\ -9.8t \end{pmatrix} = \begin{pmatrix} 18 \\ -9.8t \end{pmatrix}.$$

This shows that the velocity has components 18 and $-9.8t$ in the x- and y-directions respectively.

Notice that 18 is the derivative of $18t$ with respect to t, and $-9.8t$ is the derivative of $-4.9t^2$. This is a special case of a general rule.

> If the displacement of a projectile is $\begin{pmatrix} x \\ y \end{pmatrix}$, its velocity is $\begin{pmatrix} \dfrac{dx}{dt} \\ \dfrac{dy}{dt} \end{pmatrix}$.

This is a generalisation of the result given in M1 Section 11.2 for motion in a straight line.

Here is a good place to use the shorthand notation (dot notation) introduced in M1 Section 11.5, using $\dot{x}$ to stand for $\dfrac{dx}{dt}$ and $\dot{y}$ for $\dfrac{dy}{dt}$. You can then write the velocity vector as $\begin{pmatrix} \dot{x} \\ \dot{y} \end{pmatrix}$.

Now consider the general case, when the projectile starts with an initial speed u at an angle θ to the horizontal. Its initial velocity $\mathbf{u}$ can be described either in terms of u and θ, or in terms of its horizontal and vertical components p and q. These are connected by $p = u\cos\theta$ and $q = u\sin\theta$ (see Fig. 1.9). The notation is illustrated in Figs. 1.10 and 1.11.

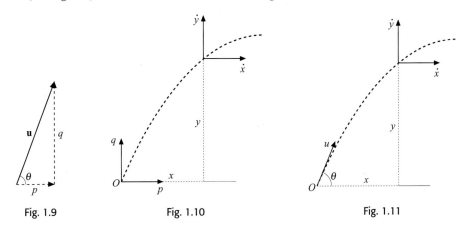

Fig. 1.9   Fig. 1.10   Fig. 1.11

The acceleration $\mathbf{g}$ is represented by $\begin{pmatrix} 0 \\ -g \end{pmatrix}$, so the equation $\mathbf{r} = \mathbf{u}t + \frac{1}{2}\mathbf{g}t^2$ becomes

$$\begin{pmatrix} x \\ y \end{pmatrix} = \begin{pmatrix} pt \\ qt \end{pmatrix} + \begin{pmatrix} 0 \\ -\frac{1}{2}gt^2 \end{pmatrix} \quad \text{or} \quad \begin{pmatrix} x \\ y \end{pmatrix} = \begin{pmatrix} u\cos\theta\, t \\ u\sin\theta\, t \end{pmatrix} + \begin{pmatrix} 0 \\ -\frac{1}{2}gt^2 \end{pmatrix}.$$

By reading along each line in turn, the separate equations for the coordinates are

$$x = pt \qquad\qquad \text{or} \quad x = u\cos\theta\, t,$$

and $\quad y = qt - \frac{1}{2}gt^2 \qquad \text{or} \quad y = u\sin\theta\, t - \frac{1}{2}gt^2.$

In a similar way, $\mathbf{v} = \mathbf{u} + \mathbf{g}t$ becomes

$$\begin{pmatrix} \dot{x} \\ \dot{y} \end{pmatrix} = \begin{pmatrix} p \\ q \end{pmatrix} + \begin{pmatrix} 0 \\ -gt \end{pmatrix} \quad \text{or} \quad \begin{pmatrix} \dot{x} \\ \dot{y} \end{pmatrix} = \begin{pmatrix} u\cos\theta \\ u\sin\theta \end{pmatrix} + \begin{pmatrix} 0 \\ -gt \end{pmatrix}.$$

So $\quad \dot{x} = p \qquad\qquad\qquad \text{or} \quad \dot{x} = u\cos\theta,$

and $\quad \dot{y} = q - gt \qquad\qquad \text{or} \quad \dot{y} = u\sin\theta - gt.$

Since g, p, q, u and θ are all constant, you can see again that $\dot{x}$ and $\dot{y}$ are the derivatives of x and y with respect to t.

Now the equations $x = pt$ and $\dot{x} = p$ are just the same as those you would use for a particle moving in a straight line with constant velocity p. And the equations $y = qt - \frac{1}{2}gt^2$ and $\dot{y} = q - gt$ are the usual constant acceleration equations $s = ut + \frac{1}{2}at^2$ and $v = u + at$ for a particle moving in a vertical line with initial velocity q and acceleration $-g$. This establishes the **independence of horizontal and vertical motion**.

> If a projectile is launched from O with an initial velocity having horizontal and vertical components p and q, under the action of the force of gravity alone and neglecting air resistance, and if its coordinates at a later time are (x, y), then
>
> the value of x is the same as for a particle moving in a horizontal line with constant velocity p;
>
> the value of y is the same as for a particle moving in a vertical line with initial velocity q and acceleration $-g$.

Most problems about projectiles are simply tackled by considering the horizontal and vertical motion separately.

Example 1.2.1
A ball is thrown in the air with speed $12\,\mathrm{m\,s^{-1}}$ at an angle of $70°$ to the horizontal. Find
(a) its position after 1.5 seconds,   (b) its velocity after 1.5 seconds.

This example shows how answers to Examples 1.1.1 and 1.1.3 can be calculated.

Take x- and y-axes through the point from which the ball is thrown.

(a) The horizontal component of the velocity of projection is $12\cos 70°\,\mathrm{m\,s^{-1}}$, which is $4.10\dots\mathrm{m\,s^{-1}}$. This stays constant so long as the ball is in the air.

After 1.5 seconds the horizontal distance travelled by the ball is $4.10\dots\times 1.5$ metres, which is 6.16 metres, correct to 3 significant figures.

The vertical component of the velocity of projection is $12\sin 70°\,\mathrm{m\,s^{-1}}$, which is $11.2\dots\mathrm{m\,s^{-1}}$. This decreases at a constant rate of $9.8\,\mathrm{m\,s^{-2}}$. After 1.5 seconds its height, y metres, is given by the equation $s = ut + \tfrac{1}{2}at^2$ as

$$y = 11.2\dots\times 1.5 - \tfrac{1}{2}\times 9.8 \times 1.5^2 = 5.89,\ \text{correct to 3 significant figures.}$$

After 1.5 seconds the displacement of the ball from the point where it is thrown is 6.16 metres horizontally and 5.89 metres vertically upwards.

(b) The horizontal component of the velocity has the constant value $4.10\dots\mathrm{m\,s^{-1}}$.

The vertical component of the velocity of the ball after 1.5 seconds, $y\,\mathrm{m\,s^{-1}}$, is given by the equation $v = u + at$ as

$$\dot{y} = 11.2\dots - 9.8 \times 1.5 = -3.42\dots.$$

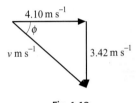

Fig. 1.12

The negative sign shows that the ball has passed its highest point and is coming down.

The two components of the velocity can now be combined by using the vector triangle in Fig. 1.12. If the ball is now moving at $v\,\mathrm{m\,s^{-1}}$ at an angle ϕ below the horizontal, then

$$v = \sqrt{4.10\dots^2 + 3.42\dots^2} = 5.34,\ \text{correct to 3 significant figures,}$$

and

$$\tan\phi = \frac{3.42\dots}{4.10\dots},\ \text{so that } \phi = 39.8°,\ \text{correct to 1 decimal place.}$$

After 1.5 seconds the ball is moving at $5.34\,\mathrm{m\,s^{-1}}$ at an angle of $39.8°$ below the horizontal.

In the example above, you could alternatively find the distance and velocity by applying the cosine and sine rules to the triangles in Figs. 1.2 and 1.6.

Example 1.2.2

A golf ball is driven with a speed of $45\,\mathrm{m\,s^{-1}}$ at $37°$ to the horizontal across a horizontal fairway.

(a) How high above the ground does the ball rise?
(b) How far away from the tee does it first land?

To a good enough approximation $\cos 37° = 0.8$ and $\sin 37° = 0.6$, so the horizontal and vertical components of the initial velocity are $p = 45 \times 0.8\,\mathrm{m\,s^{-1}} = 36\,\mathrm{m\,s^{-1}}$ and $q = 45 \times 0.6\,\mathrm{m\,s^{-1}} = 27\,\mathrm{m\,s^{-1}}$. The approximate value of g is $9.8\,\mathrm{m\,s^{-2}}$.

(a) To find the height you only need to consider the y-coordinate. To adapt the equation $v^2 = u^2 + 2as$ with the notation of Fig. 1.9, you have to insert the numerical values u (that is q) $=27$ and $a = -9.8$, and replace s by y and v by $\dot{y}$. This gives

$$\dot{y}^2 = 27^2 - 2 \times 9.8 \times y = 729 - 19.6y.$$

When the ball is at its greatest height, $\dot{y} = 0$, so $729 - 19.6y = 0$. This gives $y = \dfrac{729}{19.6} = 37.2$, correct to 3 significant figures.

(b) To find how far away the ball lands you need to use both coordinates, and the link between these is the time t. So use the y-equation to find how long the ball is in the air, and then use the x-equation to find how far it goes horizontally in that time.

Adapting the equation $s = ut + \frac{1}{2}at^2$ for the vertical motion,

$$y = 27t - 4.9t^2.$$

When the ball hits the ground $y = 0$, so that $t = \dfrac{27}{4.9} = 5.51\ldots$. A particle moving horizontally with constant speed $36\,\text{m s}^{-1}$ would go $36 \times 5.51\ldots$ m, that is $198.3\ldots$ m, in this time.

So, according to the gravity model, the ball would rise to a height of about 37 metres, and first land about 198 metres from the tee.

In practice, these answers would need to be modified to take account of air resistance and the aerodynamic lift on the ball.

Example 1.2.3

In a game of tennis a player serves the ball horizontally from a height of 2 metres. It has to satisfy two conditions (see Fig. 1.13).

(a) The ball must pass over the net, which is 0.9 metres high at a distance of 12 metres from the server.

(b) The ball must hit the ground less than 18 metres from the server.

At what speeds can the ball be hit?

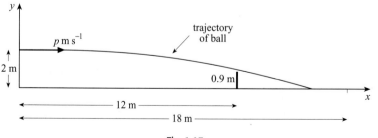

Fig. 1.13

It is simplest to take the origin at ground level, rather than at the point from which the ball is served, so add 2 to the y-coordinate given by the general formula. Since the ball is served horizontally, it falls a distance $\frac{1}{2} \times 9.8 \times t^2$ in t seconds. Therefore, if the initial speed of the ball is $p\,\mathrm{m\,s^{-1}}$,

$$x = pt \quad \text{and} \quad y = 2 - 4.9t^2.$$

Both conditions involve both the x- and y-coordinates, and the time t is used as the link.

(a) The ball passes over the net when $12 = pt$, that is $t = \dfrac{12}{p}$. The value of y is then
$$2 - 4.9\left(\frac{12}{p}\right)^2 = 2 - \frac{705.6}{p^2},$$ and this must be more than 0.9. So $2 - \dfrac{705.6}{p^2} > 0.9$.
This gives $\dfrac{705.6}{p^2} < 1.1$, which is $p > \sqrt{\dfrac{705.6}{1.1}} \approx 25.3$.

(b) The ball lands when $y = 0$, that is when $2 - 4.9t^2 = 0$, or $t = \sqrt{\dfrac{2}{4.9}}$. It has then gone a horizontal distance of $p\sqrt{\dfrac{2}{4.9}}$ metres, and for this to be within the service court you need $p\sqrt{\dfrac{2}{4.9}} < 18$. This gives $p < 18\sqrt{\dfrac{4.9}{2}} \approx 28.2$.

So the ball can be hit with any speed between about $26\,\mathrm{m\,s^{-1}}$ and $28\,\mathrm{m\,s^{-1}}$.

Example 1.2.4

A cricketer scores a six by hitting the ball at an angle of 30° to the horizontal. The ball passes over the boundary 90 metres away at a height of 5 metres above the ground, as shown in Fig. 1.14. Find the speed with which the ball was hit. (Neglect air resistance, and suppose that the ball was hit at ground level.)

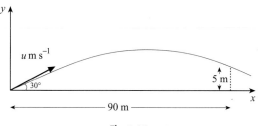

Fig. 1.14

If the initial speed was $u\,\mathrm{m\,s^{-1}}$, the equations of horizontal and vertical motion are

$$x = u\cos 30° t \quad \text{and} \quad y = u\sin 30° t - 4.9t^2.$$

You know that, when the ball passes over the boundary, $x = 90$ and $y = 5$. Using the values $\cos 30° = \frac{1}{2}\sqrt{3}$ and $\sin 30° = \frac{1}{2}$,

$$90 = u \times \tfrac{1}{2}\sqrt{3} \times t = \tfrac{1}{2}\sqrt{3}\,ut \quad \text{and} \quad 5 = u \times \tfrac{1}{2} \times t - 4.9t^2 = \tfrac{1}{2}ut - 4.9t^2$$

for the same value of t.

From the first equation, $ut = \dfrac{180}{\sqrt{3}} = 60\sqrt{3}$. Substituting this in the second equation gives

$$5 = 30\sqrt{3} - 4.9t^2,$$

so $t = \sqrt{\dfrac{30\sqrt{3} - 5}{4.9}} = 3.09\ldots .$

It follows that $u = \dfrac{60\sqrt{3}}{t} = \dfrac{60\sqrt{3}}{3.09\ldots} \approx 33.6.$

The initial speed of the ball was about $34\,\mathrm{m\,s^{-1}}$.

Example 1.2.5

A boy uses a catapult to send a squash ball through his friend's open window. The window is 7.6 metres up a wall 12 metres away from the boy. The ball enters the window descending at an angle of $45°$ to the horizontal, as shown in Fig. 1.15. Find the initial velocity of the ball.

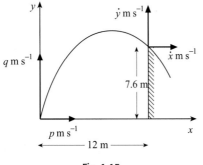

Fig. 1.15

Denote the horizontal and vertical components of the initial velocity by $p\,\mathrm{m\,s^{-1}}$ and $q\,\mathrm{m\,s^{-1}}$. If the ball enters the window after t seconds,

$$12 = pt \quad \text{and} \quad 7.6 = qt - 4.9t^2.$$

Also, as the ball enters the window, its velocity has components $\dot{x} = p$ and $\dot{y} = q - 9.8t$. Since this is at an angle of $45°$ below the horizontal, $\dot{y} = -\dot{x}$, so $q - 9.8t = -p$, or

$$p + q = 9.8t.$$

You now have three equations involving p, q and t. From the first two equations, $p = \dfrac{12}{t}$ and $q = \dfrac{7.6 + 4.9t^2}{t}$. Substituting these expressions in the third equation gives

$$\dfrac{12}{t} + \dfrac{7.6 + 4.9t^2}{t} = 9.8t, \text{ that is}$$

$$12 + (7.6 + 4.9t^2) = 9.8t^2, \quad \text{which simplifies to} \quad 4.9t^2 = 19.6.$$

So $t = 2$, from which you get $p = \dfrac{12}{2} = 6$ and

$q = \dfrac{7.6 + 4.9 \times 2^2}{2} = 13.6$.

Fig. 1.16 shows how these components are combined by the triangle rule to give the initial velocity of the ball. This has magnitude $\sqrt{6^2 + 13.6^2}\,\mathrm{m\,s^{-1}} \approx 14.9\,\mathrm{m\,s^{-1}}$ at an angle $\tan^{-1}\dfrac{13.6}{6} \approx 66.2°$ to the horizontal.

The ball is projected at about $15\,\mathrm{m\,s^{-1}}$ at $66°$ to the horizontal.

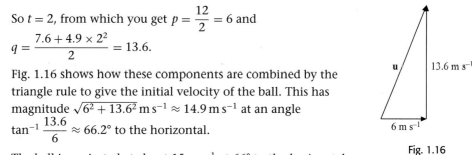

Fig. 1.16

Exercise 1B

Assume that all motion takes place above a horizontal plane unless otherwise stated.

1 A particle is projected horizontally with speed $13\,\mathrm{m\,s^{-1}}$, from a point high above a horizontal plane. Find the horizontal and vertical components of the velocity of the particle after 2 seconds.

2 The time of flight of an arrow fired with initial speed $30\,\mathrm{m\,s^{-1}}$ horizontally from a castle window was 2.5 seconds. Calculate the horizontal distance from the castle of the arrow's landing point. Calculate also the height of the castle window above the ground.

3 An arrow fired horizontally with initial speed $30\,\mathrm{m\,s^{-1}}$ struck a knight in armour after 2.5 seconds. Show that the armour protected the knight if it could be penetrated only by arrows with speed in excess of $39\,\mathrm{m\,s^{-1}}$.

4 A stone is thrown from the point O on top of a cliff with horizontal velocity $15\,\mathrm{m\,s^{-1}}$. Find the position vector of the stone after 2 seconds.

5 A particle is projected with speed $35\,\mathrm{m\,s^{-1}}$ at an angle of $40°$ above the horizontal. Calculate the horizontal and vertical components of the displacement of the particle after 3 seconds. Calculate also the horizontal and vertical components of the velocity of the particle at this instant.

6 A famine relief aircraft, flying over horizontal ground at a height of 160 metres, drops a sack of food.

   (a) Calculate the time that the sack takes to fall.

   (b) Calculate the vertical component of the velocity with which the sack hits the ground.

   (c) If the speed of the aircraft is $70\,\mathrm{m\,s^{-1}}$, at what distance before the target zone should the sack be released?

7 A particle is projected with speed $9\,\mathrm{m\,s^{-1}}$ at $40°$ to the horizontal. Calculate the time the particle takes to reach its maximum height, and find its speed at that instant.

8 A cannon fires a shot at $38°$ above the horizontal. The initial speed of the cannonball is $70\,\mathrm{m\,s^{-1}}$. Calculate the distance between the cannon and the point where the cannonball lands, given that the two positions are at the same horizontal level.

9 A girl stands at the water's edge and throws a flat stone horizontally from a height of 90 cm.

   (a) Calculate the time the stone is in the air before it hits the water.

   (b) Find the vertical component of the velocity with which the stone hits the water.

   The girl hopes to get the stone to bounce off the water surface. To do this the stone must hit the water at an angle to the horizontal of 15° or less.

   (c) What is the least speed with which she can throw the stone to achieve this?

   (d) If she throws the stone at this speed, how far away will the stone hit the water?

10 A particle projected at 40° to the horizontal reaches its greatest height after 3 seconds. Calculate the speed of projection.

11 A ball thrown with speed $18 \, \text{m s}^{-1}$ is again at its initial height 2.7 seconds after projection. Calculate the angle between the horizontal and the initial direction of motion of the ball.

12 A particle reaches its greatest height 2 seconds after projection, when it is travelling with speed $7 \, \text{m s}^{-1}$. Calculate the initial velocity of the particle. When it is again at the same level as the point of projection, how far has it travelled horizontally?

13 A batsman tries to hit a six, but the ball is caught by a fielder on the boundary. The ball is in the air for 3 seconds, and the fielder is 60 metres from the bat. Calculate

   (a) the horizontal component,   (b) the vertical component

   of the velocity with which the ball is hit.
   Hence find the magnitude and direction of this velocity.

14 A stone thrown with speed $17 \, \text{m s}^{-1}$ reaches a greatest height of 5 metres. Calculate the angle of projection.

15 A particle projected at 30° to the horizontal rises to a height of 10 metres. Calculate the initial speed of the particle, and its least speed during the flight.

16 In the first 2 seconds of motion a projectile rises 5 metres and travels a horizontal distance of 30 metres. Calculate its initial speed.

17 The nozzle of a fountain projects a jet of water with speed $10.6 \, \text{m s}^{-1}$ at 70° to the horizontal. The water is caught in a cup 4.2 metres above the level of the nozzle. Calculate the time taken by the water to reach the cup.

18 A stone was thrown with speed $15 \, \text{m s}^{-1}$, at an angle of 40°. It broke a small window 1.2 seconds after being thrown. Calculate the distance of the window from the point at which the stone was thrown.

19 A projectile reaches its greatest height after 2 seconds, when it is 35 metres from its point of projection. Determine the initial velocity.

20 A ski-jumper takes off from the ramp travelling at an angle of 10° below the horizontal with speed 72 kilometres per hour. Before landing she travels a horizontal distance of 70 metres. Find the time she is in the air, and the vertical distance she falls.

1.3 Some general formulae

Some of the results in this section use advanced trigonometry from C3 Chapter 6.

When you have more complicated problems to solve, it is useful to know formulae for some of the standard properties of trajectories. These are given in the notation of Fig. 1.11, which is repeated here as Fig. 1.17.

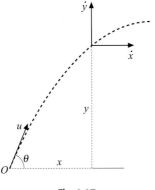

Fig. 1.17

The formulae are based on the assumption that O is at ground level. If not, adjustments will be needed to allow for this.

(i) Greatest height
This depends only on the vertical motion of the projectile, for which the component of the initial velocity is $u \sin \theta$. The greatest height is reached when the vertical component of velocity is 0. If h is the greatest height, the equation $v^2 = u^2 + 2as$ gives

$$0^2 = \left(u \sin \theta \right)^2 - 2gh.$$

Therefore

$$h = \frac{u^2 \sin^2 \theta}{2g}.$$

(ii) Range on horizontal ground
If the ground is horizontal, the time at which the projectile lands is given by putting $y = 0$ in the equation $y = u \sin \theta \, t - \frac{1}{2}gt^2$, so

$$t \left(u \sin \theta - \tfrac{1}{2}gt \right) = 0.$$

This gives $t = 0$ (when the projectile leaves O) or $t = \dfrac{2u \sin \theta}{g}$. This is called the **time of flight**. If at this time the x-coordinate is r, then

$$r = u \cos \theta \, t = \frac{u \cos \theta \times 2u \sin \theta}{g} = \frac{2u^2 \sin \theta \cos \theta}{g}.$$

It is shown in C3 Section 6.5 that $2 \sin \theta \cos \theta$ is the expanded form of $\sin 2\theta$. So you can write the formula more simply as

$$r = \frac{u^2 \sin 2\theta}{g}.$$

(iii) Maximum range on horizontal ground

Suppose that the initial speed u is known, but that θ can vary. You will see from the graph of $\sin 2\theta$ (Fig. 1.18) that r takes its greatest value when $\theta = 45°$, and that $r_{max} = \dfrac{u^2}{g}$.

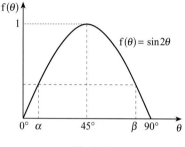

Fig. 1.18

Also, from the symmetry of the graph it follows that r has the same value when $\theta = \alpha$ and when $\theta = (90 - \alpha)°$. So any point closer than the maximum range can be reached by either of two trajectories, one with a low angle of projection ($\alpha < 45°$) and one with a high angle ($\beta = (90° - \alpha) > 45°$).

(iv) Equation of the trajectory

You can think of the equations for x and y in terms of t (given in Section 1.2) as parametric equations for the trajectory, using time as the parameter. The cartesian equation can be found by turning $x = u \cos \theta\, t$ round to give $t = \dfrac{x}{u \cos \theta}$, and then substituting for t in the equation for y:

$$y = u \sin \theta \times \frac{x}{u \cos \theta} - \frac{1}{2} g \left(\frac{x}{u \cos \theta} \right)^2.$$

You can write this more simply by replacing $\dfrac{\sin \theta}{\cos \theta}$ by $\tan \theta$. Then

$$y = x \tan \theta - \frac{g x^2}{2 u^2 \cos^2 \theta}.$$

Notice that, since u, g and θ are constant, this equation has the form $y = ax - bx^2$. You know that this is a parabola, and it is not difficult to show by differentiation that its vertex has coordinates $\left(\dfrac{a}{2b}, \dfrac{a^2}{4b} \right)$. (See C1 Section 10.1.)

Writing $a = \tan \theta$ and $b = \dfrac{g}{2 u^2 \cos^2 \theta}$, the vertex becomes $\left(\dfrac{u^2 \sin 2\theta}{2g}, \dfrac{u^2 \sin^2 \theta}{2g} \right)$.

This is another way of finding the formulae for the range and the greatest height.

Check the details for yourself.

For a projectile having initial velocity of magnitude u at an angle θ to the horizontal, under gravity but neglecting air resistance:

the greatest height reached is $\dfrac{u^2 \sin^2 \theta}{2g}$;

the time to return to its original height is $\dfrac{2u \sin \theta}{g}$;

the range on horizontal ground is $\dfrac{u^2 \sin 2\theta}{g}$;

the maximum range on horizontal ground is $\dfrac{u^2}{g}$;

the equation of the trajectory is

$$y = x \tan \theta - \frac{gx^2}{2u^2 \cos^2 \theta},$$

or $\quad y = x \tan \theta - \dfrac{gx^2 \sec^2 \theta}{2u^2}.$

The first four of these formulae are easy to work out when you need them, so they are not worth learning. But the equation of the trajectory, in one form or the other, is worth remembering.

Example 1.3.1

A basketball player throws the ball into the net, which is 3 metres horizontally from and 1 metre above the player's hands. The ball is thrown at $50°$ to the horizontal. How fast is it thrown?

Taking the player's hands as origin, you are given that $y = 1$ when $x = 3$ and that $\theta = 50°$. If you substitute these numbers into the equation of the trajectory you get

$$1 = 3 \tan 50° - \frac{9.8 \times 9}{2u^2 \cos^2 50°}.$$

This gives

$$\frac{44.1}{u^2 \cos^2 50°} = 3 \tan 50° - 1 = 2.575\ldots,$$

$$u^2 = \frac{44.1}{\cos^2 50° \times 2.575\ldots} = 41.44\ldots,$$

$$u = 6.44, \text{ correct to 3 significant figures.}$$

The ball is thrown with a speed of about $6.4 \, \text{m s}^{-1}$.

Example 1.3.2

A boy is standing on the beach and his sister is at the top of a cliff 6 metres away at a height of 4 metres. He throws her an apple with a speed of 10.5 m s^{-1}. In what direction should he throw it?

You are given that $y = 4$ when $x = 6$ and that $u = 10.5$. It is more convenient to use the second form of the equation of the trajectory. Substituting the given numbers,

$$4 = 6\tan\theta - \frac{9.8 \times 36 \times \sec^2\theta}{2 \times 10.5^2},$$

which simplifies to

$$4\sec^2\theta - 15\tan\theta + 10 = 0.$$

To solve this equation you can use the identity $\sec^2\theta \equiv 1 + \tan^2\theta$ (see C3 Section 6.2). Then

$$4(1 + \tan^2\theta) - 15\tan\theta + 10 = 0, \quad \text{that is} \quad 4\tan^2\theta - 15\tan\theta + 14 = 0.$$

This is a quadratic equation for $\tan\theta$, which factorises as

$$(4\tan\theta - 7)(\tan\theta - 2) = 0, \quad \text{so} \quad \tan\theta = \tfrac{7}{4} \text{ or } \tan\theta = 2.$$

The apple should be thrown at either $\tan^{-1}\tfrac{7}{4}$ or $\tan^{-1}2$ to the horizontal, that is either $60.3°$ or $63.4°$.

1.4* Accessible points

You may omit this section if you wish.

If you launch a projectile from O with a given initial speed u, but in an unspecified direction, you can obviously reach the points close to O, but not all points further away. You can use the method in Example 1.3.2 to find which points can be reached.

In Example 1.3.2 numerical values were given for x, y and u. If instead you keep these in algebraic form, then the equation of the trajectory can be written as

$$y = x\tan\theta - \frac{gx^2(1 + \tan^2\theta)}{2u^2}.$$

This can then be arranged as a quadratic equation for $\tan\theta$,

$$gx^2\tan^2\theta - 2u^2x\tan\theta + (gx^2 + 2u^2y) = 0.$$

Now this equation can be solved to give values for $\tan\theta$ provided that the discriminant (that is, $b^2 - 4ac$ in the usual notation for quadratics) is greater than or equal to 0. For this equation, the condition is

$$4u^4x^2 - 4gx^2(gx^2 + 2u^2y) \geqslant 0.$$

After cancelling $4x^2$, this can be rearranged as

$$y \leqslant \frac{u^2}{2g} - \frac{gx^2}{2u^2}.$$

Suppose, for example, that the initial speed is 10.5 m s^{-1}, as in Example 1.3.2. Then, in metre units, with $g = 9.8$, $\dfrac{u^2}{g} = \dfrac{45}{4}$, so this inequality becomes

$$y \leqslant \tfrac{45}{8} - \tfrac{2}{45}x^2.$$

This is illustrated in Fig. 1.19, which shows several possible trajectories with this initial speed for various angles θ. All the points on these curves lie on or underneath the parabola with equation $y = \tfrac{45}{8} - \tfrac{2}{45}x^2$. This is called the **bounding parabola** for this initial speed. It separates the points which can be reached from O from those which can't.

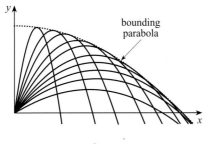

Fig. 1.19

Thus in Example 1.3.2 the coordinates of the girl were $(6,4)$. Since $\tfrac{45}{8} - \tfrac{2}{45} \times 6^2 = 4.025 > 4$, these coordinates satisfy the inequality, so it is possible for her brother to throw the apple to reach her.

Exercise 1C

Assume that all motion takes place above horizontal ground unless otherwise stated.

1 A golfer strikes the ball with speed 60 m s^{-1}. The ball lands in a bunker at the same level 210 metres away. Calculate the possible angles of projection.

2 A projectile is launched at $45°$ to the horizontal. It lands 1.28 km from the point of projection. Calculate the initial speed.

3 A footballer taking a free kick projects the ball with a speed of 20 m s^{-1} at $40°$ to the horizontal. Calculate the time of flight of the ball. How far from the point of the free kick would the ball hit the ground?

4 A stone being skimmed across the surface of a lake makes an angle of $15°$ with the horizontal as it leaves the surface of the water, and remains in the air for 0.6 seconds before its next bounce. Calculate the speed of the stone when it leaves the surface of the lake.

5 A projectile launched with speed 70 m s^{-1} is in the air for 14 seconds. Calculate the angle of projection.

6 An astronaut who can drive a golf ball a maximum distance of 350 metres on Earth can drive it 430 metres on planet Zog. Calculate the acceleration due to gravity on Zog.

7 An archer releases her arrow with speed 70 m s^{-1} at an angle of 25° to the horizontal. Calculate the range of the arrow. Determine the height of the arrow above its initial level when it has travelled a horizontal distance of 50 metres, and find the other horizontal distance for which it has the same height.

8 A particle projected at an angle of 40° passes through the point (70, 28). Find the initial speed of the particle.

9 A hockey player taking a free hit projects the ball with speed 14 m s^{-1}. A player 10 metres away intercepts the ball at a height of 1.4 metres. Calculate the angle of projection.

10 The equation of the path of a projectile is $y = 0.5x - 0.02x^2$. Determine the initial speed of the projectile.

11 A tennis player strikes the ball at a height of 0.5 metres. It passes above her opponent 10 metres away at a height of 4 metres, and lands 20 metres from the first player, who has not moved since striking the ball. Calculate the angle of projection of the ball.

12 A cricketer strikes the ball at a height of 1 metre. It passes over a fielder 7 metres from the bat at a height of 3 metres, and hits the ground 60 metres from the bat. How fast was the ball hit?

13 The greatest height reached by a projectile is one-tenth of its range on horizontal ground. Calculate the angle of projection.

14 A soldier at position P fires a mortar shell with speed $\sqrt{ag}$ at an angle θ above the horizontal, where a is a constant. P is at a vertical height b above a horizontal plane. The shell strikes the plane at the point Q, and O is the point at the level of the plane vertically below P, as shown in the diagram. Letting $OQ = x$, obtain the equation

$$x^2 \tan^2 \theta - 2ax \tan \theta + (x^2 - 2ab) = 0.$$

Show that the maximum value of x, as θ varies, is $\sqrt{a(a + 2b)}$ and that this is achieved when $\tan \theta = \sqrt{\dfrac{a}{a + 2b}}$.

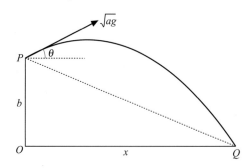

The sound of the shell being fired travels along the straight line PQ at a constant speed $\sqrt{cg}$. Given that the shell is fired to achieve its maximum range, show that if a man standing at Q hears the sound of firing before the shell arrives at Q, so giving him time to take cover, then $c > \frac{1}{2}(a + b)$.   (OCR)

Miscellaneous exercise 1

1 A girl throws a stone which breaks a window 2 seconds later. The speed of projection is 20 m s^{-1} and the angle of projection is $60°$. Assuming that the motion can be modelled by a particle moving with constant acceleration, find the horizontal and vertical components of the velocity of the stone just before impact. (OCR)

2 A ball is projected from a point on horizontal ground. The speed of projection is 30 m s^{-1} and the greatest height reached is 20 metres. Assuming no air resistance, find the angle of projection above the horizontal and the speed of the ball as it passes through the highest point. (OCR)

3 A ball is thrown with speed 28 m s^{-1} at an angle of $40°$ above the horizontal. After 3 seconds the ball is at P. Ignoring air resistance, find the magnitude and direction of the velocity of the ball as it passes through P. (OCR)

4 A particle is projected at a speed of 45 m s^{-1} at an angle of $30°$ above the horizontal.

  (a) Calculate

    (i) the speed and direction of motion of the particle after 4 seconds,
    (ii) the maximum height, above the point of projection, reached by the particle.

  (b) State one assumption made in modelling the motion of a particle. (OCR)

5 A golfer strikes a ball in such a way that it leaves the point O at an angle of elevation θ and with speed of 40 m s^{-1}. After 5 seconds the ball is at a point P which is 120 metres horizontally from O and h metres above O. Assuming that the flight of the ball can be modelled by the motion of a particle with constant acceleration, find the angle θ and the value of h. Give one force on the golf ball that this model does not allow for. (OCR)

6 An athlete throws a heavy ball. The ball is released with an initial speed of 10.3 m s^{-1} at an angle of $35°$ above the horizontal. The point of release is 1.68 metres above the ground.

  (a) Neglecting air resistance show that the equation of the path of the ball is approximately $y = 0.7x - 0.07x^2$, where y metres is the height of the ball above the release point when it has travelled a horizontal distance of x metres.

  (b) Find how far the ball has been thrown horizontally before it strikes the horizontal, flat ground.

  (c) State one further aspect of the motion of the ball which is not incorporated in the model. (OCR)

7 A fielder can throw a cricket ball faster at low angles than at high angles. This is modelled by assuming that, at an angle θ, he can throw a ball with a speed $k\sqrt{\cos\theta}$, where k is a constant.

  (a) Show that the horizontal distance he can throw is given by $\dfrac{2k^2}{g}\sin\theta\,\cos^2\theta$.

  (b) Show that this horizontal distance can be written as $\dfrac{2k^2}{g}(s - s^3)$, where $s = \sin\theta$.

  (c) Find the maximum distance he can throw the ball on level ground.

8 A boy is trying to throw a pellet of bread to a young bird sitting on a ledge in a wall, at a height of 11 metres above the ground. The boy is standing 5 metres away from the wall and throws the pellet from a height of 1.5 metres above the ground. When the pellet reaches the ledge it is moving horizontally. Treating the pellet as a particle moving with constant acceleration, find

   (a) the vertical component of the initial velocity,

   (b) the time taken for the pellet to reach the ledge,

   (c) the speed of the pellet when it reaches the ledge.

   State a force that has been neglected in the above model.   (OCR)

9 (a) At a point O on its path, a projectile has speed V and is travelling at an angle α above the horizontal. Derive the equation of the trajectory of the projectile in the form

   $$y = x \tan \alpha - \frac{gx^2}{2V^2}(1 + \tan^2 \alpha),$$

   where the x- and y-axes pass through O and are directed horizontally and vertically upwards respectively, and state briefly one simplifying assumption that is necessary in obtaining this result.

   (b) An aircraft is flown on a path given by $y = 0.28x - (2.35 \times 10^{-4})x^2$, in such a way that the acceleration of the aircraft has the constant value $9.8\,\text{m s}^{-2}$ vertically downwards. The units of x and y are metres. By comparing the equation of the aircraft's path with the standard trajectory equation in (a), find the speed and direction of motion of the aircraft at the point $(0, 0)$. Calculate the time of flight between the two points on the aircraft's path at which $y = 0$.   (OCR)

   (By flying an aircraft on a parabolic path with appropriate speed, it is possible to simulate within the fuselage a weightless environment. This has been used for astronaut training.)

10 A player in a rugby match kicks the ball from the ground over a crossbar which is at a height of 3 metres above the ground and at a horizontal distance of 30 metres from the ball as shown in the diagram. The player kicks the ball so that it leaves the ground at an angle of 25° above the horizontal.

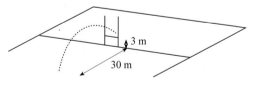

   (a) Find the minimum speed at which the ball must be kicked.

   In fact the player kicked the ball with an initial speed of $25\,\text{m s}^{-1}$.

   (b) (i) Find the time that elapsed between the ball leaving the ground and it passing vertically above the crossbar.

       (ii) Find the angle to the horizontal made by the direction of motion of the ball as it passed over the crossbar. You should make it clear whether the ball is ascending or descending at this time.

   (c) State two assumptions that you have made in modelling the motion of the ball which may not be reasonable in practice.   (OCR)

11 A particle P is projected with speed $10.1\,\mathrm{m\,s^{-1}}$ from a point O on horizontal ground. The angle of projection is α above the horizontal. At time t seconds after the instant of projection, the horizontal distance travelled by P is x metres and the height of P above the ground is y metres. Neglecting air resistance, write down expressions for x and y in terms of α and t. Hence

(a) show that P reaches the ground when $t = 2.06\sin\alpha$, approximately;

(b) find, in terms of α, the value of x when P reaches the ground;

(c) state the value of t, in terms of α, for which P is at its maximum height and show that the maximum height of P above the ground is $5.20\sin^2\alpha$ metres, approximately;

(d) find an expression for y in terms of x and α.

Given that $\alpha = 45°$, use your answer to part (d) to find the horizontal distance travelled by P when this horizontal distance is 8 times the height of P above the ground. (OCR)

12 A tennis ball A is dropped from the top of a vertical tower which is 15 metres high. At time t seconds later the tennis ball is at a height h metres above the ground. Assuming that the motion may be modelled by that of a particle, express h in terms of t.

The point O is 20 metres from the tower and is at the same horizontal level as the foot of the tower. At the instant that A is dropped, a second ball B is projected from O, towards the tower, with speed $V\,\mathrm{m\,s^{-1}}$ at an angle of elevation θ. The motion of B, before any impact, may be modelled by that of a particle, and takes place in a vertical plane containing the tower. Given that the two balls collide when $t = 1.5$ and before B hits the ground, show that $V\sin\theta = 10$ and find the value of $V\cos\theta$.

Deduce the values of V and θ. (OCR)

13 The behaviour of a water droplet in an ornamental fountain is modelled by the motion of a particle moving freely under gravity with constant acceleration. The particle is projected from the point O with speed $9.1\,\mathrm{m\,s^{-1}}$, in a direction which makes an angle of $76°$ with the horizontal. The horizontal and vertical displacements of the particle from O after t seconds are x metres and y metres respectively.

(a) Write down expressions for x and y in terms of t and hence show that $y = 4x - x^2$ is an approximation for the equation of the path of the particle.

(b) Find the range of the particle on the horizontal plane through O.

(c) Make a sketch showing the path of a particle.

The point of projection O is in the surface of a pond. The water droplets are required to hit the surface of the pond at points on a circle with centre O and diameter 7 metres. This requirement can be met, without changing the speed of projection, either by increasing the angle of projection slightly (say to about $78°$) or by reducing it considerably (say to about $12°$). In a single diagram sketch the path of the droplet in each of these cases. (OCR)

2 Work, energy and power

In this chapter the basic equations of mechanics are put together into a new form which can be applied to a wider range of problems. When you have completed it, you should

- know the definitions of work and kinetic energy
- be able to use the work–energy principle, and distinguish work done by a force from work done against a force
- know that the work–energy principle can be extended to situations in which forces are not constant
- use the fact that a force perpendicular to the direction of motion does no work
- understand the idea of power and be able to calculate it
- know and be able to use the relation between power, force and speed.

2.1 The work–energy equation

Example 2.1.1

A car and driver have a total mass of 1000 kg. The car gains speed from $7\,\mathrm{m\,s^{-1}}$ to $13\,\mathrm{m\,s^{-1}}$ with constant acceleration over a horizontal distance of 200 metres. Calculate the driving force.

> **Method 1** The acceleration of the car can be found by using the equation $v^2 = u^2 + 2as$, taking $u = 7$, $v = 13$ and $s = 200$ in SI units. This gives
>
> $169 = 49 + 2a \times 200$, so $a = \dfrac{120}{400} = 0.3$. By Newton's second law, the driving force in
>
> newtons is given by $F = 1000 \times 0.3 = 300$.

This example is typical of many problems in mechanics, in which a force of magnitude F acts on an object of mass m over a distance s, so that the speed of the object increases from u to v. You solve it by combining Newton's second law $F = ma$ with the constant acceleration equation $v^2 = u^2 + 2as$ to show that $F = m\left(\dfrac{v^2 - u^2}{2s}\right)$, which can be rearranged as

$$Fs = \tfrac{1}{2}mv^2 - \tfrac{1}{2}mu^2.$$

The expression on the left of this equation, the product of the force and the distance through which the object moves, is called the **work done by the force**. This is such an important idea in mechanics that the unit in which it is measured in the SI system has a special name, the **joule**. (James Joule was a 19th-century English physicist who played a leading part in developing the science of thermodynamics.) A joule is the work done when a force of 1 newton acts through a distance of 1 metre; that is, 1 joule = 1 newton metre. The abbreviation for joule is J.

On the right of the equation you have two terms of a similar form. If an object of mass m is moving with speed v, the quantity $\tfrac{1}{2}mv^2$ is called the **kinetic energy** of the body. So the expression $\frac{1}{2}mv^2 - \frac{1}{2}mu^2$ on the right is the increase in the kinetic energy of the object resulting from the action of the force. Kinetic energy is also measured in joules.

> **The work–energy principle** If a constant force acts on an object over a certain distance, the work done by the force is equal to the gain in the kinetic energy of the object.

You can now use the work–energy principle to shorten the solution of Example 2.1.1.

Method 2 The kinetic energy increases from $\frac{1}{2} \times 1000 \times 7^2$ J to $\frac{1}{2} \times 1000 \times 13^2$ J, that is by $500 \times (169 - 49)$ J, which is $60\,000$ J.

If the force is F newtons, the work done is $F \times 200$ J. So $F = \dfrac{60\,000}{200} = 300$.

The driving force is 300 newtons.

2.2 Some generalisations

The work–energy principle can be generalised in a number of ways. This is one reason why it is so important.

First, suppose that the force doesn't act along the line of motion, but at an angle to it. Fig. 2.1 illustrates this with an object moving along a straight track, being accelerated by a horizontal force of magnitude F at an angle θ to the track. The object is prevented from leaving the track by a normal contact force N.

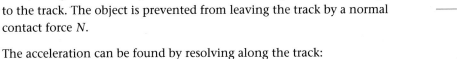

Fig. 2.1

The acceleration can be found by resolving along the track:

$$F \cos\theta = ma.$$

So, in the algebraic calculation in Section 2.1, F must be replaced by $F \cos\theta$, and the work–energy equation becomes

$$(F \cos\theta)s = \text{ gain in kinetic energy.}$$

This means that the definition of work must be generalised as follows.

> If an object moves through a distance s along a line under the action of a force of magnitude F at an angle θ to the line, the work done by the force is $Fs \cos\theta$.

It is important to notice that the force N does not appear in the work–energy equation. This is because its direction is at right angles to the direction of motion, so the work done by this force is $Ns \cos 90°$, which is zero since $\cos 90° = 0$.

> The work done by a force perpendicular to the direction of motion is zero.

The next generalisation is to introduce a resisting force R, as in Fig. 2.2. Newton's second law then becomes

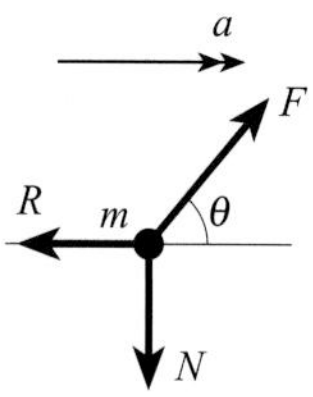

$$F \cos \theta - R = ma,$$

so that in the work–energy equation the term $(F \cos \theta)s$ is replaced by $(F \cos \theta - R)s$. Thus

$$Fs \cos \theta - Rs = \text{gain in kinetic energy.}$$

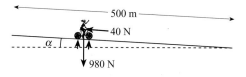

Fig. 2.2

The extra term, $-Rs$, can be described as the 'work done by the resistance', which is negative. But it is more usual to call the positive quantity Rs the 'work done against the resistance', and to extend the statement of the work–energy principle as follows.

> **The extended work–energy principle**   The work done by the force acting on an object, less the work done against resistance, is equal to the gain in the kinetic energy of the object.

Example 2.2.1

A cyclist and her machine together have a mass of 100 kg. She free-wheels down a hill of gradient 5% (1 in 20) for a distance of 500 metres. If her speed at the top was $5 \, \mathrm{m \, s^{-1}}$, and there is air resistance of 40 newtons, how fast will she be going at the bottom of the hill?

Fig. 2.3 shows the forces acting on the cyclist.

Fig. 2.3

The force accelerating the cyclist is the weight of 980 N, acting at an angle to the direction of motion of $(90° - \alpha)$, where $\sin \alpha = 0.05$. The work done by the weight is $980 \times 500 \times \sin \alpha$ J, which is $490\,000 \times 0.05$ J, or $24\,500$ J. The work done against the resistance is 40×500 J, which is $20\,000$ J. The normal contact forces on the wheels do no work. So the gain in kinetic energy is $(24\,500 - 20\,000)$ J, that is 4500 J.

At the top of the hill the kinetic energy was $\frac{1}{2} \times 100 \times 5^2$ J, which is 1250 J. The kinetic energy at the bottom is therefore $(4500 + 1250)$ J, that is 5750 J. If her speed is then $v \, \mathrm{m \, s^{-1}}$,

$$\tfrac{1}{2} \times 100 \times v^2 = 5750,$$

so $v^2 = 115$, giving $v = 10.72\ldots$.

The speed at the bottom of the hill will be $10.7 \, \mathrm{m \, s^{-1}}$, correct to 3 significant figures.

> If the amount of work is large, you may prefer to give it in kilojoules (kJ), where $1 \, \mathrm{kJ} = 1000$ J. For example, in Example 2.2.1, the work done by the weight and against the resistance could be given as 24.5 kJ and 20 kJ respectively.

There is another way in which the work–energy principle can be generalised: it enables you to talk sensibly about forces which are not constant. In the last example it is unlikely that the air resistance is constant; it will almost certainly get bigger as the cyclist gains speed. But if you think of the air resistance as having an 'average' value of 40 newtons during the descent, you can still use this to find the work done against the resistance. So the work–energy principle produces valid answers in situations when the acceleration is not constant.

Similarly, in Example 2.1.1, if the driving force is not constant, you can still use the work–energy method to deduce that the average driving force on the car is 300 newtons.

The proof of this, and a more precise definition of what is meant by the average force, involves the use of calculus. It will be discussed in more detail when motion with variable force is dealt with in M3.

Example 2.2.2

A nail is being hammered into a plank. The mass of the hammer is 200 grams, and at each stroke the hammer is raised 15 cm above the nail. If the average force used to bring the hammer down is 10 times the average force used to raise the hammer, find the speed, correct to 2 significant figures, with which the hammer hits the nail.

When the hammer is raised, the kinetic energy at both the beginning and the end of the movement is zero. So the work done in raising the hammer is equal to the work done against the force of gravity.

The weight of the hammer is $0.2 \times 9.8\,\mathrm{N}$, which is $1.96\,\mathrm{N}$, and the hammer rises by $0.15\,\mathrm{m}$. So the work done against the weight is $1.96 \times 0.15\,\mathrm{J}$, which is $0.294\,\mathrm{J}$.

On the downward stroke the work done is 10 times the work done in raising the hammer, so this is $2.94\,\mathrm{J}$. Also, as the hammer falls, its weight does work of $1.96 \times 0.15\,\mathrm{J} = 0.294\,\mathrm{J}$. So the total work done on the downward stroke is $3.234\,\mathrm{J}$.

This is equal to the kinetic energy acquired by the hammer, which is $\frac{1}{2} \times 0.2 \times v^2$, where $v\,\mathrm{m\,s^{-1}}$ is the speed with which the hammer hits the nail. This gives $0.1v^2 = 3.234$, so $v = \sqrt{32.34} = 5.68\ldots$.

The hammer hits the nail at a speed of $5.7\,\mathrm{m\,s^{-1}}$, correct to 2 significant figures.

2.3 Motion round curved paths

A further generalisation of the work–energy principle is that it is not restricted to motion along a straight line. It can also be used when an object moves round a curved path.

As an example, consider a satellite orbiting the Earth in a circular path outside the Earth's atmosphere. It is acted on by the gravitational pull from the Earth, whose direction is along the radius, perpendicular to the direction of motion. So the work done by this force is zero, which means that the kinetic energy remains constant. That is, the satellite moves at constant speed.

This is a case when it is important to distinguish between speed and velocity. The satellite doesn't, of course, move with constant velocity. It is continually changing direction because of the gravitational pull from the Earth. But in the expression for kinetic energy, v stands for the speed of the moving object. Kinetic energy is an example of what is called a 'scalar quantity'; its value doesn't depend on the direction of motion.

A similar argument applies for a particle moving on a smooth curved horizontal path, or a bead on a smooth horizontal wire. In such cases both the weight and the normal contact force are perpendicular to the velocity of the moving object. So, if there are no other forces, it moves with constant speed.

Exercise 2A

1 Find the kinetic energy of

(a) a rugby player of mass 90 kg running at $6 \, \text{m s}^{-1}$,

(b) an elephant of mass 6 tonnes charging at $10 \, \text{m s}^{-1}$,

(c) a racing car of mass 2.5 tonnes travelling at 300 km per hour,

(d) a bullet of mass 20 grams moving at $400 \, \text{m s}^{-1}$,

(e) a meteorite of mass 20 kg as it enters the Earth's atmosphere at $8 \, \text{km s}^{-1}$.

2 An object of mass 20 kg is pulled 7 metres at a constant speed across a rough horizontal floor by means of a horizontal rope. The tension in the rope is 100 N. Calculate the work done by the rope. State the work done by the weight of the object and the normal contact force between the object and the floor. State also the work done against resisting forces.

3 A gardener moves a wheelbarrow 30 metres along a level, straight path. The work done by the gardener is 120 J, and the barrow is initially and finally at rest. Calculate the average force resisting the motion.

4 A crate is moved at a steady speed in a straight line by means of a tow-rope. The work done in moving the crate 16 metres is 800 J. Calculate the resolved part of the tension in the rope in the direction of motion.

5 A ball of mass 1.2 kg moving with initial speed $20 \, \text{m s}^{-1}$ comes to rest after travelling 30 metres across a horizontal surface. Find the work done against resisting forces, and hence calculate the mean resisting force.

6 An aircraft of mass 1.8 tonnes landing on an aircraft carrier at 144 kilometres per hour is brought to rest by a parachute brake and an arrester cable. If 30% of the work is done by the parachute, calculate the work done by the cable.

7 A father pulls his children on a sledge along a level snow-covered path. The cord by which the sledge is pulled makes an angle of 20° with the horizontal, and has tension 30 N. Calculate the work done in moving the sledge 40 metres at constant speed.

8   A bicycle of mass 30 kg is pushed up a hill inclined at 15° to the horizontal. Calculate the work done in moving the bicycle 70 metres, starting and finishing with the bicycle at rest.

9   A car of mass 600 kg is pushed along a horizontal road. Initially the car is at rest, and its final speed is 4 m s^{-1}. Calculate the work done in accelerating the car.

10 A box of mass 20 kg is pulled up a ramp inclined at 30° to the horizontal. The work done in moving the box 10 metres is 1200 J. Calculate the magnitude of the average resisting force.

11 A cyclist free-wheels down a slope inclined at 15° to the horizontal, increasing his speed from 4 m s^{-1} to 10 m s^{-1} over a distance of 50 metres. Calculate the mean resistance on the cyclist, given that the mass of the cyclist and his bicycle is 60 kg.

12 A car of mass 700 kg accelerates from 10 m s^{-1} to 30 m s^{-1} over a distance of 120 metres. Neglecting resistances, calculate the work done by the car engine if the road is

(a) horizontal,   (b) rising at 10° to the horizontal,   (c) dropping at 5°.

Comment on the work done if the gradient of the road is 20° below the horizontal.

13 A parachutist of mass 70 kg falls from a stationary helicopter at an altitude of 1 km. She has speed 8 m s^{-1} on reaching the ground. Calculate the work done against air resistance.

14 A tractor of mass 500 kg pulls a trailer of mass 200 kg up a rough slope inclined at 17° to the horizontal. The resistance to the motion is 4 N per kg. Calculate the work done by the tractor engine, given that the vehicle travels at a constant speed of 1.4 m s^{-1} for 2 minutes.

2.4   Power

Competitors in a long-distance canoe race have to get past a series of locks by dragging their canoes up the towpath, a distance of 60 metres. One competitor takes 90 seconds to do this; another takes 100 seconds. The combined force of the friction and the resolved part of the weight down the slope is 75 N for both canoes. Both competitors therefore do the same amount of work in raising their canoes, 75×60 J, which is 4500 J. But the first canoeist is more powerful; she does this work in a shorter time.

The rate at which a person or an engine works is called **power**. The unit of power is the joule per second; this is given a special name, the **watt**, abbreviated to W. Thus $1 \text{ W} = 1 \text{ J s}^{-1}$. James Watt was a Scottish engineer in the second half of the 18th century, most famous for his contribution to the development of the steam engine.

In the example of the two canoeists, assuming that they work at a constant rate, the first expends power of $\frac{4500}{90}$ joules per second, on average, which is 50 watts; the second expends power of $\frac{4500}{100}$ joules per second, which is 45 watts.

Example 2.4.1

A hotel lift, of total mass 1200 kg, rises a distance of 60 metres in 20 seconds. What is the power output of the motor?

The weight of the lift is 11 760 N, so the work done in raising it 60 metres is 11 760 × 60 J, which is 705 600 J. To do this work in 20 seconds requires power of $\dfrac{705\,600}{20}$ W, which is 35 280 W.

The power output of the motor is 35 280 W, or about 35.3 kilowatts (kW).

Example 2.4.2

A car of mass 1500 kg arrives at the foot of a straight hill travelling at 30 m s^{-1}. It reaches the top of the hill 40 seconds later travelling at 10 m s^{-1}. The length of the hill is 1000 metres, and the gain in height is 120 metres. The average resistance to motion is 500 N. Find the average power developed by the engine.

The work done against the resistance is 500 × 1000 J. From Fig. 2.4 the resolved part of the weight of 14 700 N down the hill is 14 700 sin α N, where sin $\alpha = 0.12$. This is 1764 N, so the work done against the weight is 1764 × 1000 J = 1 764 000 J. The total work done against the external forces is therefore (500 000 + 1 764 000) J, which is 2 264 000 J.

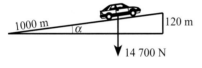

Fig. 2.4

Some of this work is accounted for by the loss in kinetic energy, which is $\left(\frac{1}{2} \times 1500 \times 30^2 - \frac{1}{2} \times 1500 \times 10^2\right)$ J = 600 000 J.

This leaves (2 264 000 − 600 000) J = 1 664 000 J to be provided by the engine.

So the engine has to produce 1 664 000 J in 40 seconds, which means that the average power developed is $\dfrac{1\,664\,000}{40}$ W, which is 41 600 W, or 41.6 kW.

2.5 Power, force and velocity

Suppose that a vehicle is travelling on a level road with constant velocity v, so that the driving force F from the engine exactly balances the resistance R. Then over an interval of time t the vehicle will travel a distance vt, and the work done by the driving force is $F \times (vt)$. The power developed by the engine is therefore $\dfrac{Fvt}{t}$, that is Fv.

You can use calculus arguments to show that this formula still holds if the velocity of the vehicle is not constant. The general result is:

> If an engine drives an object at velocity v by means of a force F in the direction of motion, the power developed by the engine is Fv.

In many cases, both for mechanical engines and for athletes, the greatest power of which they are capable is roughly constant over a range of speeds. This means that, when v gets larger, F decreases; and by Newton's second law, it follows that the acceleration decreases.

This is a familiar experience to anyone who drives a car, rides a bicycle or runs sprint races. If you are producing maximum power, then you can achieve higher acceleration at low speeds than at high speeds.

Example 2.5.1

A swimmer of mass 50 kg pushes off from the side of a pool with a speed of $0.8\,\text{m}\,\text{s}^{-1}$. She can develop power of 200 W, and the resistance of the water is 220 N.

(a) At what rate can she accelerate away from the side of the pool?

(b) Assuming the resistance remains the same, what is her greatest possible speed?

(a) At a speed of $0.8\,\text{m}\,\text{s}^{-1}$ the largest force she can produce is given by power ÷ speed, which is $\dfrac{200}{0.8}\,\text{N} = 250\,\text{N}$. The net force available for acceleration is $(250 - 220)\,\text{N}$, or 30 N. Therefore, by Newton's second law, her greatest possible acceleration is $\dfrac{30}{50}\,\text{m}\,\text{s}^{-2}$, which is $0.6\,\text{m}\,\text{s}^{-2}$.

(b) At her greatest possible speed the forward force is equal to the resistance of 220 N. Swimming at her full power of 200 W, her greatest speed is given by power ÷ force, which is $\dfrac{200}{220}\,\text{m}\,\text{s}^{-1}$, or $0.909\ldots\,\text{m}\,\text{s}^{-1}$.

At a speed of $0.8\,\text{m}\,\text{s}^{-1}$ she can accelerate away from the side at $0.6\,\text{m}\,\text{s}^{-2}$, and reach a maximum speed of about $0.9\,\text{m}\,\text{s}^{-1}$.

Example 2.5.2

A car of mass 1830 kg is being tested out at high speeds. Running at full power, it is found that the greatest speed the car can achieve is $80\,\text{m}\,\text{s}^{-1}$. With the same power output, at a speed of $64\,\text{m}\,\text{s}^{-1}$, the car accelerates at $0.5\,\text{m}\,\text{s}^{-2}$. Assuming that the resistance to motion is proportional to the square of the speed, find the acceleration of the car at full power when its speed is $75\,\text{m}\,\text{s}^{-1}$.

Let the power output of the car be P watts, and suppose that the resistance when the car is travelling at $v\,\text{m}\,\text{s}^{-1}$ is kv^2 newtons.

At $80\,\text{m}\,\text{s}^{-1}$, the driving force is $\frac{1}{80}P$ newtons. At the car's top speed the driving force is equal to the resistance of $k \times 80^2$ newtons. So

$$\tfrac{1}{80}P = k \times 80^2, \text{ which gives } P = 512\,000k.$$

At $64\,\text{m}\,\text{s}^{-1}$, the driving force is $\frac{1}{64}P$ newtons and the resistance is $k \times 64^2$ newtons, so by Newton's second law

$$\tfrac{1}{64}P - k \times 64^2 = 1830 \times 0.5.$$

Substituting $512\,000k$ for P, this equation becomes

$$8000k - 4096k = 915,$$

giving $3904k = 915$, so $k = \frac{915}{3904}$, and $P = 512\,000k = 120\,000$.

If the acceleration at $75\,\mathrm{m\,s^{-1}}$ is $a\,\mathrm{m\,s^{-2}}$, Newton's second law gives

$$\tfrac{1}{75} \times 120\,000 - \tfrac{915}{3904} \times 75^2 = 1830a,$$

so $a = \dfrac{1600 - 1318.3\ldots}{1830} = 0.154$, correct to 3 significant figures.

At full power, the acceleration of the car when its speed is $75\,\mathrm{m\,s^{-1}}$ is $0.154\,\mathrm{m\,s^{-2}}$.

Exercise 2B

1   A crane is used to raise a block of mass 2 tonnes to a height of 75 metres in 45 seconds. What is the average power output of the motor?

2   A mountaineer and her pack have mass $90\,\mathrm{kg}$. She climbs a 1200 metre mountain in 160 minutes. At what average power is she working?

3   A child of mass $30\,\mathrm{kg}$ runs up a flight of stairs in 6 seconds. The top of the flight is 3 metres above the bottom, and at the top he is running at $2\,\mathrm{m\,s^{-1}}$. What average power does he need to produce?

4   A ski-lift runs at constant speed. It raises 30 skiers a minute, of average mass $75\,\mathrm{kg}$. The top of the lift is 300 metres higher than the bottom, and the ride takes 3 minutes. What power do the motors produce?

5   The power developed by a motorcycle, as it travels on a horizontal straight road at a constant speed of $20\,\mathrm{m\,s^{-1}}$, is $12\,\mathrm{kW}$. Calculate the resistance to the motion of the motorcycle.

6   Calculate the power of the engine of a car which maintains a steady speed of $40\,\mathrm{m\,s^{-1}}$ when the motion is opposed by a constant force of $400\,\mathrm{N}$.

7   A cyclist maintains a steady speed of $11\,\mathrm{m\,s^{-1}}$ when opposed by a force of $80\,\mathrm{N}$. Calculate the power produced by the cyclist.

8   A motorcyclist is travelling on a straight level road, with the engine working at a rate of $8\,\mathrm{kW}$. The total mass of the motorcyclist and the machine is $160\,\mathrm{kg}$. Ignoring any resistance, find the acceleration at an instant when the speed is $20\,\mathrm{m\,s^{-1}}$.

9   A winch operating at $1\,\mathrm{kW}$ pulls a box of weight $980\,\mathrm{N}$ up a smooth slope at a constant speed of $2\,\mathrm{m\,s^{-1}}$. Calculate the angle the slope makes with the horizontal.

10   A car of mass $800\,\mathrm{kg}$ travels on a horizontal straight road. The resistance to motion is a constant force of magnitude $300\,\mathrm{N}$. Find the power developed by the car's engine at an instant when the car has a speed of $10\,\mathrm{m\,s^{-1}}$ and acceleration of $0.6\,\mathrm{m\,s^{-2}}$.

11   A winch is used to raise a $200\,\mathrm{kg}$ load. The maximum power of the winch is $5\,\mathrm{kW}$. Calculate the greatest possible acceleration of the load when its speed is $2.5\,\mathrm{m\,s^{-1}}$, and the greatest speed at which the load can be raised.

12 A car of mass of 950 kg moves along a horizontal road with its engine working at a constant rate of 25 kW. The car accelerates from 14 m s^{-1} to 18 m s^{-1}. Assuming that there is no resistance to motion, calculate the time taken.

13 The engine of a car of mass 1200 kg works at a constant rate of 18 kW. The car is moving on a horizontal road. Find the acceleration of the car at the instant when its speed is 25 m s^{-1} and the resistance to motion has magnitude 200 N.

14 A locomotive of mass 50 000 kg pulls a train of mass 80 000 kg up a straight slope inclined at 0.5° to the horizontal, at a constant speed of 9 m s^{-1}. The resistance to motion is a constant force of magnitude 5000 N. Calculate the power generated by the locomotive.

15 A car of mass 1200 kg is moving along a horizontal road. The engine of the car is working at a constant power of 24 kW. The frictional resistance to motion has magnitude of 400 N. When the speed of the car is v m s^{-1}, show that the acceleration is $\dfrac{60 - v}{3v}$ m s^{-2}.

16 A car of mass 900 kg descends a straight hill which is inclined at 2° to the horizontal. The car passes through the points A and B with speeds 14 m s^{-1} and 28 m s^{-1} respectively. The distance AB is 500 metres. Assuming there are no resisting forces, and that the driving force produced by the car's engine is constant, calculate the power of the car's engine at A and at B.

17 A car of mass of 960 kg moves along a straight horizontal road with its engine working at a constant rate of 20 kW. Its speed at A on the road is 10 m s^{-1}. Assuming that there is no resistance to motion, calculate the time taken for the car to travel from A until its speed reaches 20 m s^{-1}.

Assume now that there is a constant resistance to motion and that the car's engine continues to work at 20 kW. It takes 12 seconds for the car's speed to increase from 10 m s^{-1} to 20 m s^{-1}. During this time the car travels 190 metres. Calculate the work done against the resistance and hence find the magnitude of the resistance.

18 A pump, taking water from a large reservoir, is used to spray a jet of water with speed 20 m s^{-1} and radius 0.05 metres from a nozzle level with the surface of the reservoir. Calculate the power of the pump.

Miscellaneous exercise 2

1 A small block is pulled along a rough horizontal surface at a constant speed of 2 m s^{-1} by a constant force. This force has magnitude 25 N and acts at an angle of 30° to the horizontal. Calculate the work done by the force in 10 seconds.   (OCR)

2 The power developed by a motorcycle, as it travels on a horizontal straight road at a constant speed of 50 m s^{-1}, is 25 kW. Calculate the resistance to the motion of the motorcycle.   (OCR)

3 A crate of mass 5 kg is pulled directly up a rough slope, of inclination 10°, by a constant force of magnitude 20 N, acting at an angle of 30° above the horizontal. Find the work done by the force as the crate moves a distance of 3 m up the slope.   (OCR)

4 A car of mass 852 kg is moving on a horizontal road. The resistance to motion has magnitude 95 N. Find the power of the engine at an instant when the speed is $15 \, \mathrm{m \, s^{-1}}$ and the acceleration is $1.2 \, \mathrm{m \, s^{-2}}$. State where the external forces, causing the motion of the car, act, and identify their nature.   (OCR)

5 A motorcyclist is travelling on a straight level road, with the engine working at a rate of 6 kW. The total mass of the motorcyclist and her machine is 200 kg. Ignoring any air resistance, find the acceleration at an instant when the speed is $20 \, \mathrm{m \, s^{-1}}$.   (OCR)

6 A car of mass 1000 kg travels on a horizontal straight road. The resistance to motion is modelled as a constant force of magnitude 380 N. Find the power of the car's engine at an instant when the car has a speed of $12 \, \mathrm{m \, s^{-1}}$ and an acceleration of $0.7 \, \mathrm{m \, s^{-2}}$.   (OCR)

7 A barge is pulled along a straight canal by a horse on the towpath. The barge and the horse move in parallel straight lines 5 m apart. The tow-rope is 13 m long and it remains taut and horizontal. The horse and the barge each move at a constant speed of $0.78 \, \mathrm{m \, s^{-1}}$ and the tow-rope has a constant tension of 400 N. Calculate the work done by the horse on the barge in 10 minutes.   (OCR)

8 A locomotive of mass 48 900 kg pulls a train of 8 trucks, each of mass 9200 kg, up a straight slope inclined at 1° to the horizontal, at a constant speed of $8 \, \mathrm{m \, s^{-1}}$. The total of the resistances to motion of the locomotive and its trucks is modelled as a constant force of magnitude 4000 N. Calculate the power generated by the locomotive.

At a later instant the locomotive and trucks are travelling along a straight horizontal track at a speed of $20 \, \mathrm{m \, s^{-1}}$, with the locomotive continuing to work at the same rate as before. With the same model for the total of the resistances as before, find the acceleration at this instant.   (OCR)

9 A car of mass 1220 kg travels up a straight road which is inclined at an angle α to the horizontal, where $\sin \alpha = 0.05$. The resistances to motion are modelled as a constant force of magnitude 1400 N. The car travels a distance of 25.8 metres while increasing its speed from $8 \, \mathrm{m \, s^{-1}}$, at the point X, to $12 \, \mathrm{m \, s^{-1}}$ at the point Y. Calculate the work done by the car's engine in travelling from X to Y.

The car's engine works at a constant rate of 40 kW. Calculate the time taken to travel from X to Y.   (OCR)

10 A car of mass 700 kg descends a straight hill which is inclined at an angle of 3° to the horizontal. The car passes through the points P and Q with speeds of $12 \, \mathrm{m \, s^{-1}}$ and $30 \, \mathrm{m \, s^{-1}}$ respectively. The distance PQ is 500 metres. Assuming there are no resistances to motion, calculate the work done by the car's engine for the journey from P to Q.

Assuming further that the driving force produced by the car's engine is constant, calculate the power of the car's engine at P, at Q, and at the midpoint of PQ.   (OCR)

11 A resistive force acts on a cyclist, as she free-wheels down a straight hill at constant speed. The cyclist and her machine are modelled as a particle of mass 70 kg, and the resistive force as a constant force. This constant force has magnitude 48 N and acts upwards in a direction parallel to the hill. Calculate the angle of inclination of the hill to the horizontal.

The cyclist reaches the foot of the hill at a speed of $6 \, \text{m s}^{-1}$ and starts to pedal, travelling along a horizontal straight road. The cyclist works at a constant rate of 624 W. By modelling the resistive force as a constant horizontal force of magnitude 48 N, calculate the acceleration of the cyclist immediately after she starts pedalling. Show that her subsequent speed on the horizontal road cannot exceed $13 \, \text{m s}^{-1}$. (OCR)

12 A car of mass 1050 kg moves along a straight horizontal road with its engine working at a constant rate of 25 kW. Its speed at a point A on the road is $12 \, \text{m s}^{-1}$. Assuming that there is no resistance to motion, calculate the time taken for the car to travel from A until it reaches a speed of $20 \, \text{m s}^{-1}$.

Assume now that there is a constant resistance to motion and that the car's engine continues to work at 25 kW. It takes 10.7 s for the car's speed to increase from $12 \, \text{m s}^{-1}$ to $20 \, \text{m s}^{-1}$. During this time the car travels 179 m. Calculate the work done against the resistance and hence find the magnitude of the resistance.

Later the car moves up a straight hill, inclined at 2° to the horizontal. The engine works at 25 kW as before, and there is a constant resistance of the same magnitude as before. The car travels a distance of 393 m while its speed increases from $12 \, \text{m s}^{-1}$ to $20 \, \text{m s}^{-1}$. Calculate the time taken by the car to travel this distance. (OCR)

13 A car starts from rest and travels on a horizontal straight road. A resisting force acts on the car. By modelling the resisting force as a constant force of magnitude 750 N acting in the direction opposite to the motion of the car, calculate the maximum speed which the car can reach with its engine working at a constant rate of 30 kW.

The car, with its engine switched off, can easily be pushed by one person along the horizontal road. State, giving a reason, whether or not the model for the resisting force is realistic at low speeds.

The maximum power of the car is 40 kW and the mass of the car is 1250 kg. Calculate the maximum speed the car can attain after starting from rest and while travelling up a straight hill inclined at 3° to the horizontal, assuming that the resistance of 750 N continues to act. (OCR)

14 A car manufacturer plans to bring out a new model with a top speed of $65 \, \text{m s}^{-1}$ to be capable of accelerating at $0.1 \, \text{m s}^{-2}$ when the speed is $60 \, \text{m s}^{-1}$. Wind-tunnel tests on a prototype suggest that the air resistance at a speed of $v \, \text{m s}^{-1}$ will be $0.2v^2$ newtons. Find the power output (assumed constant) of which the engine must be capable at these high speeds, and the constraint which the manufacturer's requirement places on the total mass of the car and its occupants.

15 If the air resistance to the motion of an airliner at speed $v \, \text{m s}^{-1}$ is given by kv^2 newtons at ground level, then at 6000 metres the corresponding formula is $0.55kv^2$, and at 12 000 metres it is $0.3kv^2$. If an airliner can cruise at $220 \, \text{m s}^{-1}$ at 12 000 metres, at what speed will it travel at 6000 metres with the same power output from the engines?

Suppose that $k = 2.5$ and that the mass of the airliner is 250 tonnes. As the airliner takes off its speed is $80 \, \text{m s}^{-1}$ and it immediately starts to climb with the engines developing three times the cruising power. At what angle to the horizontal does it climb?

3 Potential energy

This chapter makes a distinction between two kinds of force, conservative and non-conservative, and shows how the former can be regarded as the source of a store of energy. When you have completed the chapter, you should

- know how to calculate work done by a constant force acting on an object which moves in a curved path
- know the difference between conservative and non-conservative forces
- know that the work done against a conservative force creates potential energy
- understand and be able to apply the principle of conservation of energy
- know that the total energy (potential and kinetic) can be changed by the work done by non-conservative forces.

3.1 Another expression for work

In Section 2.2 the work done by a force was defined as $(F \cos \theta) \times s$; that is, the product of the resolved part of the force and the distance moved by the object it acts on. Another way of writing this product is to link the factor $\cos \theta$ with s rather than F, as $F \times (s \cos \theta)$.

This is illustrated in Fig. 3.1. If the object moves from A to B under the action of the force, then $s \cos \theta$ is the distance AK, where K is the foot of the perpendicular from B to the line of action of the force. That is, AK is the displacement of the object in the direction of the force.

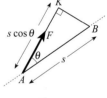

Fig. 3.1

So, if an object moves along a line under the action of a force of magnitude F, the work done by the force is equal to the product of F and the distance that the object moves in the direction of the force.

If you know about scalar products of vectors (see C4 Chapter 9), you will recognise this as the scalar product $\mathbf{F} \cdot \mathbf{r}$, where $\mathbf{r}$ denotes the displacement $\overrightarrow{AB}$.

Fig. 3.1 shows this when the object moves in a straight line, but it is also true if the object moves in a curved path, as in Fig. 3.2.

To show this, you can divide the path up into a lot of small steps AB, BC, $CD, \ldots$, for each of which the straight chord can't be distinguished from the curve. In these steps the displacements of the object in the direction of F are AK, KL, LM, $\ldots$. So the work done is

Fig. 3.2

$$F \times AK + F \times KL + F \times LM + \ldots = F(AK + KL + LM + \ldots).$$

This means that, in the statement in the third paragraph in this section, you can replace the word 'line' by 'curve':

> If an object moves along a curve under the action of a constant force of magnitude F, the work done by the force is equal to the product of F and the distance that the object moves in the direction of the force.

Example 3.1.1

A small sphere of mass m is suspended from a hook by a thread of length l. The sphere is pulled sideways so that the thread makes an angle of 60° with the downward vertical, and then released from rest. How fast is the sphere moving when the thread becomes vertical?

Fig. 3.3 shows that, after the sphere is released, there are two forces on the sphere, its weight and the tension in the thread. Since the sphere goes round part of a circle, it is always moving at right angles to the direction of the thread, so the work done by the tension is zero.

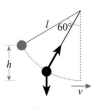

Fig. 3.3

The weight mg acts vertically downwards, so the work done by the weight is equal to mg times the distance that the sphere moves in the vertical direction. This distance is just the vertical height h of the initial position above the lowest point of the circle.

The speed v of the sphere at the lowest point can be found by using the work–energy principle,

$$(mg)\,h = \tfrac{1}{2}mv^2.$$

This gives $v^2 = 2gh$, so $v = \sqrt{2gh}$.

Now you can find h by trigonometry. From the right-angled triangle in Fig. 3.4, the initial position of the sphere is a distance $l \cos 60°$ below the hook. So
$h = l - l\cos 60° = l\left(1 - \tfrac{1}{2}\right) = \tfrac{1}{2}l.$

Substituting this in $v = \sqrt{2gh}$ gives

$$v = \sqrt{2g\left(\tfrac{1}{2}l\right)} = \sqrt{gl}.$$

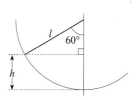

Fig. 3.4

When the thread is vertical the speed of the sphere is $\sqrt{gl}$.

3.2   Three problems with one answer

Here are three problems which you already know how to solve.

1 A stone is thrown vertically upwards with initial speed u. Find its speed v when it has risen to a height h.

2 A stone is thrown at an angle θ to the horizontal with initial speed u. Find its speed v when it has risen to a height h.

3 A stone is hit and starts to move up a smooth path at an angle α to the horizontal. If its initial speed is u, find its speed v when it is at a height h above its starting point.

The solutions are as follows.

1 This is a straight application of the constant acceleration equation $v^2 = u^2 + 2as$. Writing $a = -g$ and $s = h$ gives

$$v^2 = u^2 - 2gh$$

2 Denote the horizontal and vertical components of the velocity at height h by $\dot{x}$ and $\dot{y}$. It was shown in Section 1.2 that $\dot{x}$ has the constant value $u\cos\theta$. Also $\dot{y}$ can be found by using the constant acceleration formulae with initial velocity $u\sin\theta$, $a = -g$ and $s = h$, so $\dot{y}^2 = (u\sin\theta)^2 - 2gh$. Combining the components using $v^2 = \dot{x}^2 + \dot{y}^2$ gives

$$\begin{aligned} v^2 &= (u\cos\theta)^2 + \left((u\sin\theta)^2 - 2gh\right) \\ &= u^2\cos^2\theta + u^2\sin^2\theta - 2gh \\ &= u^2 - 2gh, \qquad \text{since} \qquad \cos^2\theta + \sin^2\theta \equiv 1. \end{aligned}$$

3 Fig. 3.5 shows the two forces acting on the stone, its weight mg and the normal contact force N. By Newton's second law,

$$\mathcal{R}(\parallel \text{to the path}) \qquad -mg\sin\alpha = ma,$$

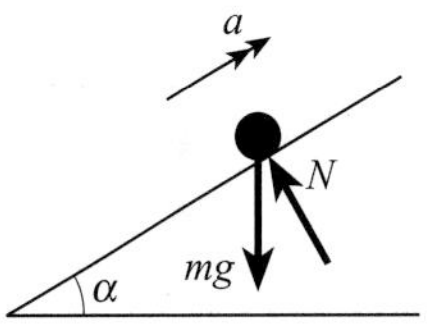

Fig. 3.5

so the stone has constant acceleration $-g\sin\alpha$ up the path. To reach a height h above its starting point it must travel a distance $\dfrac{h}{\sin\alpha}$ up the path. So, using the constant acceleration formula $v^2 = u^2 + 2as$,

$$v^2 = u^2 + 2(-g\sin\alpha) \times \frac{h}{\sin\alpha} = u^2 - 2gh.$$

The work–energy principle provides the explanation why these three problems all lead to the same answer. If you multiply each term of the equation $v^2 = u^2 - 2gh$ by $\frac{1}{2}m$, you get

$$\tfrac{1}{2}mv^2 = \tfrac{1}{2}mu^2 - mgh.$$

The terms $\frac{1}{2}mu^2$ and $\frac{1}{2}mv^2$ are the kinetic energy of the stone initially and after it has risen a height h. It remains to see why the kinetic energy is reduced by the same amount, mgh, in each case.

The stone thrown vertically upwards moves a distance h in the direction opposite to the weight mg, so mgh is the work done against the force of gravity.

The weight is still the only force for the stone thrown at an angle, but now the stone moves in a curve. The result in Section 3.1 shows that the work done against the force of gravity is equal to mg times the displacement of the stone in the direction opposite to the weight, which is again h.

For the stone moving up the smooth path there are two forces. The normal contact force does no work, because it acts at right angles to the direction in which the stone is moving. The result in Section 3.1 again provides the explanation why the work done against the force of gravity is mgh.

These examples illustrate how you can economise by using the work–energy principle. It provides a general theory which can be applied in a large number of situations which seem to be quite different.

3.3   Conservative and non-conservative forces

Here is a fourth problem which could have the same answer as those in the last section.

4   A stone is set in motion with speed u across a rough floor. The frictional force is F. Find the speed at which it is moving when it has gone a distance h horizontally.

Newton's second law gives $-F = ma$, so the acceleration has the constant value $-\dfrac{F}{m}$.

Using the formula $v^2 = u^2 + 2as$ with $a = -\dfrac{F}{m}$ and $s = h$ gives

$$v^2 = u^2 - 2\frac{F}{m}h.$$

Now suppose that F has the value mg. The equation would then become $v^2 = u^2 - 2gh$. This can again be expressed in work–energy form, as $\frac{1}{2}mv^2 = \frac{1}{2}mu^2 - mgh$, but this time the term mgh is the work done against the frictional force mg over the horizontal displacement h.

But there is an important difference between this example and those in Section 3.2. For the stones thrown into the air or hit up the smooth path, kinetic energy has been temporarily lost, but you will eventually get it all back when the stone returns to the same level as it started. For this reason the force of gravity is called a **conservative** force. You can think of gaining height as a way in which the stone can store up energy, which it can use later to recover its original kinetic energy.

It is quite different with the frictional force. In the fourth example, if the stone is allowed to continue across the floor, it will go on losing speed until it stops. The kinetic energy which it had to start with is lost, and there is no way of getting it back. The frictional force is said to be **non-conservative**.

3.4   The conservation of energy

Fig. 3.6 shows part of a roller-coaster ride. Consider an idealised model in which there is no friction or air resistance. At four points A, B, C and D on the ride the car has speeds p, q, r and s, and it is at heights a, b, c and d above ground level. The car has mass m and weight W, where $W = mg$.

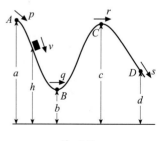

Fig. 3.6

The two forces on the car (with passengers) are its weight and the normal contact force from the track. The contact force does no work, because it always acts at right angles to the direction in which the car is moving.

Between A and B the car is descending with increasing speed. The car loses height of amount $a - b$, so the work done by the weight is $W(a - b)$. Therefore, by the work–energy principle,

$$W(a - b) = \tfrac{1}{2}mq^2 - \tfrac{1}{2}mp^2.$$

This equation can be rearranged as

$$Wa + \tfrac{1}{2}mp^2 = Wb + \tfrac{1}{2}mq^2.$$

Between B and C the car climbs and the speed decreases. Work is done against the weight of amount $W(c - b)$, so there is a decrease of kinetic energy of amount

$$\tfrac{1}{2}mq^2 - \tfrac{1}{2}mr^2 = W(c - b).$$

Rearranging,

$$Wb + \tfrac{1}{2}mq^2 = Wc + \tfrac{1}{2}mr^2.$$

Between C and D the car descends again, so

$$Wc + \tfrac{1}{2}mr^2 = Wd + \tfrac{1}{2}ms^2.$$

What these equations show is that, as the car goes up and down, its height h and speed v at any point vary so that the sum

$$Wh + \tfrac{1}{2}mv^2$$

remains constant. As h increases, v decreases, and vice versa.

The quantity Wh represents the car's store of energy, which can be traded in for increased kinetic energy by reducing h. It is called **potential energy**, and the property illustrated by the roller-coaster example is called the conservation of energy principle.

> **The conservation of energy principle**   For an object moving along a path, if there is no work done by external forces other than the force of gravity, the sum of the potential energy and the kinetic energy is constant.

The terms 'potential energy' and 'kinetic energy' are often abbreviated to their initials p.e. and k.e.

The idea of storing energy in the form of potential energy has many practical applications. For example, in mountainous areas valleys are often dammed to create a reservoir of water at a height above the surrounding land. This allows water to be released when required so that, as it loses height, it gains speed which can be used to drive a turbine and generate electricity.

Another example is in clock mechanisms. If you look inside the case of a grandfather clock you will find a heavy weight attached to a chain. The energy needed to keep the clock going is provided by raising the weight to the top of the case, thus creating a store of potential energy.

You can also think of Example 3.1.1 in terms of the conservation of energy. When the sphere is pulled aside, so that it is at a height $\tfrac{1}{2}l$ above the lowest point of the circle, potential energy of amount $mg\left(\tfrac{1}{2}l\right)$ is created. When the sphere is released, this is converted into kinetic energy of amount $\tfrac{1}{2}mv^2$.

Example 3.4.1

Fig. 3.7 shows the profile of a hill. The points A, B and C are at heights 80, 40 and 50 metres respectively above D. A snowmobile of mass 250 kg starts from rest at A and descends the hill without power. Neglecting any resistances, calculate how fast it is travelling at B, C and D.

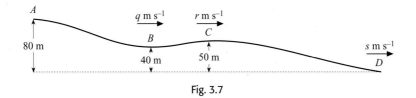

Fig. 3.7

Denote the speeds at B, C and D by q m s^{-1}, r m s^{-1} and s m s^{-1} respectively. The weight of the snowmobile is 2450 N, so the potential energy at a height of h metres is 2450h joules. The conservation of energy principle gives the equations

$$2450 \times 80 = 2450 \times 40 + 125q^2 = 2450 \times 50 + 125r^2 = 125s^2.$$

Notice that at the beginning there is no kinetic energy, and at the end there is no potential energy. At B and C there is both potential and kinetic energy.

From these equations you can calculate $q^2 = 784$, $r^2 = 588$ and $s^2 = 1568$, so $q = 28$, $r = 24.2\ldots$ and $s = 39.5\ldots$.

At B, C and D the snowmobile is travelling at about 28 m s^{-1}, 24 m s^{-1} and 40 m s^{-1} respectively.

In working this example all the heights have been taken to be measured above D, so that the potential energy at D is zero. But in fact you can take any level to be at 'zero height', so long as you are consistent right through the calculation. For example, D might be 600 m above sea level; if you choose to take the potential energy above sea level, then the potential energy terms in the equations would be 2450×680, 2450×640, 2450×650 and 2450×600.

Alternatively, you could choose to take the potential energy above B. In that case the heights at A, B, C and D would be 40, 0, 10 and -40. The conservation of energy equations would then be

$$2450 \times 40 = 125q^2 = 2450 \times 10 + 125r^2 = 2450 \times (-40) + 125s^2.$$

You can easily check that in either case you get the same answers as before. This is because, in a conservation of energy equation, measuring from a different level simply adds or subtracts the same amount on both sides of the equation, which doesn't affect the answer.

For instance, in Example 3.1.1 you could measure all the heights from the level of the hook. The sphere is initially $\frac{1}{2}l$ below the hook, and you want the speed v when it is l below the hook. The conservation of energy equation would then be

$$mg\left(-\tfrac{1}{2}l\right) = mg(-l) + \tfrac{1}{2}mv^2,$$

which gives the answer $v = \sqrt{gl}$, as before.

Exercise 3A

1 A particle of mass 2 kg falls freely from rest. Calculate the kinetic energy of the particle after it has descended 20 metres.

2 A stone of mass 0.8 kg is thrown vertically upwards with speed $10\,\mathrm{m\,s^{-1}}$. Calculate the initial kinetic energy of the stone, and the height to which it will rise.

3 A helicopter of mass 800 kg rises to a height of 170 metres in 20 seconds, before setting off in horizontal flight. Calculate the potential energy gain of the helicopter, and hence estimate the mean power of its engine. State a form of kinetic energy that has been ignored in this model.

4 A child of mass 25 kg slides 15 metres down a water-chute inclined at 30° to the horizontal, starting from rest. Calculate the speed the child would have at the foot of the chute, assuming no energy is lost during the descent.

5 A mountaineer of mass 65 kg scales a peak 3.2 km high. Calculate her gain in potential energy.

6 If no mechanical energy were lost, a skier descending a straight 40 metre slope would arrive at its foot with speed $15\,\mathrm{m\,s^{-1}}$. Calculate the angle the slope makes with the horizontal.

7 A boy reaches the foot of a helter-skelter ride with speed $7\,\mathrm{m\,s^{-1}}$, after starting from rest. Because of friction, only 25% of his initial potential energy has been converted into kinetic energy. Calculate the vertical distance the boy has descended.

8 A 160 kg barrel of bricks is raised vertically by a 2 kW engine. Calculate the distance the barrel will move in 7 seconds travelling at a constant speed.

9 A stone of mass 0.5 kg is attached to one end of a light inextensible string of length 0.4 metres. The other end of the string is attached to a fixed point O. The stone is released from rest with the string taut, and inclined at an angle of 40° below the horizontal through O. Calculate the speed of the particle as it passes beneath O. Calculate also the speed of the stone when the string makes an angle of 20° with the vertical through O.

10 A simple pendulum is modelled as a thread of length 0.7 metres, fixed at one end and with a particle (called the 'bob') attached to the other end. As the pendulum swings, the greatest speed of the bob is $0.6\,\mathrm{m\,s^{-1}}$. Calculate the angle through which the pendulum swings.

11 A particle of mass 0.2 kg is attached to one end of a light rod of length 0.6 metres. The other end of the rod is freely pivoted at a fixed point O. The particle is released from rest with the rod making an angle of 60° with the upward vertical through O. Calculate the speed of the particle when the rod is

(a) horizontal,   (b) vertical.

12 A bead is threaded on a smooth circular wire hoop. The radius of the hoop is a metres. The bead is projected from the lowest point of the hoop with speed $u\,\mathrm{m\,s^{-1}}$, and just reaches the top of the hoop. Express u in terms of a and g.

13 A particle is projected with speed $4\,\mathrm{m\,s^{-1}}$ up a line of greatest slope of a smooth ramp inclined at 30° to the horizontal. It reaches the top of the ramp with speed $1.2\,\mathrm{m\,s^{-1}}$. Calculate the length of the ramp.

14 A cyclist of mass 90 kg arrives at the top of a hill travelling at $4\,\mathrm{m\,s^{-1}}$. Free-wheeling, he descends to a bridge and then climbs up to his house on the other side of the valley. The heights above sea level of the three points are 432, 350 and 387 metres respectively. Use a model which neglects resistances to estimate the cyclist's speed as he crosses the bridge and as he reaches his house. (See also Exercise 3B Question 10.)

3.5 Application to systems of connected objects

Conservation of energy can also be used to solve problems about a pair of objects connected by a string.

Example 3.5.1
A child constructs a toy in which a truck of mass 4 kg can run on a track at an angle of 30° to the horizontal. A light chain attached to the truck runs parallel to the track to a light pulley at its upper end, and then hangs vertically (see Fig. 3.8). A counterweight of mass 3 kg is attached to the free end of the chain. The system is released from rest with the counterweight at a height $\frac{1}{2}$ m above the floor. Assuming that no energy is lost in overcoming friction, find how fast the truck is moving when the counterweight hits the floor.

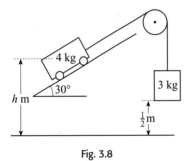

Fig. 3.8

Suppose that the truck is originally h metres above the floor. Let the speed with which the truck is moving as the counterweight hits the floor be $v\,\mathrm{m\,s^{-1}}$. If the chain is inextensible, the counterweight will also be moving at $v\,\mathrm{m\,s^{-1}}$.

At the start there is no kinetic energy, but both the truck and the counterweight have potential energy, of amounts $(4g)h$ joules and $(3g)\frac{1}{2}$ joules respectively, where $g = 9.8$. When the counterweight hits the floor, the truck has moved a distance $\frac{1}{2}$ m up the track, so it has gained a height of $\frac{1}{2}\sin 30°$ m, which is $\frac{1}{4}$ m. So, equating the total energy at the beginning and the end,

$$4gh + \tfrac{3}{2}g = 4g\left(h + \tfrac{1}{4}\right) + \tfrac{1}{2} \times 4 \times v^2 + \tfrac{1}{2} \times 3 \times v^2.$$

Cancelling the terms $4gh$ on each side, this can be simplified as

$$\left(\tfrac{3}{2} - 1\right)g = \tfrac{7}{2}v^2, \qquad \text{so} \qquad v^2 = \tfrac{1}{7}g, \qquad \text{and} \qquad v = 1.18\ldots.$$

The truck is moving at about $1.2\,\mathrm{m\,s^{-1}}$ as the counterweight hits the floor.

In this example you might wonder whether the tension in the chain contributes to the energy equation. The answer is that when you consider the system as a whole the tension does no work. As the truck and the counterweight move $\tfrac{1}{2}$ m, the tension of T newtons acting up the plane on the truck does work $T \times \tfrac{1}{2}$ J, and the tension of T newtons acting upwards on the counterweight does work $(-T) \times \tfrac{1}{2}$ J. These add up to zero.

You can, though, find the tension by writing a work–energy equation for the truck by itself. During the motion the truck gains potential energy $4g \times \tfrac{1}{4}$ J and kinetic energy $\tfrac{1}{2} \times 4 \times v^2$. So, equating the gain in energy to the work done by the tension,

$$\tfrac{1}{2}T = g + 2\left(\tfrac{1}{7}g\right),$$

which gives $T = \tfrac{18}{7}g = 25.2$. The tension in the chain is therefore $25.2\,\mathrm{N}$.

> You can check for yourself that this is the same answer as you get using the method described in M1 Chapter 7.

3.6 Including non-conservative forces in the equation

The speeds calculated in Example 3.4.1 are unrealistic, since resistance is not taken into account. Because some of this will be air resistance, it is likely to be greater at higher speeds. The next example tries to model the motion of the snowmobile more realistically.

Example 3.6.1
Suppose that in Example 3.4.1 the distances AB, BC and CD measured along the hill are $200\,\mathrm{m}$, $100\,\mathrm{m}$ and $300\,\mathrm{m}$. Estimate the average resistance to motion along these stretches of the hill to be $280\,\mathrm{N}$, $360\,\mathrm{N}$ and $380\,\mathrm{N}$. For the uphill stretch from B to C the motor is activated, producing a driving force of $700\,\mathrm{N}$. Calculate the speeds at B, C and D using this model.

Between A and B the work done against the resistance is 280×200 J, and the effect of this is to reduce the total energy (potential and kinetic) at B. So the first equation in Example 3.4.1 is replaced by

$$2450 \times 80 - 280 \times 200 = 2450 \times 40 + 125q^2.$$

Between B and C there are two extra terms in the equation, the work done by the driving force, which is 700×100 J, and the work done against the resistance, which is 360×100 J. So the equation is

$$2450 \times 40 + 125q^2 + 700 \times 100 - 360 \times 100 = 2450 \times 50 + 125r^2.$$

For the final stretch the work done against the resistance is 380×300 J, so

$$2450 \times 50 + 125r^2 - 380 \times 300 = 125s^2.$$

These equations give $125q^2 = 42\,000$, $125r^2 = 51\,500$ and $125s^2 = 60\,000$, so $q = \sqrt{336} = 18.3\ldots$, $r = \sqrt{412} = 20.2\ldots$ and $s = \sqrt{480} = 21.9\ldots$.

At B, C and D the snowmobile is moving at about $18\,\mathrm{m\,s^{-1}}$, $20\,\mathrm{m\,s^{-1}}$ and $22\,\mathrm{m\,s^{-1}}$.

This example shows that the conservation of energy principle has to be modified to take account of the driving force and the resistance, which are the non-conservative forces in the situation. Notice, though, that the work done by the weight no longer appears as a separate term in the equations, since this has already been included in the form of the potential energy.

> For an object moving along a path, the total energy (potential and kinetic) is increased by the work done by the non-conservative external forces.

In Example 3.6.1 the work done by the driving force between B and C is positive, but the work done by the resistance is negative, equal to minus the work done against the resistance.

Notice that potential energy can be used up either by conversion into kinetic energy, or in overcoming resistance. In Examples 3.4.1 and 3.5.1, all the potential energy lost is converted into kinetic energy. In Example 3.6.1 some of it is converted into kinetic energy and some is lost in work done against resistance. In the example of the grandfather clock, raising the weight inside the case doesn't make the clock run faster; the potential energy created when the weight is raised is all used to overcome the resistance inside the clock mechanism.

Example 3.6.2

Abe and Ben have mass $30\,\mathrm{kg}$ and $40\,\mathrm{kg}$ respectively. Abe is standing on the ground holding one end of a rope. Ben is 5 metres up a tree. Abe tosses the other end of his rope over a high branch. Ben grabs it, pulls it tight and then uses it to descend to the ground. As he does so, Abe keeps hold of the rope and goes up. As Ben reaches ground level, both boys are moving at $3\,\mathrm{m\,s^{-1}}$. How much work is done against the frictional force between the rope and the branch?

In the descent Ben loses potential energy of $40 \times 9.8 \times 5\,\mathrm{J}$, and Abe gains potential energy of $30 \times 9.8 \times 5\,\mathrm{J}$, so the net loss of potential energy is $(40 - 30) \times 9.8 \times 5\,\mathrm{J}$, which is $490\,\mathrm{J}$.

Both boys gain kinetic energy. Abe gains $\frac{1}{2} \times 30 \times 3^2\,\mathrm{J}$, and Ben gains $\frac{1}{2} \times 40 \times 3^2\,\mathrm{J}$, so the total gain is $\frac{1}{2} \times (30 + 40) \times 3^2\,\mathrm{J}$, which is $315\,\mathrm{J}$.

The only non-conservative force is the friction between the rope and the branch, so the loss of energy of $175\,\mathrm{J}$ must be accounted for by the work done against this frictional force.

Notice that in this example various minor complications have been neglected, such as the mass of the rope, air resistance and the possibility that the rope might stretch. None of these factors is likely to have much effect, and the calculated answer would give a good estimate of the loss of energy due to the friction.

Exercise 3B

1 Two particles of mass 0.3 kg and 0.5 kg are connected by a light inextensible string passing over a smooth rail. The particles are released from rest with the string taut and vertical except where it is in contact with the rail. Calculate the velocity of the particles after they have moved 1.3 metres.

2 Two children of mass 40 kg and 50 kg are holding on to the ends of a rope which passes over a thick horizontal branch of a tree. The parts of the rope on either side of the branch are vertical and the heavier child is moving downwards. A model is to be used in which the children may be considered as particles, and in which the rope is light and inextensible and is moving freely in a smooth groove on the branch. When the heavier child is moving at $2\,\text{m s}^{-1}$, she lets go of the rope. Calculate the further upward distance moved by the other child before falling back to the ground.

The motion described began with both children stationary. Calculate the distance they travelled before one let go of the rope.   (OCR, adapted)

3 Particles of mass 1.2 kg and 1.4 kg hang at the same level, connected by a long light inextensible string passing over a small smooth peg. They are released from rest with the string taut. Calculate the separation of the particles when they are moving with speed $0.5\,\text{m s}^{-1}$.

4 A particle of mass 1.2 kg is at rest 2 metres from the edge of a smooth horizontal table. It is connected by a light inextensible string, passing over a light pulley on smooth bearings at the edge of the table, to a particle of mass 0.7 kg which hangs freely. The system is released from rest.

Calculate

(a) the distance moved by the particles when their speed is $3\,\text{m s}^{-1}$,

(b) the speed of the particles just before the heavier particle reaches the pulley.

5 An object of mass 1.6 kg rests on a smooth slope inclined at 10° to the horizontal. It is connected by a light inextensible string passing over a smooth rail at the top of the slope to an object of mass 0.8 kg which hangs freely.

After their release from rest, calculate

(a) their speed when they have moved 0.5 metres,

(b) the distance they have moved when their speed is $3\,\text{m s}^{-1}$.

6 Two particles of mass 0.1 kg and 0.2 kg are attached to the ends of a light inextensible string which passes over a smooth peg. Given that the particles move vertically after being released from rest, calculate their common speed after each has travelled 0.6 m. Deduce the work done on the lighter particle by the string, and use this to calculate the tension in the string.

7 A particle of mass 2.2 kg rests on a smooth slope inclined at 30° to the horizontal. It is connected by a light inextensible string passing over a smooth rail at the top of the slope to a particle of mass 2.7 kg which hangs freely. The particles are set in motion by projecting the lighter down a line of greatest slope with speed 4 m s^{-1}. Find the distance the particles travel before their direction of motion is reversed. Find the total energy gained by the hanging mass during this part of the motion, and hence find the tension in the string.

8 An airliner of mass 300 tonnes is powered by four engines, each developing 15 000 kW. Its speed at take-off is 75 m s^{-1}, and it takes 11 minutes to reach its cruising speed of 210 m s^{-1} at a height of 10 000 metres. Calculate the work done against air resistance during the climb.

9 A and B are two points 1 km apart on a straight road, and B is 60 metres higher than A. A car of mass 1200 kg passes A travelling at 25 m s^{-1}. Between A and B the engine produces a constant driving force of 1600 newtons, and there is a constant resistance to motion of 1150 newtons. Calculate the speed of the car as it passes B.

10 A more realistic model for the cyclist's motion in Exercise 3A Question 14 includes a resistance force of constant magnitude, which produces a value of 15 m s^{-1} for the speed of the cyclist as he crosses the bridge. The road lengths of the downhill and uphill stretches of his ride are 820 metres and 430 metres respectively. Calculate the resistance force. Show that he won't be able to complete the journey without pedalling, and find the constant force necessary on the uphill stretch to produce the energy to reach his house.

Miscellaneous exercise 3

1 A particle is at rest at the apex A of a smooth fixed hemisphere whose base is horizontal. The hemisphere has centre O and radius a. The particle is then displaced very slightly from rest and moves on the surface of the hemisphere. At the point P on the surface where angle $AOP = \theta$ the particle has speed v. Find an expression for v in terms of a, g and θ.   (OCR)

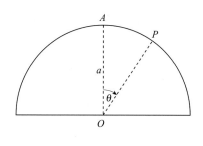

2 A smooth plane AB is 10 metres long. It is inclined at 30° to the horizontal with the lower end, B, 6 metres vertically above horizontal ground. A particle is placed on the plane at the upper end, A, and then released from rest so that it slides down the plane. Find the speed of the particle as it strikes the ground.   (OCR)

3 A skier of mass 70 kg set off, with initial speed of 5 m s^{-1}, down the line of greatest slope of an artificial ski-slope. The ski-slope is 80 metres long and is inclined at a constant angle of 20° to the horizontal. During the motion the skier is to be modelled as a particle.

(a) Calculate the potential energy that the skier loses in sliding from the top to the bottom of the slope.

(b) Ignoring air resistance and friction, calculate the speed of the skier at the bottom of the slope.

The skier actually reaches the bottom of the slope with speed $6\,\mathrm{m\,s^{-1}}$. Calculate the magnitude of the constant resistive force along the slope which could account for this final speed.   (OCR)

4 Two bodies, of mass $3\,\mathrm{kg}$ and $5\,\mathrm{kg}$, are attached to the ends of a light inextensible string. The string passes over a smooth fixed rail and the particles are moving vertically with both vertical parts of the string taut. Find the speed of the particles when they have travelled 0.4 metres, and deduce the magnitude of their acceleration.

5 The diagram shows a light inextensible string passing over a fixed smooth pulley. Particles A, of mass $4\,\mathrm{kg}$, and B, of mass $3\,\mathrm{kg}$, are attached to the ends of the string and each of the two parts of the string that are not in contact with the pulley is vertical. The system is released from rest with the string taut, with A at a height of 1.4 m above the horizontal step, and with B on the floor. The modelling assumption is made that the acceleration of each particle is constant. Calculate the speed with which A hits the step. State a physical force that has been neglected in the above model.   (OCR)

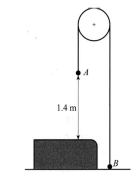

6 Particles, of mass $1.5\,\mathrm{kg}$ and $2\,\mathrm{kg}$, are attached to the ends of a light inextensible string. The string passes over a light pulley on smooth bearings, fixed at the top of the smooth, sloping face of a fixed wedge. The $2\,\mathrm{kg}$ mass is at rest on the sloping face, which is inclined at 30° to the horizontal. The $1.5\,\mathrm{kg}$ mass hangs freely and the string is taut. The particles are released. Find the speed of the particles when they have travelled 0.7 metres, and state the direction of motion of the $1.5\,\mathrm{kg}$ mass.

7 A car of mass $650\,\mathrm{kg}$ is travelling on a straight road inclined to the horizontal at 5°. At a certain point P on the road the car's speed is $15\,\mathrm{m\,s^{-1}}$. The point Q is 400 metres down the hill from P, and at Q the car's speed is $35\,\mathrm{m\,s^{-1}}$. For the motion from P to Q, find

(a) the increase in kinetic energy of the car,

(b) the decrease in gravitational potential energy of the car.

Neglecting any resistances to the car's motion, and assuming that the car's engine produces a constant tractive force on the car as it moves down the hill from P to Q, calculate the magnitude of the tractive force and the power of the car's engine when the car is at Q.

Assume instead that resistance to the car's motion between P and Q may be represented by a constant force of magnitude $900\,\mathrm{N}$. Given that the acceleration of the car at Q is zero, show that the power of the car's engine at this instant is approximately $12\,\mathrm{kW}$.

Assuming that the power of the car's engine is the same when the car is at P as it is when the car is at Q, calculate the car's acceleration at P.   (OCR)

8 A smooth wire is bent into the shape of the graph of $y = x + 2\sin x$ for $0 < x < 2\pi$, the units being metres. Points A, B and C on the wire have coordinates $(0, 0)$, (π, π) and $(2\pi, 2\pi)$. A bead of mass m kg is projected along the wire from A with speed u m s^{-1} so that it has enough energy to reach B but not C. Prove that u is between 8.66 and 11.10, to 2 decimal places, and that the speed at B is at least 3.66 m s^{-1}.

If $u = 10$, the bead comes to rest at a point D between B and C. Find

(a) the greatest speed of the bead between B and D,

(b) the coordinates of D, correct to 1 decimal place.

What happens after the bead reaches D?

9 A block of mass M is placed on a rough horizontal table. A string attached to the block runs horizontally to the edge of the table, passes round a smooth peg, and supports a sphere of mass m attached to its other end. The motion of the block on the table is resisted by a frictional force of magnitude F, where $F < mg$. The system is initially at rest.

(a) Show that, when the block and the sphere have each moved a distance h, their common speed v is given by $v^2 = \dfrac{2\,(mg - F)\,h}{M + m}$.

(b) Show that the total energy lost by the sphere as it falls through the distance h is $\dfrac{m\,(Mg + F)\,h}{M + m}$. Hence find an expression for the tension in the string.

(c) Write down an expression for the energy gained by the block as it moves through the distance h. Use your answer to check the expression for the tension which you found in part (b).

10 A tube is bent into the form of a semicircle with centre O and radius r. It is fixed in a vertical plane with its diameter horizontal, as shown in the diagram. A steel ball is held at one end A of the tube, and released. Throughout its motion the ball experiences a resistance of constant magnitude R. The ball first comes to rest at B, where OB makes an angle of $\frac{1}{3}\pi$ with the vertical. It then runs back down the tube and next comes to rest at C, where OC makes an angle α with the vertical.

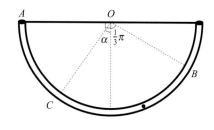

(a) Show that $R = \dfrac{3mg}{5\pi}$.

(b) Find the speed of the ball at the lowest point of the tube
    (i) as it moves from A to B,
    (ii) as it moves from B to C.

(c) Show that $0.6\alpha = \pi\,(\cos\alpha - 0.7)$.

(d) Explain why the ball will continue to oscillate after reaching C if $\alpha > \sin^{-1}\left(\dfrac{0.6}{\pi}\right)$, and determine whether this condition is satisfied.

4 Moments

The objects in this chapter are not particles but rigid objects, which can turn about a point such as a hinge. When you have completed the chapter, you should

- understand the model of a rigid object
- understand that a rigid object has a centre of mass
- know that the turning effect of a force is measured by its moment
- be able to calculate moments of forces
- be able to solve problems about the equilibrium of rigid objects by taking moments about chosen points.

4.1 Rigid objects

You have probably used a spoon to open a tin of coffee. You slide the end of the handle into the gap between the rim of the tin and the lid, and prise the lid up by pushing down on the bowl of the spoon, as in Fig. 4.1.

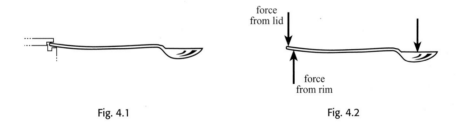

Fig. 4.1   Fig. 4.2

There are three main forces acting on the spoon (Fig. 4.2):

- the force pushing down on the bowl of the spoon;
- the contact force from the underside of the lid, which is the reaction to the force from the spoon pushing the lid up;
- the contact force from the rim of the tin.

A fourth force is the weight of the spoon, but this is likely to be small compared with the other three. It could be neglected in an approximate calculation.

You couldn't use any old spoon to do this. The handle of a cheap metal spoon would probably bend when you push down on the bowl, and a plastic spoon would snap. You need a strong spoon which will keep its shape when you apply enough force to lift the lid.

An object which stays the same shape when forces are applied to it is said to be **rigid**.

The idea of a rigid object is another example of a mathematical model. In reality, it is impossible to make an object whose shape is completely unaffected by the forces applied to it. Geologists have shown that even the hardest rocks will compress and shear under the forces to which they are subjected by earth movements. But there are many objects whose behaviour approximates very closely to the rigid model.

Up to now you have modelled all the objects in mechanics problems as particles. This does not mean that they are necessarily small. A tree trunk, an aircraft, or even the Earth can be treated as a particle so long as you are only interested in equilibrium or motion without rotation, with all the forces acting through the point where the particle is located.

But there is no way in which the spoon in Fig. 4.1 could be modelled as a particle. The whole point of using it is to apply a force acting along one line to produce a much larger force which acts along a different line. And when the lid starts to lift, the spoon will not move along a line but will rotate about the rim of the tin.

So the rigid object model is quite different from the particle model, and new principles and equations will be needed to solve problems about rigid objects.

4.2   Centres of mass

An important property of rigid objects is that they have a point at which, for many purposes, the whole mass may be supposed to be concentrated. This point is called the **centre of mass** of the object.

Take a rigid object with an irregular shape, such as a tennis racket. Lay it over the arm of a chair with the handle at right angles to the arm and the frame horizontal. Adjust the position of the racket on the arm until it balances, and then stick a piece of tape at the point of balance. The point on the central axis of the racket under the tape is the centre of mass.

Now fix a nail into a wall and hang the racket over the nail at some point of the string mesh. Whichever point you choose, you should find that the racket hangs with the centre of mass directly below the nail.

Go out to a playing field, hold the racket by its handle and throw it into the air across the grass. The racket will probably spin round quite erratically, but ignore this and keep your eye on the motion of the tape. This will move along quite a smooth trajectory, just like a ball thrown in a similar way. (If you have a camcorder or a cine-camera, you can show this more precisely. Keep the camera still, and plot the path of the tape from a sequence of stills.)

Every rigid object has a centre of mass, but it can be quite complicated to calculate where it is. However, the centre of mass for objects with simple shapes is usually where you would expect it to be.

If an object is made of the same material with the same density all the way through, it is said to be **uniform**. For any uniform rigid object with a centre of geometrical symmetry, the centre of mass is at the centre of symmetry.

For example, the centre of mass of a uniform cylinder is at the midpoint of the axis; the centre of mass of a uniform cuboid is at the point where the diagonals meet; and so on.

Notice, though, that the centre of mass of an object may not actually be at a point of the physical object. For example, the centre of mass of a uniform hollow pipe lies on its axis, which is in open space.

4.3   The moment of a force

Take a strip of wood just over a metre long, the heavier the better so long as it is uniform. Mark a metre scale symmetrically on it, so that it can be used as a ruler. Drill a hole at the zero point of the scale (as in Fig. 4.3). Pin the ruler to a wall with a nail through the hole. (Make the diameter of the hole larger than that of the nail.)

Left alone, the ruler will hang vertically, its weight supported by the contact force at the nail.

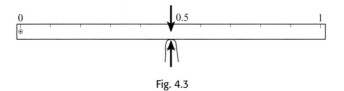

Fig. 4.3

Now support the ruler in a horizontal position by placing a finger underneath it at the midpoint of the scale, directly below the centre of mass, as in Fig. 4.3. The weight will then be completely supported by the contact force from your finger. If you look at the hole, you should find that the nail no longer exerts any force on the ruler.

Move your finger to the right end of the scale. You will now need to exert less force to support the ruler. If you look at the hole, you will see that the nail is in contact with the ruler at the top of the hole. The contact force from the nail is providing some of the force holding the ruler up, as in Fig. 4.4.

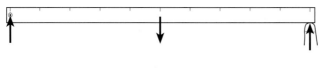

Fig. 4.4

Move your finger near to the left end of the scale. You will now have to exert a much larger force to keep the ruler horizontal. If you look at the hole, you will see that the nail is in contact with the ruler at the bottom of the hole. So you are having to push not only to support the weight of the ruler, but also against the contact force from the nail, as in Fig. 4.5.

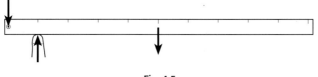

Fig. 4.5

To make this experiment more precise, you could replace your finger by a spring balance and measure the magnitude of the force. For a metre rule with a weight of 5 newtons, you might get a set of readings such as those in Table 4.6.

Distance of support from nail (m)	0.5	1.0	0.1
Supporting force (N)	5	2.5	25

Table 4.6

So if you double the distance of your finger from the nail (measured horizontally) from 0.5 m to 1 m, the force is halved from 5 N to 2.5 N. If you reduce the distance to one-fifth of its first value, from 0.5 m to 0.1 m, you multiply the force by five, from 5 N to 25 N.

The effect of a force varies according to the line along which it acts (see M1 Section 10.2). The experiment shows that if you multiply the magnitude of the supporting force by the distance of its line of action from the nail, you always get the same answer:

$$5 \times 0.5 = 2.5, \quad 2.5 \times 1.0 = 2.5, \quad \text{or} \quad 25 \times 0.1 = 2.5.$$

The interpretation of this is that the product of the force and the distance is a measure of the turning effect of the force about the nail. This is called the 'moment' of the force about the nail.

> The **moment** of a force about a point is calculated as the product of the magnitude of the force and the distance of its line of action from the point.

In the SI system of units the moment of a force is measured in units of 'newton metres' (abbreviated to N m) because it is calculated by multiplying a number of newtons by a number of metres.

In the experiment with the ruler there is one force which stays the same: the weight of the ruler. This acts at a distance of 0.5 m from the nail and has magnitude 5 N, so its moment about the nail is 5×0.5 N m. The turning effect of the weight is clockwise, of magnitude 2.5 N m.

This has to be balanced by the turning effect of the force from your finger, which is a moment of 2.5 N m anticlockwise.

Suppose now that you place your finger under the ruler one-quarter of the way along, below the 0.25 m mark on the scale, and that the force from your finger is F newtons. Then the moment of this force is $F \times 0.25$ N m anticlockwise, so you can write an equation

$$F \times 0.25 = 2.5.$$

This equation is described as **taking moments** about the nail. A useful shorthand for showing where your equation comes from is to write

$$\mathcal{M}(\text{nail}) \qquad F \times 0.25 = 5 \times 0.5.$$

That is, the anticlockwise moment of the force from your finger about the nail is equal to the clockwise moment of the weight. It follows that $F = 10$, so that in this position your finger must exert a force of 10 newtons.

Some people prefer to write equations of moments in the form

'anticlockwise moments – clockwise moments = 0'

rather than

'anticlockwise moments = clockwise moments.'

For example, the $\mathcal{M}$(nail) equation above would be written as $F \times 0.25 - 5 \times 0.5 = 0$. If you go on to study the mechanics of rotation (in M4) you will need to get used to putting all the moments on the left side of the equation. The drawback is the complication of having minus signs in the equation. Whichever form you use, it is very important to consider for each force whether its moment is anticlockwise or clockwise.

Example 4.3.1

A door is kept closed by a wedge, placed under the door at a distance of 75 cm from the hinge. A person tries to open the door by applying a force of 40 N at 60 cm from the hinge, but it doesn't move. Calculate the friction force between the wedge and the floor.

Fig. 4.7 shows the forces on the door which act horizontally. You must remember to put in the force from the hinge, even though it is not asked for.

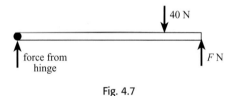

Fig. 4.7

There are also some vertical forces, the weight of the door and a vertical component of the hinge force. These have not been included in the diagram; they have no turning effect about the hinge.

It is simplest to use units of newton centimetres (N cm) for the moments. If the friction force is F newtons,

$\mathcal{M}$(hinge) $\qquad F \times 75 = 40 \times 60.$

So $\quad F = \dfrac{40 \times 60}{75} = 32.$

The friction force between the wedge and the floor is 32 newtons.

If you prefer to stick with basic SI units, with forces in newtons and distances in metres, then the equation of moments would be $F \times 0.75 = 40 \times 0.6$. Using centimetres instead of metres avoids the need for decimals, so the arithmetic is simpler. In the next example the masses are very large, so it is simpler to work with mass in tonnes rather than kilograms, and force in kilonewtons rather than newtons, to avoid having too many zeros in the numbers. But whenever you are doing mechanics with numerical data, it is important to remember what units you are working in. If you use non-standard units, it helps to indicate this by writing a note about units alongside your solution.

Example 4.3.2

Fig. 4.8 shows a simplified model of the horizontal arm of a crane which is being used to lift a load of 8 tonnes at a distance of 30 metres from the vertical column. The arm itself has a mass of 1.4 tonnes, distributed uniformly; its length is 50 metres, of which 10 metres extends on the opposite side of the column. Equilibrium is maintained by a counterbalance whose centre of mass is 9 metres from the column. Calculate the mass of the counterbalance.

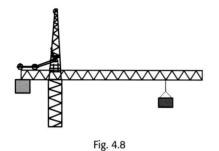

Fig. 4.8

In a numerical example like this, where you are given the masses of the components and have to find the weights, it often makes the arithmetic easier if you use the letter g to stand for the number 9.8. (This was discussed in M1 Section 7.5.) In this example you will find that g cancels out from the equations, so the answer is the same whatever value is taken for the acceleration due to gravity.

The forces on the arm, in kilonewtons, are shown in Fig. 4.9.

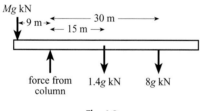

Fig. 4.9

Notice that although the arm extends on both sides of the column, it is still possible to take its weight of $1.4g$ kN to be concentrated at the centre of mass, which is 15 metres to the right of the column. Let the mass of the counterbalance be M tonnes, so that its weight is Mg kN.

Two of the forces, the weights of the arm and the load, have clockwise moments, and these are balanced by the anticlockwise moment of the weight of the counterbalance.

$\mathcal{M}$(column) $(Mg) \times 9 = 1.4g \times 15 + 8g \times 30.$

This gives $M = \dfrac{(21 + 240)\,g}{9g} = 29.$

To maintain equilibrium, a counterbalance of mass 29 tonnes is needed.

In all the examples so far the forces have been at right angles to the object on which they act. When this is not the case, you may need to use trigonometry to find the distance from the hinge to the line of action of the force.

Example 4.3.3

A beam of weight 400 N is attached to a fixed point by a hinge. The other end of the beam is supported by a smooth platform. The beam is at an angle of 20° to the horizontal. The beam is 5 metres long, and its centre of mass is 3 metres from the hinge, as shown in Fig. 1.10. Calculate the force from the platform on the beam.

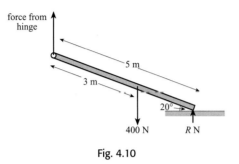

Fig. 4.10

Because the platform is smooth, the force from the platform on the beam acts vertically upwards. Let its magnitude be R N.

From the definition, the moment of the weight about the hinge is the product of its magnitude 400 N and the distance of its line of action from the hinge. This distance is measured perpendicular to the line of action, that is horizontally, as shown in Fig. 4.11(a). From the right-angled triangle, this distance is 3 cos 20° m.

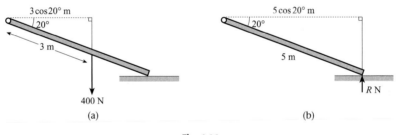

Fig. 4.11

Similarly, from Fig. 4.11(b), the distance from the hinge to the line of action of the normal contact force is 5 cos 20° m.

You can now write the equation of moments as

$\mathcal{M}$(hinge) $R \times 5 \cos 20° = 400 \times 3 \cos 20°$.

So $R = \dfrac{400 \times 3 \cos 20°}{5 \cos 20°} = 240.$

The force from the platform on the beam is 240 N vertically upwards.

You will see that in this example the factor cos 20° cancels out in the calculation of R. The answer would be the same if the beam were at any angle θ to the horizontal. The equation of moments would then be

$R \times 5 \cos \theta = 400 \times 3 \cos \theta,$

which still gives $R = 240$.

Exercise 4A

1 A closed carpark barrier is modelled as a rod of weight 40 N which is pivoted at a point. The centre of mass of the rod is 0.8 metres from the pivot, and it is supported horizontally at a point 2 metres from the pivot. Find the magnitude of the vertical force exerted on the rod by the support.

2 A steeplejack rides at one end of a uniform beam which is being moved into position in the skeleton of a high building, as shown in the diagram. The weight of the beam is 4200 N and the weight of the steeplejack is 800 N. Given that the length of the beam is 12 m, find the distance between the steeplejack and the crane's vertical chain when the beam is horizontal and the crane and the beam are at rest.

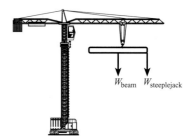

3 The total mass of two children is 60 kg. Find their separate masses, given that the children are balanced on a seesaw when one is 1.6 metres from the centre and the other is 1.4 metres from the centre.

When the heavier child sits 1.6 metres from the centre and the lighter child sits 1.4 metres from the centre, the seesaw is balanced by applying a vertically downward force, behind the lighter child, at a distance of 2 metres from the centre. Find the magnitude of this downward force.

4 The diagram shows a door being pushed on one side with a force of magnitude 60 N, at a distance of 69 cm from the hinged edge, and on the other side by a force of magnitude 90 N. The forces act at the same height, and both act at right angles to the plane of the door. Given that the door does not move, find the distance from the hinged edge at which the force of magnitude 90 N acts.

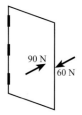

5 In each of the following cases a bone or collection of bones is modelled by a light rod. The rod is pivoted at P and carries a vertical load W newtons. The rod is held in position by the tension, acting vertically, in a tendon which connects the bone to a muscle. The magnitude of the tension is T newtons.

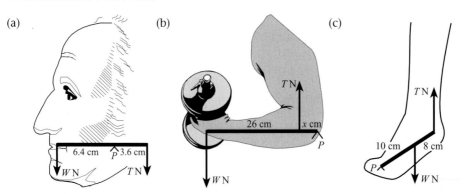

(a) Find the value of T given that $W = 27$.

(b) Given that $W = 40$ and $T = 300$, find x.

(c) Given that $T = 200$, find W.

6 Two men, each of mass 80 kg, and a woman of mass 64 kg, are walking on a horizontal straight path which forms an edge of a lake. The woman's expensive hat is blown into the lake, and is caught by reeds at a distance of 4 metres from the path. A rigid plank, of length 6 metres and whose weight can be ignored, is available for use in retrieving the hat, by allowing it to rest on the path while overhanging the lake, with two people standing on the part of the plank which is in contact with the path, and the third person effecting the recovery. Determine whether

(a) one of the men can effect the recovery, (b) the woman can effect the recovery.

7 A uniform rectangular hatch $ABCD$, of mass 12 kg, is hinged along its edge AB, and is horizontal when closed. A vertical force acting upwards through the midpoint of CD keeps the hatch open at a fixed angle. Assuming the weight of the hatch acts through the centre of $ABCD$, find the magnitude of the vertical force.

4.4 Forces from supports

In the experiment with the ruler in the last section, the supporting force from your finger was calculated from an equation of moments about the nail. But there are other ways of looking at it.

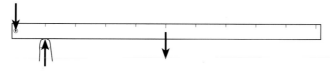

Fig. 4.12

Fig. 4.12, which is a copy of Fig. 4.5, shows the forces in the case when your finger is close to the nail, and it was found that at the hole the nail exerted a downward force on the ruler. You could calculate this force from the nail directly by resolving vertically for the forces on the ruler. It was shown earlier in Table 4.6 that the upward force from your finger is 25 N, and this must equal the sum of the weight of 5 N and the force from the nail. So the force from the nail is 20 N.

But you could also calculate this force by imagining your finger as the hinge about which the ruler could turn. In this case the weight of the ruler, 5 N, is acting along a line 0.4 m from your finger, so that it has a clockwise moment of 5×0.4 N m, that is 2 N m. This is balanced by the anticlockwise moment of the force from the nail, at a distance of 0.1 m from your finger. This force is therefore $\frac{2}{0.1}$ N, that is 20 N.

This is an example of a more general way of thinking about equations of moments.

> **The principle of moments**   If a rigid object is in equilibrium, the sum of the anticlockwise moments about any point must equal the sum of the clockwise moments.

The word to notice in this statement is 'any'. It is not necessary for there to be a hinge about which the object is able to turn. You can take moments about any point you like.

Example 4.4.1

A horizontal uniform plank of length 10 m and mass 50 kg is supported by two vertical ropes, attached at A, 2 m from the left end, and at B, 3 m from the right end. Two children stand on the plank: Jane (44 kg) 4 m from the left end, and Ken (36 kg) 2 m from the right end, as shown in Fig. 4.13. Find the tension in the ropes.

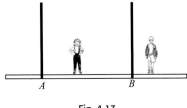

Fig. 4.13

As in Example 4.3.2, it helps to use the letter g to stand for the number 9.8.

There is no hinge here, but you can still take various points of the plank and consider the turning effects of the forces about them. Let the tensions in the ropes at A and B be S and T newtons respectively, as shown in Fig. 4.14.

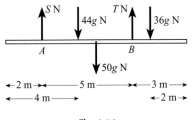

Fig. 4.14

For example, the tension T newtons has an anticlockwise moment about A, and this is balanced by the clockwise moments of the three weights.

$\mathcal{M}(A)$ $T \times 5 = 44g \times 2 + 50g \times 3 + 36g \times 6,$

which gives $T = 90.8g$.

Now substitute $g = 9.8$ to find the numerical value $T = 889.84$.

Now consider the turning effects about B. The weights of Jane and the plank have anticlockwise moments, but the moment of Ken's weight is clockwise.

$\mathcal{M}(B)$ $44g \times 3 + 50g \times 2 = 36g \times 1 + S \times 5,$

which gives $S = 39.2g = 392 \times 9.8 = 384.16.$

So the tensions in the ropes at A and B are 384 N and 890 N, correct to 3 significant figures.

As a check, note that the sum of the two tensions is $130g$ N, which is equal to the sum of the three weights.

In an example such as this, you are not restricted to taking moments about points at which the plank is attached to a rope. You could, for example, consider the moments about the left end of the plank. The three weights have a combined clockwise moment of $(44g \times 4 + 50g \times 5 + 36g \times 8)$ N m, that is $714g$ N m, and the two tensions have a combined anticlockwise moment of $(S \times 2 + T \times 7)$ N m. You can check that, with the values calculated, $S \times 2 + T \times 7 = (39.2g) \times 2 + (90.8g) \times 7 = 714g$.

You can in fact get a correct equation by taking moments about any point you like. The advantage of taking moments about A and B is that only one of the unknown forces comes into the equations. This is an example of a general strategy.

> You can remove an unknown or unwanted force from an equation by taking moments about a point on its line of action.

Example 4.4.2
A heavy rod AB of length 3 m lies on horizontal ground. To lift the end B off the ground needs a vertical force of 200 N. To lift A off the ground needs a force of 160 N. Find the weight of the rod, and the position of its centre of mass.

Let the weight of the rod be W newtons, and let the centre of mass be x metres from A. The two situations described are illustrated in Fig. 4.15.

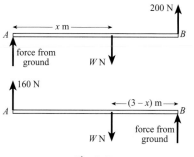

Fig. 4.15

When the end B is lifted:

$\mathcal{M}(A)$ $W \times x = 200 \times 3.$

When the end A is lifted:

$\mathcal{M}(B)$ $W \times (3 - x) = 160 \times 3.$

Adding these equations gives $W \times 3 = 1080$, so that $W = 360$. Then, from the first equation, $x = \dfrac{600}{360} = \dfrac{5}{3}$.

The rod has a weight of 360 N, and its centre of mass is $1\frac{2}{3}$ m from A.

Example 4.4.3

A car with front-wheel drive has mass 1000 kg, including the driver and passengers. The front wheels are 2.5 m in front of the rear wheels, and the centre of mass is 1.5 m in front of the rear wheels. The engine may be taken to have unlimited power. The coefficient of friction between the tyres and the road surface is 0.4.

(a) What is the maximum acceleration of which the car is capable?

(b) What difference would it make if bicycles of mass 75 kg were strapped to the back of the car 0.8 m behind the rear wheels?

The forward force on the car is produced by the friction at the front tyres. This cannot be more than 0.4 times the normal force S newtons between the front tyres and the ground. The normal force can be found by taking moments about the contact P between the rear tyres and the ground.

(a) The forces are shown in Fig. 4.16.

$$\mathcal{M}(P) \qquad S \times 2.5 = 9800 \times 1.5,$$

so $S = 5880$. Since the coefficient of friction is 0.4, the maximum forward force is 0.4×5880 N, that is 2352 N.

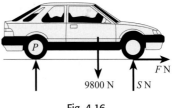

Fig. 4.16

Therefore, by Newton's second law, the maximum acceleration is $\frac{2352}{1000}$ m s^{-2}, that is 2.35 m s^{-2}, correct to 3 significant figures.

(b) There is now an additional anticlockwise moment of $(75 \times 9.8) \times 0.8$ N m.

$$\mathcal{M}(P) \qquad S \times 2.5 + 735 \times 0.8 = 9800 \times 1.5,$$

which reduces the value of S to 5644.8 N. The maximum forward force is therefore 0.4×5644.8 N, and the total mass is 1075 kg. The maximum acceleration is then

$$\frac{0.4 \times 5644.8}{1075} \text{ m s}^{-2}, \text{ or about } 2.10 \text{ m s}^{-2}.$$

Exercise 4B

1 The objects in these diagrams are in equilibrium.

(a) Find X and Y.   (b) Find X and y.

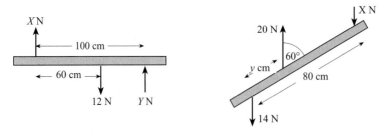

(c) Find X and Y.

(d) Find x and Y.

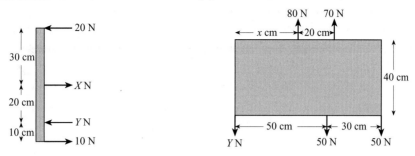

2 A uniform plank of length 4 m and weight 200 N rests on two supports, 0.8 m from one end and 1.2 m from the other. Find the vertical forces on the plank from the supports.

3 A log of wood is 6 m long and weighs 750 N. It rests on two trestles. Its centre of mass is 2 m from one end. One of the trestles is 1 m from that end, and this supports three-fifths of the weight. How far from the other end is the other trestle?

4 An oar is hung up by two vertical chains, attached to points 0.6 m and 3 m from the end of the shaft. The tensions in the chains are 25 N and 95 N respectively. How far from the end of the shaft is the centre of mass of the oar?

5 A metal rod 2 m long is lying on a smooth ice rink. The centre of mass of the rod is 0.8 m from one end. The rod is picked up by that end, which is held 1 m above the ice with a force of 15 N. Explain why this force is vertical, and find the weight of the rod.

6 A cyclist sits astride her stationary machine, with her feet lightly touching the ground and her hands lightly touching the handlebar. The mass of the machine is 14 kg, and the line of action of its weight is the perpendicular bisector of $O_f O_r$, where O_f and O_r are the centres of the front and rear wheels respectively. The mass of the cyclist is 80 kg and her weight acts in a line through the saddle. Given that the distance $O_f O_r$ is 1020 mm and that the vertical line through the saddle is 240 mm in front of O_r, find the magnitude of the force exerted by the ground on

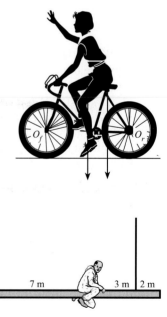

(a) the front wheel,   (b) the rear wheel.

7 A steeplejack rides on a structural beam which is being moved into position in the skeleton of a high building, as shown in the diagram. The mass of the beam and the mass of the steeplejack are 2000 kg and 80 kg respectively. The length of the beam is 12 m, and chains which hang vertically from the crane are attached at the left end of the beam and at a distance of 10 m from the left end. The steeplejack sits at a distance of 7 m from the left end. Find the tension in each of the chains when the beam is horizontal and at rest.

8 A uniform beam, of mass 16 kg and length 12 m, rests horizontally on supports at 2 m from its left end and 4 m from its right end. Find the force exerted on the beam by each of the supports, when a child of mass 32 kg and an adult of mass 70 kg stand on the beam at the left end and the right end respectively, as shown in the diagram.

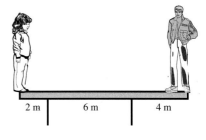

2 m   6 m   4 m

Find also the mass which the adult would need to be carrying for the beam to be just on the point of tilting.

9 Two men *A* and *B* carry a boat horizontally over their heads along a shore. The length of the boat is 17.5 m. One end of the boat overhangs *A*'s point of support by 2.5 m, and *B*'s point of support is at the other end of the boat. *A* supports a load of 720 N and *B* supports a load of 480 N. Calculate the distance from *B*'s end of the point through which the weight of the boat acts.

10 A uniform curtain rail of length 2.5 m and mass 5 kg rests horizontally on supports at its ends. Two curtains, each of mass 4 kg, hang from the rail. The left curtain is drawn across to the middle of the rail and the right curtain is drawn back to within 20 cm of the right support, as shown in the diagram. Assuming the weight of the left curtain acts at a distance of 0.625 m from the left end of the rail, and that the weight of the right curtain acts at a distance of 10 cm from the right end of the rail, find the magnitude of the vertical force exerted by each of the supports on the rail.

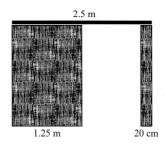

2.5 m

1.25 m   20 cm

The right curtain is now drawn partially across the window with the effect that the magnitude of the vertical force exerted by the right support decreases by 4.71 N. Making a suitable assumption, which should be stated, find the distance from the right support to which the right curtain is now drawn.

11 A light rigid rod rests horizontally on supports at its ends. The rod carries two equal point loads, one at distance x from one end and the other at distance x from the other end. Show that the magnitude of the vertical force acting on the rod at each of the supports is independent of x.

A light clothes rail of length 2.5 m rests horizontally on supports at its ends. The rail has 25 identical garments hanging on it, at points distant $(10n - 5)$ cm from one end, for $n = 1, 2, \ldots, 25$. The total weight of the garments is 250 N. State the magnitude of the vertical force acting on the rod at each of the supports.

The garments 5th and 14th from one end are removed. Find the magnitude of the vertical force now acting on the rod at each of the supports.

12 A cyclist and her machine have total mass 90 kg. The distance O_fO_r, where O_f and O_r are the centres of the front and rear wheels respectively, is 1 m. The total weight of the cyclist and her machine acts in a line 0.3 m in front of O_r.

(a) Find the magnitude of the normal contact force exerted by the ground on the rear wheel.

The coefficient of friction between the rear wheel and the ground is 0.45.

(b) Find the maximum possible frictional force exerted by the ground on the rear wheel.

(c) Hence find the maximum possible acceleration of the cyclist and her machine.

4.5 Forces in different directions

The examples so far have all involved forces in parallel directions, but the principle of moments applies whatever the direction of the forces.

Imagine for example a merry-go-round on a children's playground. You can turn this by exerting a horizontal force around the circumference. The turning effect of this force is the same, whatever way you are facing as you push.

Example 4.5.1
A uniform rectangular plate of weight W is held in a vertical plane as shown in Fig. 4.17. The plate has width a and height b. It is hinged at the lower left corner, and kept in equilibrium by a horizontal force F applied at the upper right corner. Find F in terms of a, b and W.

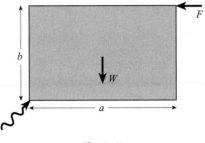

Fig. 4.17

When you show the forces in the diagram, it is important to include the force from the hinge as well as W and F. Draw it with a wavy line, as you do not know the exact direction in which it acts. For this reason take moments about the hinge, so this unknown force does not come into the equation.

The distances from the hinge to the lines of action of W and F are $\frac{1}{2}a$ and b respectively.

$\mathcal{M}(\text{hinge}) \qquad Fb = W\left(\frac{1}{2}a\right).$

It follows directly that $F = \dfrac{Wa}{2b}.$

Example 4.5.2

A drawbridge of weight W newtons is 4 metres long, and is supported by horizontal hinges along one edge. It is raised by a cable attached to the opposite edge which passes over a pulley 8 metres above the hinge. Find the tension in the cable which will support the weight of the bridge

(a) when it is horizontal (Fig. 4.18),

(b) when the cable is perpendicular to the bridge (Fig. 4.19).

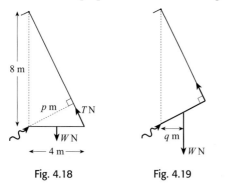

Fig. 4.18   Fig. 4.19

Denote the tension in the cable by T newtons. The force at the hinge is unknown, so T is calculated by taking moments about the hinge.

(a) The moment of the weight is $2WN$ m, but to find the moment of the tension needs trigonometry. Begin by noticing that the length of the cable up to the pulley is $4\sqrt{5}$ m. So, if the cable makes an angle x with the vertical,

$$\cos x = \frac{2}{\sqrt{5}} \text{ and } \sin x = \frac{1}{\sqrt{5}}.$$

There are two ways of calculating the moment of the tension.

Method 1   The perpendicular distance, p metres, from the hinge to the cable is $8 \sin x \text{ m} = \dfrac{8}{\sqrt{5}}$ m. So the moment of the tension is $\dfrac{8T}{\sqrt{5}}$ N m.

Method 2   Split the tension into two components, $T \cos x$ N vertically and $T \sin x$ N horizontally, as in Fig. 4.20. The vertical component has moment $4T \cos x \, \mathrm{N\,m} = \dfrac{8T}{\sqrt{5}} \, \mathrm{N\,m}$. The horizontal component has zero moment, since its line of action passes through the hinge.

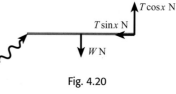

Fig. 4.20

Using either method,

$$\mathcal{M}(\text{hinge}) \qquad \frac{8T}{\sqrt{5}} = 2W.$$

Therefore $T = \frac{1}{4}\sqrt{5}\,W.$

(b) When the cable is perpendicular to the bridge, the angle between the bridge and the vertical is $\cos^{-1}\frac{4}{8} = 60°$. The perpendicular distance from the hinge to the cable is 4 metres, so the moment of the tension is $4T$ N m. To find the moment of the weight you need the perpendicular distance, q metres, from the hinge to its line of action, which is $2\cos 30°$ metres, that is $\sqrt{3}$ metres.

$\mathcal{M}$(hinge) $4T = \sqrt{3}\,W.$

Therefore $T = \frac{1}{4}\sqrt{3}\,W.$

Example 4.5.3
A crate of weight W newtons is 1.8 m long and 0.8 m high. It is carried up a staircase at an angle of 10° to the horizontal by men supporting the crate by vertical forces at its two lower corners A and B. What proportion of the total load is carried by the lower man?

Since only the force from the lower man is asked for, take moments about the corner B held by the upper man. Let the supporting forces be P newtons and Q newtons, as shown in Fig. 4.21; the weight of the crate is W newtons. Although all the forces are vertical, it is quite complicated to calculate the moments.

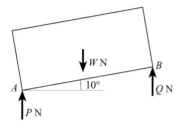

Fig. 4.21

Method 1   The moments about B of the forces P newtons and the weight are Px N m and Wy N m, where x metres and y metres are the distances marked in Fig. 4.22.

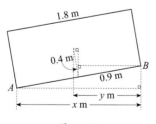

Fig. 4.22

These can be calculated from the right-angled triangles as

$x = 1.8\cos 10°$

and $y = 0.9\cos 10° + 0.4\sin 10°.$

$\mathcal{M}(B)$ $W(0.9\cos 10° + 0.4\sin 10°) = P(1.8\cos 10°).$

Method 2   Split the forces into components parallel to the sides of the crate, as in Fig. 4.23. The force of $P \sin 10°$ N has no moment about B, since its line of action passes through B.

$\mathcal{M}(B)$ $P \cos 10° \times 1.8 = W \cos 10° \times 0.9 + W \sin 10° \times 0.4.$

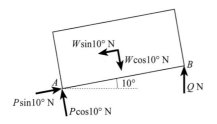

Fig. 4.23

You can easily see that both equations are the same and give

$$P = \frac{W}{1.8} \times (0.9 + 0.4 \tan 10°) = 0.539 \, W, \text{ correct to 3 significant figures.}$$

The man supporting the crate at A must exert a force of about $0.54 \, W$, which is 54% of the total load.

Exercise 4C

1 Find the moment of the force shown, about the point O, in each of the following cases.

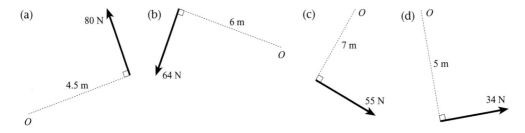

2 Find the total moment about O of the forces shown, in each of the following cases.

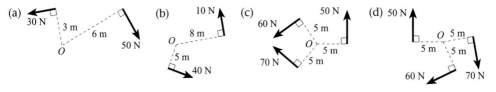

3 Find the moment of the force shown, about the point O, in each of the following cases.

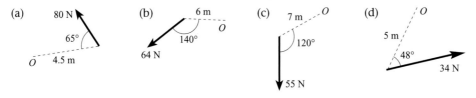

4 Find the value of *d* in each of the following cases, given that the moment about *O* is 480 N m clockwise.

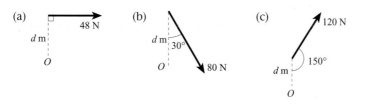

(a)   48 N

d m

O

(b)   *d* m 30°

O   80 N

(c)   120 N

150°

d m

O

5 Find the angle θ in each of the following cases, given that the moment about *O* is 480 N m anticlockwise. Give your answers in degrees, to 1 decimal place.

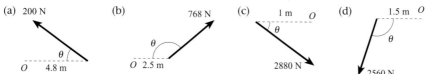

(a) 200 N

θ

O   4.8 m

(b)   768 N

θ

O 2.5 m

(c)   1 m   *O*

θ

2880 N

(d)   1.5 m *O*

θ

2560 N

6 A capstan is used to wind a cable attached to a boat. It rotates round a vertical axis, and the radius of the drum on which the cable winds is 10 cm. Power is provided by six men pushing on the arms of the capstan at 90 cm from the axis, each exerting a force of 200 N. Calculate the tension in the cable.

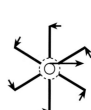

7 A mirror of mass 24 kg is supported by two screws 80 cm apart symmetrically placed along the top edge. One of the screws breaks, and while it is being replaced a helper keeps the mirror in position by a horizontal force applied 120 cm below the level of the screws. How large must this force be?

8 A uniform rod of length 2 metres and weight 40 newtons is hinged at one end. It is pulled aside at 50° to the downward vertical by a horizontal force applied at the other end. Find the magnitude of this force.

9 In the diagram *OA* represents a uniform porch roof of weight *W* newtons. It is hinged at *O* so that it can be set at different angles, and kept in position by a chain *AB* attached to a point *B* vertically above *O*. The lengths *OA* and *OB* are both 2 metres. Find the tension in the chain in terms of *W* when the angle between *OA* and the upward vertical is

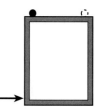

(a) 60°,   (b) 90°.

Show that, when the angle between *OA* and the upward vertical is 2θ, the tension in the chain is $W \sin\theta$ newtons.

10 The diagram shows a uniform rectangular sign $ABCD$ weighing $50\,\text{N}$ which is being fixed to a vertical frame. The lengths AD and AB are $120\,\text{cm}$ and $80\,\text{cm}$ respectively. The corner A is already attached to the frame by a horizontal nail, so that the sign can rotate about A in a vertical plane. While the corner B is being attached an assistant temporarily holds the sign steady at C by a force at $40°$ to the horizontal. Find the size of this force.

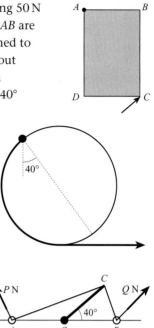

11 A hoop of weight 20 newtons can rotate freely about a pin fixed in a wall. A string has one end attached to the pin, runs round the circumference of the hoop to its lowest point, and is then held horizontally at its other end. A gradually increasing horizontal force is now applied to the string, so that the hoop begins to rotate about the pin. Find the tension in the string when the hoop has rotated through $40°$.

12 On a model ship, the mast OC has length $50\,\text{cm}$ and weight 20 newtons. The mast is hinged to the deck at O, so that it can rotate in the vertical fore-and-aft plane of the ship. Small smooth rings are fixed at points A and B on the deck in this plane such that $AO = OB = 50\,\text{cm}$.

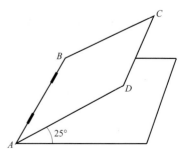

Threads from C are passed through these rings, and held at their ends by two children who exert forces of P newtons and Q newtons respectively. If $Q = 10$, calculate the value of P needed to hold the mast in equilibrium at $40°$ to the horizontal deck.

13 A chest, 2.4 metres long and 0.8 metres high, of weight 1500 newtons, stands on a rough floor. It is tilted about one edge of the base so that the length of the chest makes an angle of $8°$ with the horizontal. It is supported in this position by a prop at the midpoint of the parallel edge of the base. The prop is set perpendicular to the base of the chest, with its other end on the floor. Calculate the thrust in the prop.

14 In Greek myth Sisyphus was condemned for eternity to push a boulder up a hill. The boulder is modelled as a sphere of weight W and radius r. The hill slopes at an angle α to the horizontal, and Sisyphus exerts a force directed along a radius at an angle β to the hill. Prove that, to hold the boulder in equilibrium, he must exert a force of magnitude $\dfrac{W\sin\alpha}{\cos\beta}$.

15 A uniform rectangular hatch $ABCD$, of mass $12\,\text{kg}$, is hinged along its edge AB, and is horizontal when closed. A force acting through the midpoint of CD keeps the hatch open at a fixed angle of $25°$. Find the magnitude of the force, given that its acts

(a) vertically,

(b) horizontally,

(c) at right angles to $ABCD$.

16 A carpark barrier is modelled as a light rod which is pivoted
at a point. The rod carries a weight of 200 N at a point 0.25 m
from the pivot. The rod is held open at 80° to the horizontal
by a fixed arm, which prevents further upward movement of
the rod by obstructing it at a point 0.25 m from the pivot, as
shown in the diagram. Find the force exerted on the rod by
the fixed arm.

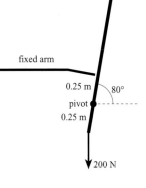

Find the magnitude of the force applied at a distance of 2 m
from the pivot which will just start to move the rod
downwards to its closed position, given that its direction is

(a) vertical,   (b) horizontal,   (c) at right angles to the rod.

Miscellaneous exercise 4

1 A rigid goal frame of mass 100 kg consists of two identical
posts, P_1 and P_2, and a uniform crossbar. When the frame
is placed in suitably constructed holes in a playing field,
the posts are vertical and the crossbar is horizontal. The
contact forces on the frame, which are assumed to act
vertically at the base of the holes, have magnitudes
R_1 newtons and R_2 newtons, as indicated in the diagram.
State the value of R_1.

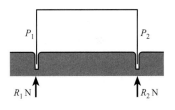

A goalkeeper of mass 75 kg hangs by one hand, without moving, from a point of the
crossbar 2 m from the corner where P_1 meets the crossbar. Given that the length of the
crossbar is 7 m, calculate the new values of R_1 and R_2.   (OCR)

2 The diagram shows a gym bench of length 2.5 m,
which stands on horizontal ground. The two supports
of the bench are of the same height; they are 2 m
apart and each is 0.25 m from an end of the bench.
The centre of mass of the bench is equidistant from
its ends. When a girl of weight 376 N stands on one
end, the bench is on the point of toppling. Calculate
the weight of the bench.   (OCR)

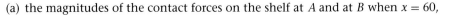

3 A horizontal rigid shelf AB, of mass 2.3 kg and length
80 cm, is supported at its ends. The supports are smooth.
An ornament of mass 0.4 kg is placed in such a way that
its centre of mass is vertically above the point X on the
shelf, where $AX = x$ cm. By treating the shelf as a uniform
rod, calculate

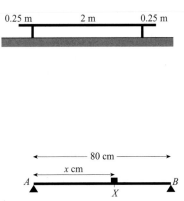

(a) the magnitudes of the contact forces on the shelf at A and at B when $x = 60$,

(b) the value of x for which the magnitude of the contact force at B is 1.25 times the
magnitude of the contact force at A.   (OCR)

4   A uniform sphere, of radius 0.2 m and mass 0.7 kg, rests on
    a uniform horizontal beam, of length 0.8 m and mass
    2.0 kg. The ends of the beam rest on smooth supports.
    The sphere overhangs the beam at one end by 0.07 m, as
    shown in the diagram. Find the magnitudes of the forces
    exerted on the beam by the two supports.   (OCR)

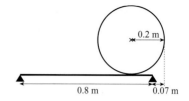

5   The diagram shows a non-uniform rod AB of length 1.2 m
    hanging in equilibrium, suspended by two vertical strings.
    In the equilibrium position shown, the tension in the
    string attached to A is 1.5 times the tension in the string
    attached to B. Find the distance of the centre of mass of
    the rod from A.   (OCR)

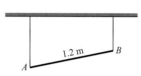

6   An open rectangular door $ABCD$ is smoothly hinged at
    the points P and Q of the vertical edge AB (see diagram).
    $AB = 2$ m, $BC = 0.75$ m, $AP = BQ = 0.25$ m, and the weight
    of the door is 200 N. By modelling the door as a uniform
    lamina, find the horizontal components of the forces on the
    door at P and Q.

    A wedge is placed between the door and the floor at D, exerting
    a vertically upward force of magnitude F newtons on the door.
    Given that the horizontal components of the forces on the door
    at P and Q are now both zero, calculate F.   (OCR)

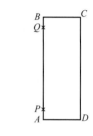

7   In the diagram, AB is a uniform rod of mass 2.5 kg and
    length 0.8 m which is smoothly hinged at B to a fixed vertical
    wall. The rod is held in equilibrium, making an angle of 40°
    with the wall, by means of a force of magnitude T newtons
    acting at A. The force acts in a direction making an angle
    of 110° with the rod. By taking moments about B, or
    otherwise, find T.   (OCR)

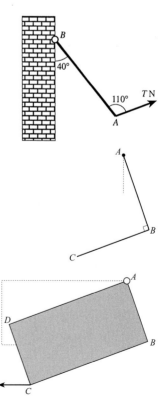

8   Two uniform rods, each of weight W and length l, are welded
    together so that angle ABC is a right angle. The diagram
    shows the rods hanging in equilibrium from a fixed point
    at A by a hinge which allows the rods to swing in a vertical
    plane. By taking moments about the hinge, find the angle
    that AB makes with the vertical.

9   A uniform rectangular panel $ABCD$ is being attached
    to the frame of a building. The panel has mass 80 kg and
    the lengths AD and AB are 4 m and 2 m respectively.
    The corner A is already bolted to the frame, so that
    the panel can rotate about A in a vertical plane. What
    horizontal force at C is needed to support the panel
    when the edge AD makes an angle of 20° with the
    horizontal?

10 A simple lift-bridge is modelled as a uniform rod AD of length 4.2 m and weight 5000 N. The rod is freely hinged at B and rests on a small support at C; $AB = 1.5$ m and $BC - 2.4$ m as shown in the first figure. The closed position of the bridge is represented by the rod being horizontal. Calculate the forces acting on the bridge due to the hinge at B and support at C.

A lump of concrete of mass M kg is placed at A to 'counterbalance' the bridge to make it easier to open. For the bridge to stay firmly closed, the force at C must be 25 N vertically upwards. Calculate the value of M.

With the lump of concrete attached, the bridge is held open at 60° to the horizontal by means of a light rope of negligible mass attached to D. The rope pulls upwards at an angle of 10° to the horizontal, as shown in the second diagram. Calculate the tension in the rope.   (MEI)

5 Centre of mass

This chapter shows how to find the centre of mass for objects made up of several simple parts. When you have completed it, you should

- be able to find the centre of mass for objects made up of parts whose centres of mass you already know
- understand how the procedure is justified by the theory of moments
- know the weighted mean formula for finding centres of mass
- know how to use the centre of mass to determine equilibrium positions for objects standing on a surface, hanging from a hook or suspended by a string.

5.1 One-dimensional objects

Example 5.1.1
A portable radio has a telescopic aerial, consisting of three parts of masses 0.05 kg, 0.03 kg and 0.02 kg, each of length 20 cm. The first part is hinged to the radio at one end, and the other two parts slide inside it. All three parts are uniform. Find the distance of the centre of mass from the hinge when

(a) the aerial is closed up,

(b) the second and third parts are pulled out together to make an aerial of length 40 cm,

(c) the aerial is fully extended.

Suppose that the aerial is pointed in a horizontal direction. Then the weight of the aerial has a moment about the hinge. You can calculate this moment either by taking the parts separately, or by supposing that the total weight acts along a line through the centre of mass.

(a) When it is closed up, as in Fig. 5.1a, the aerial is in effect a single object of mass 0.1 kg with its centre of mass at its geometrical centre, 10 cm from the hinge.

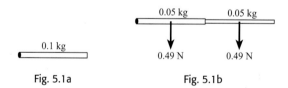

Fig. 5.1a   Fig. 5.1b

(b) With the two inside parts pulled out together, as in Fig. 5.1b, the aerial consists of two sections, each of mass 0.05 kg and length 20 cm. Although not geometrically symmetrical, this is in effect a single uniform rod of mass 0.1 kg and length 40 cm, with its centre of mass 20 cm from the hinge.

You can check this by considering the moments of the weights separately. Treated as two sections, with weights 0.49 N and centres of mass 10 cm and 30 cm from the hinge, the total moment is $0.49 \times 10 + 0.49 \times 30$ N cm. A single rod of weight 0.98 N at 20 cm from the hinge has a moment of 0.98×20 N cm. Either way, the calculation gives a moment of 19.6 N.

(c) Fig. 5.1c shows the aerial fully extended.

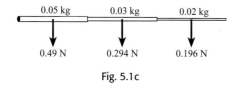

0.05 kg   0.03 kg   0.02 kg

0.49 N   0.294 N   0.196 N

Fig. 5.1c

You can't now appeal to symmetry to find the centre of mass, so you must use the moment argument. The three sections have weights of 0.49 N, 0.294 N and 0.196 N, acting at distances of 10 cm, 30 cm and 50 cm from the hinge. The total moment of these weights is $0.49 \times 10 + 0.294 \times 30 + 0.196 \times 50$ N cm, that is 23.52 N cm.

This can be equated to the moment of a weight of 0.98 N acting through the centre of mass. The centre of mass must therefore be $\frac{23.52}{0.98}$ cm, or 24 cm, from the hinge.

The calculation in part (c) of this example can be written in a more general form using algebra. Suppose that the masses of the three sections are denoted by m_1, m_2 and m_3, and that the centres of mass are at distances x_1, x_2 and x_3 from the hinge. Then the total moment of the weights about the hinge is $(m_1 g) x_1 + (m_2 g) x_2 + (m_3 g) x_3$, which you can write more simply as $(m_1 x_1 + m_2 x_2 + m_3 x_3) g$.

Let M denote the total mass $m_1 + m_2 + m_3$. It is usual to denote the coordinate of the centre of mass (in this case the distance from the hinge) by $\bar{x}$. The moment of the total weight can then be written as $(Mg)\bar{x}$, or $(M\bar{x})g$. Since these have to be equal,

$$(M\bar{x})g = (m_1 x_1 + m_2 x_2 + m_3 x_3)g.$$

Cancelling g, and then dividing by M, gives

$$\bar{x} = \frac{m_1 x_1 + m_2 x_2 + m_3 x_3}{M}.$$

This expression for $\bar{x}$ is called a **weighted mean**. It is an average of the distances x_1, x_2 and x_3 in which the distances are 'weighted' according to the masses at the corresponding points.

You may already have used weighted means in statistics. For example, if in a charity collection f_1 people give £x_1, f_2 people give £x_2 and f_3 people give £x_3, the average donation is £$\frac{f_1 x_1 + f_2 x_2 + f_3 x_3}{N}$, where N is the total number of contributors, so that $N = f_1 + f_2 + f_3$. This is the same formula, but in a quite different context.

If an object is made up of n sections of masses $m_1, m_2, \ldots, m_n$, each with its centre of mass on a line and having coordinates $x_1, x_2, \ldots, x_n$, then the centre of mass has coordinate $\bar{x}$ where

$$\bar{x} = \frac{m_1 x_1 + m_2 x_2 + \cdots + m_n x_n}{M} \quad \text{and} \quad M = m_1 + m_2 + \cdots + m_n.$$

It is often convenient to set out centre of mass calculations in tabular form, as in Table 5.2. On the left of the vertical line are the separate masses and distances, and on the right is the total mass at the centre of mass.

Mass	m_1	m_2	m_3	$\ldots$	m_n	M
Distance	x_1	x_2	x_3	$\ldots$	x_n	$\bar{x}$

Table 5.2

For example, Table 5.3 gives a summary of the data for Example 5.1.1(c).

Mass (kg)	0.05	0.03	0.02	0.1
Distance (cm)	10	30	50	$\bar{x}$

Table 5.3

From this you can write down at once the equation

$$0.05 \times 10 + 0.03 \times 30 + 0.02 \times 50 = 0.1\bar{x},$$

so $\qquad \bar{x} = \dfrac{2.4}{0.1} = 24.$

Before leaving Example 5.1.1, there is one further point to notice. In the solution the aerial was placed horizontally, but this wasn't necessary. If it had been at an angle α to the horizontal, then the moment of the weight $m_1 g$ would have been calculated (using either Fig. 5.4 or 5.5, whichever you find easier) as $(m_1 g) x_1 \cos\alpha$ or as $(m_1 g \cos\alpha) x_1$, and similarly for the weights $m_2 g$, $m_3 g$ and Mg.

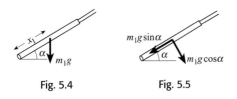

Fig. 5.4   Fig. 5.5

In simplifying the equation, you would then have cancelled out the factor $g \cos\alpha$ rather than just g, and the final result would have been the same as before. It is an important property of a rigid object that, if it is moved around in space, the position of the centre of mass relative to the object remains the same.

Example 5.1.2

The bird table shown in Fig. 5.6 is made by glueing together three pieces of wood: the base, the column and the feeding table. These three components each have square cross-section; their dimensions are shown in Fig. 5.7. They are assembled with their centres in the same vertical line. How high above the ground is the centre of mass of the bird table?

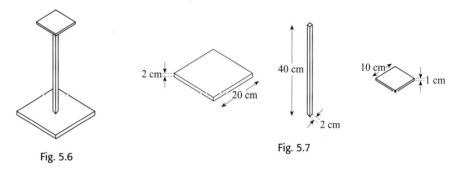

Fig. 5.6

Fig. 5.7

The bird table may not look like a one-dimensional object. But since it is made up of three parts with their centres of mass in line, only one coordinate is involved; that is, the height above the ground. So for the purposes of locating the centre of mass, the calculation can be treated as one-dimensional.

The components have volume $20^2 \times 2 \, \text{cm}^3$, $2^2 \times 40 \, \text{cm}^3$ and $10^2 \times 1 \, \text{cm}^3$. So, if the mass of $1 \, \text{cm}^3$ of the wood is k kg, the components have mass $800k$ kg, $160k$ kg and $100k$ kg respectively. The heights of their centres of mass above the ground are 1 cm, $(2 + 20)$ cm and $(2 + 40 + 0.5)$ cm. This information is summarised in Table 5.8.

Let the height of the combined centre of mass above the ground be $\bar{h}$ cm.

Mass (kg)	800k	160k	100k	1060k
Height (cm)	1	22	42.5	$\bar{h}$

Table 5.8

Using the formula in the blue box,

$$\bar{h} = \frac{800k \times 1 + 160k \times 22 + 100k \times 42.5}{1060k}$$

$$= \frac{800 + 3520 + 4250}{1060} = 8.08, \text{ correct to 3 significant figures.}$$

The centre of mass of the bird table is 8.08 cm above the ground.

5.2 Two-dimensional objects

If you have an object which extends in two dimensions, you will need two coordinates to describe the position of the centre of mass, and of the parts which make it up. For a rigid object you can choose a pair of axes which are fixed relative to the object, so that as the object moves the axes move with it.

The formulae giving $(\bar{x}, \bar{y})$, the coordinates of the centre of mass, are then a direct extension of the formula for one-dimensional objects.

> If an object is made up of n sections of masses $m_1, m_2, \ldots, m_n$, each with its centre of mass in a plane and having coordinates $(x_1, y_1), (x_2, y_2), \ldots, (x_n, y_n)$, then the centre of mass has coordinates $(\bar{x}, \bar{y})$, where
>
> $$\bar{x} = \frac{m_1 x_1 + m_2 x_2 + \cdots + m_n x_n}{M}, \qquad \bar{y} = \frac{m_1 y_1 + m_2 y_2 + \cdots + m_n y_n}{M}$$
>
> and $M = m_1 + m_2 + \cdots + m_n$.

It is worth noting that this can also be written using vectors.

> If the centres of mass of the sections have position vectors $\mathbf{r}_1, \mathbf{r}_2, \ldots, \mathbf{r}_n$, then the centre of mass has position vector $\bar{\mathbf{r}}$, where
>
> $$\bar{\mathbf{r}} = \frac{m_1 \mathbf{r}_1 + m_2 \mathbf{r}_2 + \cdots + m_n \mathbf{r}_n}{M}.$$

If you write each position vector in column form, $\mathbf{r}_1 = \begin{pmatrix} x_1 \\ y_1 \end{pmatrix}, \ldots$ and $\bar{\mathbf{r}} = \begin{pmatrix} \bar{x} \\ \bar{y} \end{pmatrix}$, and read along each line in turn, you get back to the cartesian forms in the previous blue box.

Example 5.2.1
A letter F is drawn on graph paper, as in Fig. 5.9, and a piece of thin card is then cut out to this shape. Find the centre of mass of the card.

The letter F has no symmetry, but there are several ways of splitting it up into rectangles. One way is to split it into three rectangles, as shown by the dotted lines on Fig. 5.9.

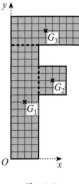

Fig. 5.9

The centres of mass of the rectangles are at the points labelled G_1, G_2 and G_3. You do not know the masses of the rectangles, but if the card is of uniform thickness the masses will be proportional to their areas. Suppose that the card has a mass of k units for each small square. Since the rectangles are made up of 64, 16 and 40 small squares, their masses are $64k$, $16k$ and $40k$ units.

Then, taking the origin at the bottom left corner of the letter, and axes across and up the page, the data can be laid out as in Table 5.10.

Mass	$64k$	$16k$	$40k$	$120k$
x-coordinate	2	6	5	$\bar{x}$
y-coordinate	8	11	18	$\bar{y}$

Table 5.10

The formulae then give

$$\bar{x} = \frac{64k \times 2 + 16k \times 6 + 40k \times 5}{120k} = \frac{53}{15},$$

$$\bar{y} = \frac{64k \times 8 + 16k \times 11 + 40k \times 18}{120k} = \frac{176}{15}.$$

The coordinates of the centre of mass are $\left(3\frac{8}{15}, 11\frac{11}{15}\right)$.

Example 5.2.2

A thin wire of uniform thickness is bent into a triangle with sides of length 30 cm, 40 cm and 50 cm. Find the position of the centre of mass.

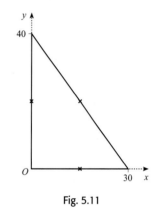

Fig. 5.11

The triangle has sides in the ratio 3 : 4 : 5, so it is right-angled. In Fig. 5.11 the origin is taken at the right angle, with x- and y-axes along the 30 cm and 40 cm sides respectively.

Each straight section of wire has mass proportional to its length, with centre of mass at its midpoint. Let the wire have mass k kg per centimetre. Then the data are shown in Table 5.12.

Mass (kg)	30k	40k	50k	120k
x-coordinate (cm)	15	0	15	$\bar{x}$
y-coordinate (cm)	0	20	20	$\bar{y}$

Table 5.12

The formulae give

$$\bar{x} = \frac{30k \times 15 + 40k \times 0 + 50k \times 15}{120k} = 10,$$

$$\bar{y} = \frac{30k \times 0 + 40k \times 20 + 50k \times 20}{120k} = 15.$$

The centre of mass is 15 cm from the 30 cm side, and 10 cm from the 40 cm side.

Exercise 5A

Keep your answers to Questions 2, 4, 9, 10 and 13 for use in Questions 9, 10 and 11 in Exercise 5B.

1 A stepped rod has three uniform sections, each of length 40 cm. The masses of the sections are 0.6 kg, 0.3 kg and 0.1 kg, as shown in the diagram. Find the distance of the centre of mass from the heavier end of the rod.

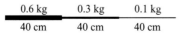

2 The frame shown in the diagram is made by welding a uniform rod, of mass 1 kg and length 1.2 m, to a uniform circular hoop, of mass 3.6 kg and radius 0.6 m. Find the distance of the centre of mass of the frame from the rod.

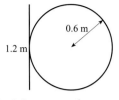

3 For some astronomical purposes it is useful to consider the Earth and the Moon together as a single system. Given that the mass of the Earth is 82.45 times the mass of the Moon, and that the mean distance of the Moon from the Earth is 384 400 km, find the distance of the centre of mass of the Earth–Moon system from the centre of the Earth.

4 A uniform lamina has the shape and dimensions shown in the diagram. Find the distance of the centre of mass of the lamina from *AB*.

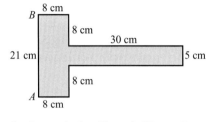

5 A badminton racket consists of a frame 28 cm long attached to a shaft of length 38 cm. For the last 16 cm of its length the shaft is surrounded by the grip. If the frame, the shaft and the grip have mass 70 grams, 40 grams and 30 grams respectively, and the centre of mass of each part is at its geometrical centre, find the distance of the centre of mass of the racket from the end of the shaft.

6 A fishing rod is made of three parts clipped together, each uniform and of length 1.2 metres. The separate parts have mass 60 grams, 40 grams and 25 grams. Half of the heaviest part is wrapped in a sleeve to which a reel is attached, with total mass 75 grams and centre of mass 40 cm from the end of the rod. Find the distance of the centre of mass of the whole rod from this end.

7 The vase shown in the figure is made of sheet metal of uniform thickness. It is open at the top. Find the height of the centre of mass above the base.

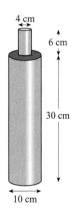

8 An oar consists of a uniform shaft of length 3 metres and a blade of length 70 cm, whose centre of mass is 40 cm beyond the shaft. The oar passes through a rowlock 80 cm from the end of the shaft. If the mass of the shaft is 4 kg, and the mass of the blade is 0.3 kg, find the distance of the centre of mass of the oar from the rowlock.

9   The diagram shows a uniform lamina; all the corners are right
    angles. Using the axes shown, find the coordinates of the centre
    of mass of the lamina.   (OCR)

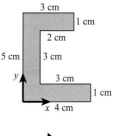

10 A frame, in the form of the quadrilateral shown in the diagram,
    is made from a piece of uniform wire of length 54 cm. Find
    the distance of the centre of mass of the frame from

    (a) the side of length 18 cm,

    (b) the side of length 12 cm.

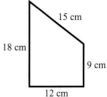

11 A pair of trousers on a hanger is modelled as a rectangular
    lamina attached to a horizontal rod. Another two rods, which
    are connected to each other, are attached to the ends of the
    horizontal rod, as shown in the diagram. All three rods are
    uniform. The mass of the lamina is 550 grams and its centre of
    mass is 30 cm below the horizontal rod. The mass of the
    horizontal rod is 100 grams and its length is 40 cm. Each of
    the other rods has mass 75 grams and length 25 cm. Find the
    distance of the centre of mass of the combined hanger and
    trousers, below the horizontal bar of the hanger.

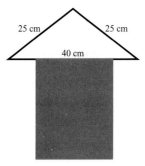

12 A stone sculpture consists of a 2 m × 1.6 m × 1 m cuboid
    surmounted by a cylinder of radius x metres and length 1 m,
    as shown in the diagram. The centre of mass of the sculpture
    is a point of contact between the two parts. Find x.

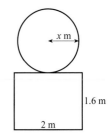

13 One end of a circular cylinder of mass 0.8 kg, radius 3 cm
    and length 25 cm is attached to a circular disc of
    mass 0.45 kg and radius 15 cm. The axis of the cylinder
    is at right angles to the disc and 10 cm from its centre,
    as shown in the diagram. Find the distance of the centre
    of mass of the combined cylinder and disc from

    (a) the plane of the disc,

    (b) the axis of the disc.

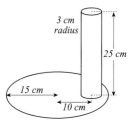

14 An ice-hockey stick is modelled as a pair of parallelograms, with dimensions as shown in the figure. Taking the mass per unit area to be constant, find the distances of the centre of mass of the stick above and to the right of the heel H.

15 C is the centre of mass of the uniform lamina shown in the diagram. Given that $\bar{y} = 3$, find z and $\bar{x}$.

16 A sheet of metal has uniform thickness and uniform density. A lamina having the shape shown in the diagram is cut from the sheet of metal. Find the coordinates $(\bar{x}, \bar{y})$ of the centre of mass C of the lamina.

5.3   Hanging and balancing

Take the aerial in Example 5.1.1 and extend it. Suppose that it could be unhooked from the hinge and balanced on your finger. Where along the aerial would it balance?

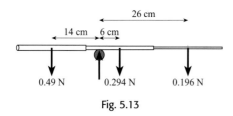

Fig. 5.13

The answer is, of course, at the centre of mass. Fig. 5.13 shows the situation with the finger 24 cm from the thick end. The weight of the 0.05 kg section has an anticlockwise moment of 0.49×14 N cm; the weights of the other two sections have a total clockwise moment of $(0.294 \times 6 + 0.196 \times 26)$ N cm. So there are moments of 6.86 N cm both anticlockwise and clockwise, and the aerial is in equilibrium.

If you have any object standing on a surface in equilibrium, there are only two forces acting: the weight acting vertically through the centre of mass, and the resultant contact force from the surface. These must therefore act along the same line, so that the centre of mass must be directly above a point at which the resultant contact force can act.

For example, if the contact is at a single point, the centre of mass must be above that point. If the contact is bounded by a circle, the centre of mass must be above a point inside or on the boundary of the circle; similarly for a rectangle or a triangle.

Example 5.3.1
Fig. 5.14 shows a design for a piece of table sculpture which is to be carved out of a single uniform piece of marble. The dimensions are in centimetres. What is the largest possible value for the length labelled d?

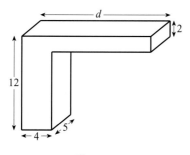

Fig. 5.14

Although the sculpture is three-dimensional, it has a vertical plane of symmetry in which the centre of mass must lie. Fig. 5.15 shows the cross-section in this plane of symmetry.

The dotted line suggests one way of splitting the sculpture into two cuboids. If the marble has density k kg per cm^3, the mass of the upright column is $(4 \times 10 \times 5)\,k$ kg, and the mass of the flat slab is $(2 \times d \times 5)\,k$ kg. The data are summarised in Table 5.16.

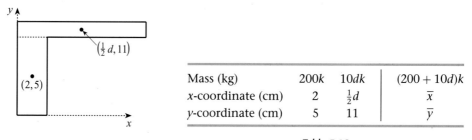

Mass (kg)	$200k$	$10dk$	$(200 + 10d)k$
x-coordinate (cm)	2	$\frac{1}{2}d$	$\bar{x}$
y-coordinate (cm)	5	11	$\bar{y}$

Fig. 5.15   Table 5.16

The sculpture will stand unsupported if the centre of mass lies above a point of the rectangular base, that is if $\bar{x} \leqslant 4$. The value of $\bar{y}$ doesn't matter. The formula gives

$$\bar{x} = \frac{400k + 5d^2k}{(200 + 10d)\,k} = \frac{80 + d^2}{40 + 2d}.$$

The value of d must therefore satisfy the condition

$$\frac{80 + d^2}{40 + 2d} \leqslant 4, \quad \text{that is} \quad d^2 - 8d \leqslant 80.$$

To complete the square, add 16 to both sides, which gives $(d - 4)^2 \leqslant 96$, so that $d \leqslant 4 + \sqrt{96} = 13.8$, correct to 3 significant figures.

The maximum length of the sculpture is about 13.8 cm.

Example 5.3.2
A plastic tumbler has the shape of a cylindrical tube whose height is twice the diameter of its base. The sides and the base have the same thickness. It is placed on a rough surface at 20° to the horizontal. Will it topple over if placed
(a) the right way up,   (b) upside down?

The tumbler is made of thin plastic, so it can be modelled as a surface of negligible thickness. If the base has radius r, the height of the tumbler is $2(2r) = 4r$, so the area of the curved surface is $(2\pi r) \times 4r = 8\pi r^2$, which is 8 times the area of the base. So if the base has mass m, the curved surface has mass $8m$.

The centre of mass lies on the axis of symmetry, so you only need to find the height above the base. The data are summarised in Table 5.17.

Mass	m	$8m$	$9m$
Height above base	0	$2r$	$\bar{y}$

Table 5.17

So $\bar{y} = \dfrac{16mr}{9m} = \tfrac{16}{9}r$.

(a) Fig. 5.18 shows the tumbler on the sloping surface the right way up. Note that the axis of the tumbler is at 20° to the vertical.

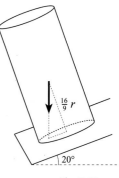

Fig. 5.18

The vertical line through the centre of mass meets the base of the tumbler at a distance $\left(\tfrac{16}{9}r\right)\tan 20°$ from the centre, which is about $0.65r$. Since this is less than r, the contact force from the surface can act along this line, so that the tumbler will not topple over. (Note that the contact force has been omitted from Fig. 5.18.)

(b) Now turn the tumbler upside down. Since the height of the tumbler is $4r$, the centre of mass is now $\tfrac{20}{9}r$ above the rim. When it is placed on the sloping surface, the vertical line through the centre of mass meets the plane of the rim at a distance $\left(\tfrac{20}{9}r\right)\tan 20°$ from the centre, which is about $0.81r$. The tumbler still will not topple over; the resultant contact force can act along this line, even though it doesn't pass through a point where the tumbler is physically in contact with the surface. It is enough for the line of action to meet the surface at a point inside the rim of the tumbler.

In this example the contact must also be rough enough for the tumbler not to slide down the surface. You already know that this means that the coefficient of friction has to be more than $\tan 20°$. See M1 Experiment 5.3.2.

The same principle applies when an object hangs from a hook. The weight is then opposed by the contact force from the hook. So in equilibrium the object rests with its centre of mass directly below the hook.

Example 5.3.3
The triangular wire in Example 5.2.2 hangs from a hook at the sharpest corner. Find the angle which the 40 cm side makes with the vertical.

In Fig. 5.19 G is the centre of mass. You know that $GN = 10\,\text{cm}$ and $GM = 15\,\text{cm}$, so that $AN = 25\,\text{cm}$. Since G must be directly below A, the angle required is GAN, which is equal to $\tan^{-1}\dfrac{10}{25} = 21.8\ldots°$.

The 40 cm side hangs at about 22° to the vertical.

A similar situation is when the object hangs by a string. The upward force is then provided by the tension in the string, so the centre of mass must lie on the line of the string produced.

Sometimes it is quite difficult to draw diagrams with the hanging object at an angle. The next example illustrates a useful trick which can be used to get round this difficulty.

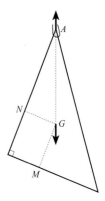

Fig. 5.19

Example 5.3.4
An open box has five square faces of side 10 cm, each having mass m kg. Initially it stands with its base on the floor. A string is then fixed to one of the upper corners, and the box is lifted by the string until it is clear of the floor. Find the angle now made with the vertical by the edges which were originally vertical.

Fig. 5.20 shows the box in its initial position. The four vertical faces have a total mass of $4m$ kg, and their combined centre of mass is 5 cm above the centre of the base. The

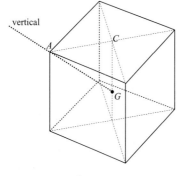

Fig. 5.20

base has mass m kg. So the height of G, the centre of mass of the box, above the base is $\dfrac{4m \times 5 + m \times 0}{5m}$ cm, which is 4 cm.

Let C be the middle of the top of the box, and A the corner at which the string is fixed. When the box hangs from the string, the line AG is vertical. Instead of drawing the box again in its new position, you can simply join AG and label it 'vertical'. It is only a convention that vertical lines are drawn up the page!

The angle wanted is equal to the angle AGC. It is easy to calculate that $GC = (10 - 4)$ cm $= 6$ cm and $AC = \frac{1}{2}\sqrt{10^2 + 10^2} = 5\sqrt{2}$ cm, so this angle is $\tan^{-1}\frac{5}{6}\sqrt{2} = 49.68\ldots°$

When the box hangs from A by a string, the edges are at about $50°$ to the vertical.

5.4*   The theory justified

It was stated at the end of Section 5.1 that, if a rigid object is moved around in space, the position of the centre of mass relative to the object remains the same. It is now time to explore this statement more precisely. You may, if you wish, omit this section and go straight to Exercise 5B.

The object is rigid, so it keeps the same shape as it is moved around. This means that you can set up axes fixed in the object, which move around with it. The object is made up of parts with masses denoted by m_i (where the suffix i takes values $1,\ 2, \ldots, n$) located at points P_i whose coordinates remain constant as it moves.

To avoid too much complication, the proof in this section will be restricted to two-dimensional objects in a vertical plane, so that you only need two coordinates (x_i, y_i).

What can then be shown is:

> In any equation of resolving or moments, the weights of the separate parts can be replaced by the weight of a mass M located at the point G with coordinates $(\bar{x}, \bar{y})$, where $M, \bar{x}, \bar{y}$ are defined as in Section 5.2.

The proof for resolving equations is trivial. If you are resolving in a direction making an angle θ with the vertical, the resolved parts of the weights contribute an amount $m_1 g \cos\theta + m_2 g \cos\theta + \cdots + m_n g \cos\theta$, which you can write as $(m_1 + m_2 + \cdots + m_n) g \cos\theta$, which is $Mg \cos\theta$.

To prove the result for moments equations it helps to use the trick introduced in Example 5.3.4, setting the axes in their conventional position and tilting the line representing vertical. In Fig. 5.21 the weights are drawn at an angle α to the x-axis; this corresponds to a position in which the rigid object is turned so that the x-axis makes an angle α with the vertical.

Suppose that you are taking moments about a point H with coordinates (a, b). The moment of the weight $m_i g$ is $p_i m_i g$, where p_i denotes the perpendicular distance from H to the line

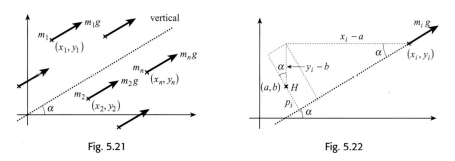

Fig. 5.21   Fig. 5.22

of action of the weight. You can see from Fig. 5.22 that this distance is equal to

$$(x_i - a) \sin \alpha - (y_i - b) \cos \alpha.$$

So the total moment of all the weights is the sum of terms of the form

$$m_i g \left((x_i - a) \sin \alpha - (y_i - b) \cos \alpha \right),$$

which you can write as

$$m_i x_i g \sin \alpha - m_i a g \sin \alpha - m_i y_i g \cos \alpha + m_i b g \cos \alpha.$$

Adding up these moments for $1, 2, \ldots, n$ and replacing $m_1 + m_2 + \cdots + m_n$ by M, $m_1 x_1 + m_2 x_2 + \cdots + m_n x_n$ by $M \bar{x}$, and $m_1 y_1 + m_2 y_2 + \cdots + m_n y_n$ by $M \bar{y}$, this becomes

$$M \bar{x} g \sin \alpha - M a g \sin \alpha - M \bar{y} g \cos \alpha + M b g \cos \alpha,$$

which is $Mg((\bar{x} - a) \sin \alpha - (\bar{y} - b) \cos \alpha)$, the moment of the force Mg at an angle α acting through G.

This completes the proof. The property is so basic in mechanics that G was once commonly called the **centre of gravity**. But since the point G has other properties which continue to hold even where there is no gravity, it is better to stick with the term centre of mass.

Exercise 5B

1 Find by experiment the position of the centre of mass of

   (a) a snooker cue,   (b) a squash racket,   (c) a cricket bat.

2 A straight rigid rod AB is suspended by a string attached at a point P of its length. The centre of mass of the rod is at G. Describe how the rod would hang

   (a) if P is between A and G,   (b) if P is between G and B,   (c) if P is at G.

3 The stepped rod of Question 1 of Exercise 5A is held in a horizontal position, suspended by two vertical strings. One of the strings is attached to the end A of the rod, as shown in the diagram. Find the tension in each of the strings when the other string is attached to the rod

   (a) at its centre of mass,   (b) at its end B.

4 Carry out the following experiment. Begin by standing to attention. Then try to carry out the following movements, keeping the rest of your body upright.

(a) Raise your right arm sideways to a horizontal position.

(b) Raise your right leg sideways as far as you can.

(c) Raise your right arm and your right leg sideways at the same time.

(d) Raise your left arm and your right leg sideways at the same time.

Describe and explain what happens in each case.

5 A thick sheet of plywood in the shape of a parallelogram has sides of length 30 cm and 50 cm, with an angle α between them. What can you say about α if the sheet can stand upright in equilibrium with one of its shorter edges on a horizontal surface?

6 These letters are made up from pieces of the same thin metal rod. They are all 12 cm high and 8 cm wide. They are suspended in equilibrium from the points marked with a dot. Find the angle made with the vertical by the rod attached to the point of suspension.

7 The object shown is made of two plates of the same width and thickness welded together. The object is placed on a horizontal floor with the plates at equal angles to the horizontal. If *BD* is of length 10 cm, what is the greatest possible length for *AC* if the object is able to stand on the floor in equilibrium?

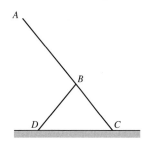

8 The L-shaped figure in the diagram is the cross-section of an object carved out of polystyrene and placed on a very rough slope. The angle of inclination of the slope is increased until the object tips over. At what angle to the horizontal does this occur?

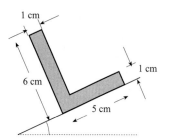

9 The structures in Question 10 and Question 2 of Exercise 5A are hung in equilibrium from a string as shown in the following diagrams. Find the angles α, β, γ and δ.

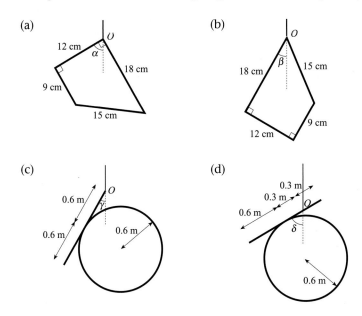

(a)

(b)

(c)

(d)

10 The laminas in Question 4 and Question 9 of Exercise 5A are suspended in equilibrium as shown in the following diagrams. Find the angles α, β, γ and δ.

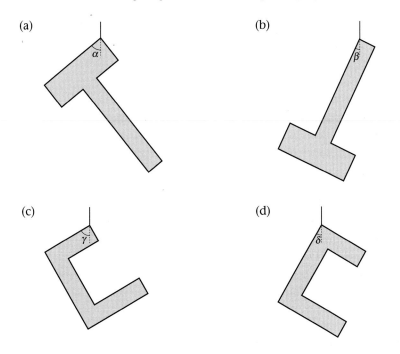

(a)

(b)

(c)

(d)

11 The combined cylinder and disc in Question 13 of Exercise 5A is suspended as shown in the diagram. Find the angle α.

12 A walking stick is made in three straight sections of the same small diameter, with dimensions as shown in the figure. What angle will the upright part of the stick make with the vertical if it is supported in the palm of a person's hand

(a) at A,   (b) at B?

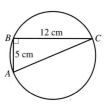

Miscellaneous exercise 5

1 The structure having the shape shown in the diagram, consisting of a right-angled triangle inscribed in a circle, is made of uniform wire. Calculate the distance of the centre of mass of the structure from

(a) AB,   (b) BC.

2 A simplified model of a spade consists of a handle joined by a shaft to a metal plate $ABCD$, as shown in the diagram. The handle is a uniform cylinder with mass 0.5 kg and diameter 4 cm. The shaft is a uniform cylinder with mass 2.0 kg and length 70 cm. The metal plate is uniform and rectangular, with mass 2.5 kg, and $BC = 24$ cm. Using this model, calculate the distance of the centre of mass of the spade from AB.   (OCR)

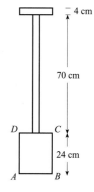

3 Two uniform solid spheres are rigidly joined to the ends of a uniform rod lying along the line containing their centres. One sphere has mass 3 kg and diameter 10 cm; the other has mass 10 kg and diameter 16 cm. The rod has mass 2 kg and length 32 cm (see diagram). The midpoint of the rod is M, and G is the centre of mass of the combined body (consisting of the two spheres and the rod). Calculate the distance MG.   (OCR)

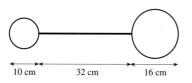

4 In a fairground ride, a cabin is attached to one end of an arm of mass 100 kg and length 7.2 m. The total mass of the cabin and passengers is 300 kg. A counterweight of mass 200 kg is attached to the other end of the arm. The ride is modelled as a uniform rod AB, with particles attached at A and B, which is free to rotate, without resistance, in a vertical plane about a fixed horizontal axis through the mid-point O of AB (see diagram). Find the distance of the centre of mass of the system from O. (OCR)

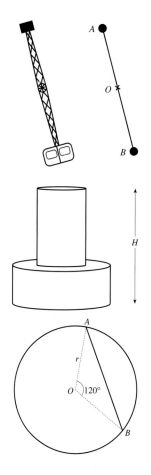

5 Two uniform cylinders, made from the same material, are arranged one on top of the other as shown in the diagram. The radius of the upper cylinder is half that of the lower, and the height of the upper cylinder is twice that of the lower. The overall height of the structure is H. Find, in terms of H, the distance of the centre of mass from the base.

6 A structure made of a uniform wire consists of a circular piece, of radius r, and a straight piece. The straight piece forms a chord AB of the circle, which subtends an angle of $120°$ at the centre O of the circle, as shown in the diagram. Show that the distance, from the chord, of the centre of mass of the structure is $\dfrac{\pi r}{2\pi + \sqrt{3}}$. The structure is suspended from the point A. Find the angle that the chord makes with the downward vertical.

7 Two blocks, one rectangular and one L-shaped, are of uniform thickness and made of the same material. The dimensions of the blocks are as shown in the diagram. Find the value of x when

(a) the blocks are unattached and the L-shaped block is on the point of toppling from the rectangular block,

(b) the blocks are attached and the combined blocks are on the point of toppling.

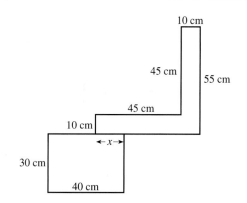

8 An L-shaped block of uniform thickness has the corners of one of its faces labelled A, B, C, D, E and F, as shown in the diagram. The block stands on a plane which is inclined at an angle α to the horizontal. In which of the following configurations P, Q, R and S is the block on the point of toppling when $\tan\alpha$ is

(a) $\frac{1}{7}$, (b) $\frac{5}{7}$, (c) 1, (d) $\frac{7}{5}$?

P AB coincides with a line of greatest slope of the plane with B above A.

Q BC coincides with a line of greatest slope of the plane with C above B.

R CD coincides with a line of greatest slope of the plane with D above C.

S DE coincides with a line of greatest slope of the plane with E above D.

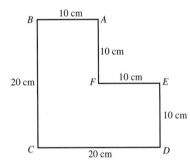

9 A uniform square lamina $ABCD$ is freely suspended from the point E on AB, where $AE = \frac{1}{4}AB$. The lamina hangs in equilibrium. Find the angle between AB and the vertical.   (OCR)

10 A uniform rectangular block, one of whose faces has corners labelled A, B, C and D, can rest in equilibrium with the edge AB along a line of greatest slope of a rough plane inclined at an angle α to the horizontal (see diagram). $AB = 25$ cm and $BC = 15$ cm. Show that $\tan\alpha \leqslant \frac{5}{3}$.

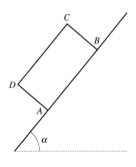

The block cannot rest in equilibrium with the face $ABCD$ vertical and the edge BC along a line of greatest slope of the plane. Given that the plane is rough enough to prevent sliding, show that $\tan\alpha > \frac{3}{5}$.   (OCR)

11 An L-shaped block of uniform thickness 10 cm has dimensions as shown in the first diagram. Two cylindrical 'handles', each of radius 4 cm and length 40 cm and made of the same material as the block, are attached so that they have a common axis which is at right angles to the face $ABCDEF$, as shown in the second diagram. This axis is 5 cm from AB and 5 cm from AF. Determine whether the block topples when placed on a horizontal surface with BC vertical, and DC in contact with the surface.

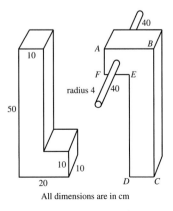

Find whether the result would be the same if the length of the cylinders was 39.5 cm.

12 Toy bricks, all uniform cubes of the same size, are contained in a box. With the box open a child builds a column of the bricks in its lid, as shown in the diagram. With eight bricks used the column does not topple, but when the ninth brick is added the column topples. Show that the angle the lid makes with the horizontal lies between $\tan^{-1}\frac{1}{9}$ and $\tan^{-1}\frac{1}{8}$.

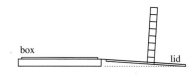

6 Rigid objects in equilibrium

This chapter establishes the conditions for a rigid object to be in equilibrium under the action of a number of coplanar forces. When you have completed it, you should

- know and be able to apply general conditions for the equilibrium of a rigid object
- be able to determine how equilibrium is broken as a force is increased
- be able to find lines of action of forces needed to maintain equilibrium
- recognise that some problems are indeterminate and do not have a unique solution.

6.1 Equilibrium equations

Suppose that a ladder is put up against the wall of a building, and that both the ground and the wall are so smooth that friction can be neglected. You would expect the ladder to slide down until it lies flat on the ground.

Fig. 6.1 explains in terms of the forces on the ladder why it can't rest against the wall in equilibrium. There are only three forces: the weight, and the normal contact forces (R and S) from the ground and the wall. Although the forces would balance vertically if R were equal to W, there is no horizontal force to counteract S.

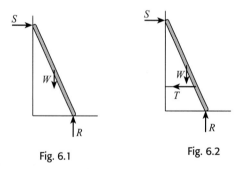

Fig. 6.1   Fig. 6.2

For the ladder to be in equilibrium there has to be some other force with a horizontal resolved part. This could be provided for example by attaching a rope from the ladder to an anchor on the wall. Fig. 6.2 shows the forces with the addition of a tension in a horizontal rope attached to the ladder one-quarter way up its length.

You could now write down two equations, resolving horizontally and vertically:

$$\mathcal{R}(\rightarrow) \quad S = T, \quad \text{and} \quad \mathcal{R}(\uparrow) \quad R = W.$$

The weight of the ladder is presumably known, so you know the value of R. But you don't know either S or T, so you need a third equation to find these. This is provided by an equation of moments about some point. You can choose any point you like, for example the foot of the ladder.

Denote the length of the ladder by l and the angle with the vertical by α. Fig. 6.3 shows the distances of the foot of the ladder from the lines of action of the forces S, W and T.

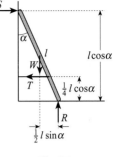

$$\mathcal{M}(\text{foot of ladder}) \quad S \times l \cos \alpha = W \times \tfrac{1}{2} l \sin \alpha + T \times \tfrac{1}{4} l \cos \alpha.$$

Dividing through by l and substituting $S = T$ from the $\mathcal{R}(\rightarrow)$ equation,

$$T \cos \alpha = \tfrac{1}{2} W \sin \alpha + \tfrac{1}{4} T \cos \alpha,$$

so

$$\tfrac{3}{4} T \cos \alpha = \tfrac{1}{2} W \sin \alpha.$$

Fig. 6.3

It follows that $T = \tfrac{2}{3} W \tan \alpha$. Since $S = T$, all three unknown forces have now been found in terms of W and α.

This is a typical way of finding the forces which keep a rigid object in equilibrium. You can write down two resolving equations and one moments equation, and then solve these for the unknown forces.

Example 6.1.1
A rectangular wooden platform $ABCD$ has edges $AB = 5\,\text{m}$, $BC = 3\,\text{m}$. It is lying horizontally, and being manoeuvred into position by horizontal forces at A, B, C and D directed along the edges, as shown in Fig. 6.4. The force at A has magnitude $75\,\text{N}$, and the forces at B, C and D are X, Y and Z newtons respectively. Calculate the values of X, Y and Z needed to keep the platform in equilibrium.

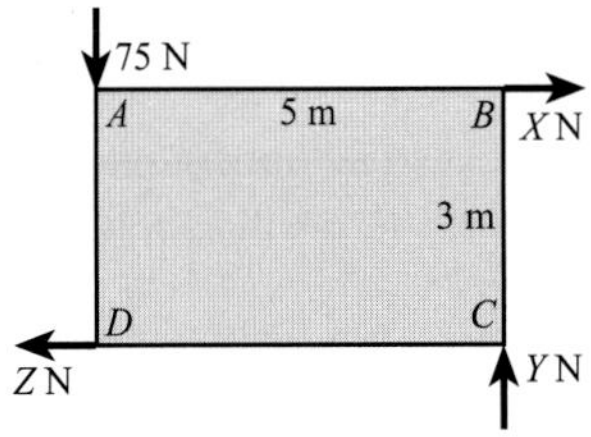

Fig. 6.4

Two resolving equations are

$$\mathcal{R}(\rightarrow) \quad X - Z = 0, \qquad \mathcal{R}(\uparrow) \quad Y - 75 = 0.$$

These give the value of Y, and show that X and Z are equal. But to find the actual values of X and Z you need one more equation, which must be an equation of moments. There is no obvious point to take moments about, so choose B. The forces X and Y have no moment about B, so

$$\mathcal{M}(B) \quad 75 \times 5 - Z \times 3 = 0.$$

This gives $Z = 125$, and it follows that $X = 125$.

The forces at B, C and D are $125\,\text{N}$, $75\,\text{N}$ and $125\,\text{N}$ respectively.

Choose some other point (not necessarily a corner of the platform) and check for yourself that the moments of the four forces balance about that point.

Example 6.1.2

A high diving board is a uniform horizontal plank of length 2 metres and weight 100 N. It is hinged to the step tower at one end, and supported at 0.5 metres from that end by a strut which produces a thrust at 20° to the vertical. Find the magnitude of the thrust and the force from the hinge when a diver of weight 700 N stands at the other end of the board.

It would seem that the hinge has to pull the board in towards the tower and also exert a downward force on the board. In Fig. 6.5 the force from the hinge is therefore towards the left and downwards. It is simplest to find these as two components, X newtons and Y newtons, and then to combine them. Let the thrust in the strut be S newtons.

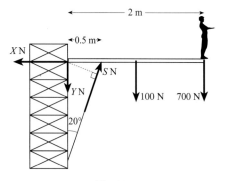

Fig. 6.5

The natural choices for the three equations are to take moments about the hinge and to resolve in horizontal and vertical directions.

You need to calculate the distance from the hinge to the line of action of the thrust from the strut. The perpendicular to the strut is at 20° to the horizontal, so this distance is $0.5 \cos 20°$ m.

$\mathcal{M}(\text{hinge})$ $S(0.5 \cos 20°) = 100 \times 1 + 700 \times 2.$
$\mathcal{R}(\rightarrow)$ $S \cos 70° = X.$
$\mathcal{R}(\uparrow)$ $S \cos 20° = Y + 100 + 700.$

Working to 4 significant figures, the first equation gives $S = 3193$, and then $X = 1092$ and $Y = 2200$. Finally, X and Y can be combined, using Fig. 6.6, to show that the force from the hinge is 2456 N at an angle of 63.60° to the horizontal.

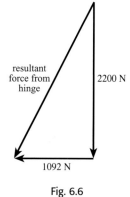

Fig. 6.6

So the thrust from the strut is about 3190 N, and the force from the hinge is about 2460 N at 63.6° to the horizontal.

In Example 6.1.2, if you do the calculations for yourself, you will find that the value $Y = 2200$ is exact. This is because another way of calculating Y is to take moments about the point where the strut meets the board, giving the equation $0.5Y = 0.5 \times 100 + 1.5 \times 700$. There is always the possibility of replacing one, or even both, of the resolving equations by an equation of moments.

Example 6.1.3

A student has on her desk a glass paperweight in the shape of a hemisphere of radius 4 cm. She rests a uniform pen 12 cm long against it, at 30° to the horizontal, with its lower end on the desk, as shown in Fig. 6.7. The paperweight does not move. If the contact between the pen and the paperweight is smooth, how large must the coefficient of friction between the pen and the desk be to maintain equilibrium?

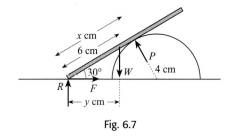

Fig. 6.7

You are not given the weight of the pen, so denote it by W. The other forces on the pen are the normal contact force P from the paperweight, and the friction F and normal contact force R from the desk.

It is simplest to begin by taking moments about the end of the pen on the desk, which will give P in terms of W. You can then find F and R by resolving horizontally and vertically.

To calculate the distance, x cm, from the end of the pen to the line of action of P, note that $\dfrac{4}{x} = \tan 30°$. Since $\tan 30° = \dfrac{1}{\sqrt{3}}$, $x = 4\sqrt{3}$. The distance, y cm, from the end of the pen to the line of action of W is given by $\dfrac{y}{6} = \cos 30° = \tfrac{1}{2}\sqrt{3}$, so $y = 3\sqrt{3}$.

So, using centimetre units for length,

$\mathcal{M}(\text{end of pencil}) \quad P \times 4\sqrt{3} = W \times 3\sqrt{3}, \qquad \text{giving } P = \tfrac{3}{4}W.$

$\mathcal{R}(\rightarrow) \quad F = P \cos 60°, \quad \text{so } F = \tfrac{1}{2}P = \tfrac{3}{8}W.$

$\mathcal{R}(\uparrow) \quad R + P \cos 30° = W, \quad \text{so } R = W - \tfrac{3}{4}W \times \tfrac{1}{2}\sqrt{3} = W\left(1 - \tfrac{3}{8}\sqrt{3}\right).$

If μ denotes the coefficient of friction between the pen and the desk, it is necessary for equilibrium to be possible that $F \leqslant \mu R$, so

$$\tfrac{3}{8}W \leqslant \mu W\left(1 - \tfrac{3}{8}\sqrt{3}\right),$$

$$\mu \geqslant \frac{\tfrac{3}{8}}{1 - \tfrac{3}{8}\sqrt{3}} = \frac{3}{8 - 3\sqrt{3}} = 1.07, \text{ correct to 3 significant figures.}$$

For the pen to rest in equilibrium against the paperweight at an angle of 30°, the coefficient of friction between the pen and the desk must be at least 1.07.

In the next example two equations of moments are used, so that the contact forces can each be found from a single equation.

Example 6.1.4

A quarry truck has wheels 4 metres apart. When fully loaded with stone, the centre of mass is 1.2 metres from the tracks and midway between the wheels. A brake can be used to lock one of the pairs of wheels when the truck is on a slope. Is it better for the brake to be on the lower or the upper wheels? If the coefficient of friction between the wheels and the rails is 0.4, what is the steepest slope on which the truck can stand when fully loaded?

Fig. 6.8 shows the truck on a slope of angle α. You don't yet know whether the frictional force F acts on the lower or the upper wheels. It is simpler to write the equations of moments if you split the weight W into components $W \sin \alpha$ and $W \cos \alpha$ parallel and perpendicular to the slope. The contact forces at the upper and lower wheels are R and S.

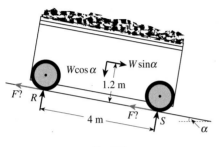

Fig. 6.8

$\mathcal{M}$(lower wheel) $4R + 1.2W \sin \alpha = 2W \cos \alpha.$

$\mathcal{M}$(upper wheel) $4S = 1.2W \sin \alpha + 2W \cos \alpha.$

So $R = W(0.5 \cos \alpha - 0.3 \sin \alpha)$ and $S = W(0.5 \cos \alpha + 0.3 \sin \alpha)$. It follows that $S > R$. Since the greatest frictional force is proportional to the contact force, you can get more friction by having the brake on the lower wheels. Let F be the frictional force.

$\mathcal{R}$(∥ to slope) $F = W \sin \alpha.$

For the truck not to move down the slope, $F < 0.4S$, so that

$$W \sin \alpha < 0.2W \cos \alpha + 0.12W \sin \alpha.$$

Therefore $0.88 \sin \alpha < 0.2 \cos \alpha$, which gives $\tan \alpha < \dfrac{0.2}{0.88}$. The maximum angle of slope is $\tan^{-1} \dfrac{0.2}{0.88}$, which is 12.80°, correct to 2 decimal places.

The lower wheels should be braked, and the angle of slope cannot exceed 12.8°.

Notice in this example that, if you add the two equations of moments and divide by 4, you get $R + S = W \cos \alpha$, which is the equation of resolving at right angles to the slope. So to get any new information by resolving, you have to choose a direction which is not at right angles to the line joining the two points about which you take moments.

For a similar reason, if you choose to take moments about a third point, you will only get new information if this point is not in line with the first two.

The equations for the equilibrium of a rigid object acted on by coplanar forces can be obtained by

- taking moments about one point and resolving in two different directions; or

- taking moments about two points and resolving in a direction which is not perpendicular to the line joining them; or

- taking moments about three points which are not collinear.

Exercise 6A

1   The diagrams show rigid objects in equilibrium under the action of a number of forces. Find the unknown forces and distances.

(a)   Find P, Q and R.

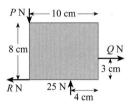

(b)   Find P, Q and x.

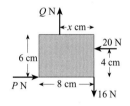

(c)   Find P, Q and x.

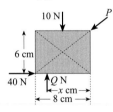

(d)   Find P, Q and R.

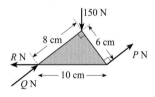

(e)   Find P, Q and x.

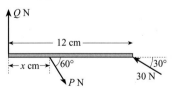

(f)   Find P, Q and R.

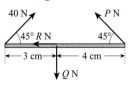

2   A uniform rectangular picture $ABCD$, 3 metres wide and 2 metres high, has weight 400 newtons. It is supported on a trestle at a point E of DC, 1 metre from D, and kept upright by means of a rope attached to the picture at A. Calculate the tension in the rope and the normal and frictional forces at E

(a)   if the rope is horizontal,

(b)   if the rope is held at 40° to the vertical.

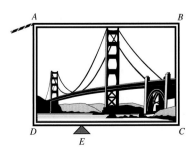

3 (a) A uniform metal bar, of length 4 metres and weight
    2000 newtons, is being pushed horizontally from one
    end across two supports 2 metres apart. The support
    closer to the pushing force is a light rail which can rotate smoothly about a horizontal
    axis. The other support is fixed, and the coefficient of friction at this support is 0.6.
    Calculate the force necessary to push the bar at constant speed when x metres of its
    length projects beyond the fixed support.

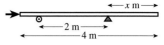

  (b) The fixed support is now raised so that the metal bar is inclined at 10° to the horizontal.
    The distance between the two supports is still 2 metres. Find the least value of x which
    will enable the bar to rest in equilibrium on the two supports without any externally
    applied force.

4 In a stretching exercise two men, of the same height and
    weight, stand toe-to-toe, each grasping the other's wrists.
    Both lean backwards, so that their arms are stretched, and
    both keep their bodies straight. One of the men is modelled
    as a rod having one end A in contact with the ground,
    which is horizontal. The weight of 800 N acts through the
    point 100 cm from A. The rod is kept at an angle of 66° to
    the horizontal by a horizontal force of magnitude P newtons
    applied at the point which is 150 cm from A, as shown in the
    diagram. Find P.

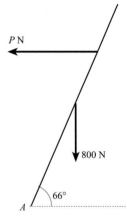

   Given that the men are on the point of slipping and that their feet
   do not touch each other, use the model to estimate the coefficient
   of friction between the men's shoes and the floor.

5 A rectangular platform $ABCD$ of weight 200 N is smoothly
   hinged, along its edge AB, to a vertical wall. The platform is
   kept horizontal by two parallel chains, inclined at 45° to
   the horizontal, connecting the points P and Q of the wall
   to the points D and C respectively, as shown in the
   diagram. P and Q are vertically above A and B respectively.
   A man of weight 850 N stands on the edge of the platform
   midway between D and C. Find

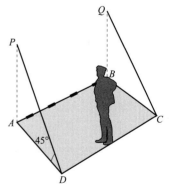

  (a) the tension in each of the chains,

  (b) the magnitude of the total force exerted on the hinge by
      the wall.

6   A gardener is taking a wheelbarrow down a path which
slopes at 6° to the horizontal. She puts it down for a rest.
The rear legs of the barrow are 120 cm behind the front
wheel. The weight of the barrow and its load is 300
newtons, and the centre of mass, G, is 40 cm from the
path and 50 cm behind the front wheel. There is no
friction at the contact between the wheel and the path.
What is the least coefficient of friction between the legs
and the path which will enable the barrow to rest in
equilibrium?

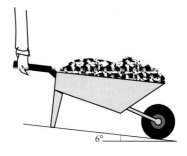

The gardener now lifts up the barrow and starts to wheel it down the path at a steady speed.
She holds the handles at points 150 cm behind the front wheel and 60 cm from the path.
Find the components parallel and perpendicular to the path of the total force from her two
arms. Hence find the tension in each arm and the angle between her arm and the direction
of the slope.

7   A uniform beam AB has length 3.5 m and weight 200 N. The
beam has its end A in contact with horizontal ground and is
at rest propped against a marble slab of height 0.7 m, as
shown in the diagram. A is 2.4 m from the nearest face of
the slab. Assuming the contact between the beam and the
slab is smooth, find the normal and frictional components
of the contact force at A, and hence find the least possible
value of the coefficient of friction between the beam and
the ground.

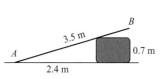

8   A car of weight W is parked facing downwards on a straight road inclined at angle α to the
horizontal. The handbrake is on, which has the effect of locking the back wheels. The total
normal contact force on the front wheels is S and the total normal contact force on the
back wheels is R. Given that $S + R = \frac{24}{25} W$, find the value of $\cos \alpha$ and of the total frictional
force, in terms of W, on the rear wheels.

The distance between the front and rear wheels is L. The distance of the centre of mass of
the car behind the front wheels is kL, and from the road surface is h. Show that
$$R = \tfrac{1}{25} W \left(24k - \frac{7h}{L} \right).$$
Given that $k = 0.4$ and that $\dfrac{h}{L} = 0.3$, find the ratio $\dfrac{S}{R}$.

6.2   Breaking equilibrium by sliding or toppling

Suppose that you are trying to push a box across the floor by applying a force along the top
edge. If the floor is not too rough, there should be no problem so long as you push hard
enough. But if the floor is very rough, the box may topple over about the opposite edge.

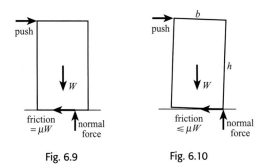

Fig. 6.9   Fig. 6.10

In practice you would probably start with quite a small force, and gradually increase it until the box starts to move. Fig. 6.9 illustrates what you hope will happen, assuming that the box has not yet toppled over. If the box has weight W and you push horizontally, the normal force is also W. You must therefore push with a force greater than the limiting friction μW.

Fig. 6.10 illustrates what you hope will not happen, assuming that the box has not started to slide. If the clockwise moment of the push about the edge of the box exceeds the anticlockwise moment of the weight, the box will start to topple over. Suppose that the box has height h and width b, and the pushing force is P. Then the critical value of P is when the two moments are equal; that is,

$$\mathcal{M}(\text{edge of box}) \qquad Ph = W\left(\tfrac{1}{2}b\right),$$

which gives $P = \dfrac{Wb}{2h}$.

So if μW is less than $\dfrac{Wb}{2h}$, then as the push is increased the box will start to slide before the push reaches a value large enough to make it topple. But if $\dfrac{Wb}{2h}$ is less than μW, the box will start to topple before the push reaches a value large enough to overcome the friction. That is, as the push is increased, the box will slide if $\mu < \dfrac{b}{2h}$, but it will topple if $\mu > \dfrac{b}{2h}$.

Example 6.2.1
A table lamp has a circular base of radius 10 cm, and its centre of mass is 15 cm above the centre of the base. The lamp is placed on a hinged desk lid which is inclined at an angle α to the horizontal. The coefficient of friction between the base of the lamp and the desk lid is 0.6. State the conditions for the lamp to rest on the lid in equilibrium. If the angle α is gradually increased, will equilibrium be broken by sliding or toppling?

Fig. 6.11 shows the forces on the lamp while it is in equilibrium. The weight is not given, so denote it by W N. The other two forces are the normal contact force of R N and a frictional force of F N acting up the slope.

The forces must satisfy two equations of resolving and one of moments.

$\mathcal{R}(\perp \text{ to the slope}) \quad R = W\cos\alpha.$
$\mathcal{R}(\text{up the slope}) \qquad F = W\cos(90° - \alpha), \quad \text{which is} \quad F = W\sin\alpha.$

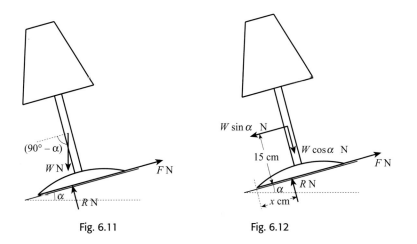

Fig. 6.11   Fig. 6.12

The equation of moments is most easily written by splitting the weight into components $W\cos\alpha$ N perpendicular to the slope and $W\sin\alpha$ N down the slope, as in Fig. 6.12.

There is one other unknown, which is the point of the base at which the resultant normal contact force is taken to act. If the lid were horizontal, this point would be at the centre of the base. But when the lid is tilted, this point shifts down the slope. In Fig. 6.12 the force is shown acting at a distance of x cm from the lowest point of the base.

> You can demonstrate this shift of the contact force experimentally by standing on a slope facing downhill, leaning forward so that your body is perpendicular to the slope. You will find that in this position more of your weight is taken by the ball of the foot and less by the heel. This is because the resultant normal contact force has shifted down the slope.

The equation of moments about the lowest point of the base is then

$$Rx + (W\sin\alpha) \times 15 = (W\cos\alpha) \times 10.$$

The three equations are based on the assumption that the lamp is in equilibrium. But for this to be possible two conditions have to be satisfied: the lamp must not slide down the lid, and it must not topple about the lowest point of the base.

The condition for the lamp not to slide is that $\dfrac{F}{R} \leqslant 0.6$, that is

$$\frac{W\sin\alpha}{W\cos\alpha} \leqslant 0.6,$$

which gives

$$\tan\alpha \leqslant 0.6.$$

The condition for the lamp not to topple is that $x \geqslant 0$, so from the third equation

$$(W \sin \alpha) \times 15 \leqslant (W \cos \alpha) \times 10.$$

So
$$\frac{W \sin \alpha}{W \cos \alpha} \leqslant \frac{10}{15},$$

which gives

$$\tan \alpha \leqslant \frac{2}{3}.$$

Now as the angle α is gradually increased, $\tan \alpha$ increases until one or other of these conditions is broken. Since 0.6 is less than $\frac{2}{3}$, the first condition to fail is that $\tan \alpha \leqslant 0.6$. This means that equilibrium is broken by sliding, and that this occurs as soon as $\tan \alpha$ exceeds 0.6. So the lamp will begin to slide down the lid when the lid makes an angle of 31.0° with the horizontal.

Example 6.2.2

A small boy of weight 300 N sits on a square table, dangling his legs over the edge. His centre of mass G_B is directly above the line of the legs, 120 cm above the floor. The table has weight 200 N, and its centre of mass G_T is 70 cm above the floor. The feet of the legs form a square of side 160 cm. The floor is very rough, and the coefficient of friction between the seat of the boy's trousers and the table is 0.3. His sister starts to tilt the table about the legs above which the boy is sitting. Will he slide off the table, or will the boy and the table topple over together?

Fig. 6.13 shows the situation before the table begins to tilt, and Fig. 6.14 shows the situation when the table is at an angle θ to the floor and is about to topple over.

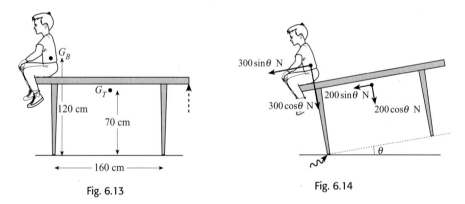

Fig. 6.13   Fig. 6.14

Suppose that the boy is still on the table when it starts to topple over. To make the calculation of moments easier, the weights of the boy and the table have been split into components parallel and perpendicular to the table-top.

$\mathcal{M}$(feet of legs on floor) $300 \sin \theta \times 120 + 200 \sin \theta \times 70 = 200 \cos \theta \times 80.$

This gives $\tan \theta = \dfrac{16\,000}{36\,000 + 14\,000} = 0.32.$

Now you know that, for an object on a sloping surface, sliding takes place when $\tan\theta = \mu$. (See M1 Experiment 5.3.2.) So, if the table has not already toppled, the boy will slide off the table when $\tan\theta = 0.3$.

As the table is tilted, the value of $\tan\theta$ increases from zero. It will reach the value 0.3 first, so the boy will start to slide off the table before it topples over with him on it.

Example 6.2.3

In a forest, after trees have been felled and trimmed, the trunks are towed to a central collection point. A cable is attached to the narrow end of each trunk, and the tension is then increased by a winch on the towing truck. One such trunk is 10 metres long, and its centre of mass is 6 metres from the end to which the cable is attached. The coefficient of friction of the trunk with the ground is 0.6. What angle should the cable make with the horizontal if the trunk is to be lifted clear of the ground rather than dragged along?

Let T_1 newtons be the tension in the cable needed to lift the end from the ground, supposing that the trunk has not started to drag. The forces are shown in Fig. 6.15.

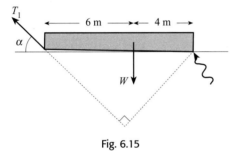

Fig. 6.15

If the cable is at an angle α to the horizontal, and the weight of the trunk is W newtons,

$$\mathcal{M}(\text{thick end}) \qquad T_1(10\sin\alpha) = 4W.$$

That is, $T_1 = \dfrac{2W}{5\sin\alpha}.$

Let T_2 newtons be the tension in the cable needed to drag the trunk along the ground, supposing that it has not started to lift clear of the ground. Friction is then limiting, and the forces are as shown in Fig. 6.16.

If the normal contact force is R newtons,

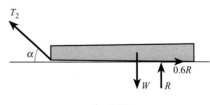

Fig. 6.16

$$\mathcal{R}(\leftarrow) \qquad T_2\cos\alpha = 0.6R, \quad \text{and}$$
$$\mathcal{R}(\uparrow) \qquad T_2\sin\alpha + R = W.$$

Eliminating R from these equations,

$$T_2\cos\alpha = 0.6(W - T_2\sin\alpha),$$

so $T_2 = \dfrac{0.6W}{\cos\alpha + 0.6\sin\alpha}.$

As the tension in the cable is increased, the trunk will lift off the ground first if $T_1 < T_2$, that is if

$$\frac{2}{5 \sin \alpha} < \frac{0.6}{\cos \alpha + 0.6 \sin \alpha},$$

which gives $2 \cos \alpha + 1.2 \sin \alpha < 3 \sin \alpha$, or $2 \cos \alpha < 1.8 \sin \alpha$, leading to $\tan \alpha > \dfrac{2}{1.8}$, and $\alpha > 48.0°$, correct to 3 significant figures.

So to lift the trunk clear of the ground before it starts to drag, the cable should make an angle of at least 48° with the horizontal.

6.3 Locating lines of action

In many problems you know the points at which the various forces act, but what is not known is their magnitude or their direction. However, this is not always the case.

Look back at Fig. 6.9. What is shown as the normal force from the floor on the box is in fact the resultant of small forces acting at all the points where the box and the floor are in contact. Before you start to push the box, this resultant acts at the centre of the base, directly below the centre of mass of the box. When the force is applied at the top edge, the contact forces get bigger on the right side of the base and smaller on the left side, so the resultant normal force moves to the right.

Fig. 6.17 shows the situation when you push with a horizontal force of magnitude P, before the box starts to either slide or topple. Suppose that the resultant normal force then acts at a point X on the base of the box, at a distance x from the centre. If you take moments about X, then neither the normal force nor the friction come into the equation.

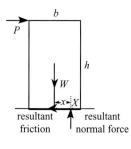

Fig. 6.17

$\mathcal{M}(X)$ $Wx = Ph$.

It follows that $x = \dfrac{Ph}{W}$. Since h and W are constant, this shows that, as P increases, x increases and X moves to the right.

If the floor is rough enough, then x eventually reaches $\frac{1}{2}b$, when $P = \dfrac{Wb}{2h}$. The box is then just about to start to topple.

Example 6.3.1
A raft is stuck on a hidden obstruction in a river-bed (see Fig. 6.18). Ropes are attached to one edge of the raft at A, B and C, where $AB = 6$ m and $BC = 2$ m. The crew pull on these ropes with forces of 400 N, 350 N and 450 N at right angles to the edge of the raft, but fail to move it. Where is the obstruction?

Suppose that the obstruction lies along a line through X perpendicular to the edge of the raft, where X is the point of the edge x metres from A, as shown in Fig. 6.18. If you take moments about the obstruction, the force which it produces will not appear in the equation.

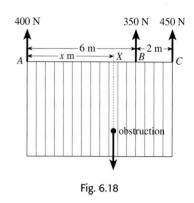

$\mathcal{M}(\text{obstruction})$

$$400x = 350(6 - x) + 450(8 - x).$$

This gives $1200x = 5700$, so $x = 4\frac{3}{4}$.

The obstruction is somewhere along the perpendicular to the edge through a point X, $4\frac{3}{4}$ metres from A.

Fig. 6.18

In this example you could just as well have taken moments about any point of the edge. For example, $\mathcal{M}(A)$ would have given the equation $1200x = 6 \times 350 + 8 \times 450$ directly. To use this, you have to begin by finding the force from the obstruction by resolving, but this is not difficult!

However, an advantage of taking moments about the unknown point is that just one of the unknown quantities appears in each equation. You can see this in the next example, which has forces in two dimensions.

Example 6.3.2
In a mechanism a rectangular plate $ABCD$ is subjected to forces at A, B and D as shown in Fig. 6.19. Where should a fourth force be applied to keep the plate in equilibrium?

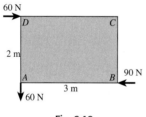

Fig. 6.19

A convenient method is to use coordinates, shown in Fig. 6.20. Let the fourth force, acting at the point P with coordinates (x, y), have components X and Y parallel to the axes. Then you can write down three equations.

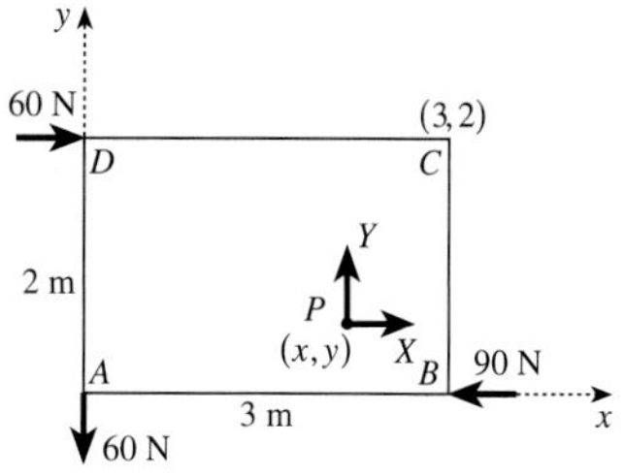

$\mathcal{R}(x\text{-direction}) \quad X + 60 = 90,$

so $X = 30$.

$\mathcal{R}(y\text{-direction}) \quad Y = 60.$

$\mathcal{M}(P) \quad\quad 60x = 90y + 60(2 - y),$

which can be simplified to $y = 2x - 4$.

Fig. 6.20

Notice that there are four unknowns but only three equations. You should expect this; $y = 2x - 4$ is the equation of the line of action of the force, and it doesn't matter where along the line of action the fourth force is applied.

As a check, Fig. 6.21 shows the force with components $X = 30$ and $Y = 60$ combined to give a single resultant force. You will see that this makes an angle $\tan^{-1} 2$ with the x-direction, so it is parallel to the line of action with gradient 2.

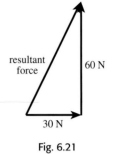

The fourth force, of magnitude $30\sqrt{5}$, should be applied at some point along the line $y = 2x - 4$. The most convenient points would be where this line cuts the boundary of the plate, that is either at C with coordinates $(3,2)$, or at $(2,0)$, 2 metres from A along the edge AB.

Fig. 6.21

6.4*   Indeterminate problems

You may omit this section if you wish.

Suppose that a uniform shelf AC of length 4 metres and weight W newtons rests on supports at both ends and at B, 1 metre from C. How much of the weight is taken by each support?

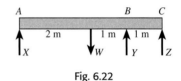

Fig. 6.22

Let the forces at A, B and C be (in newtons) X, Y and Z (Fig. 6.22).

There are three unknowns, so you need three equations. You might try

$\mathcal{R}(\uparrow)$ $X + Y + Z = W,$
$\mathcal{M}(A)$ $3Y + 4Z = 2W,$ and
$\mathcal{M}(C)$ $4X + Y = 2W.$

But if you try to solve these for X, Y and Z, you will be unlucky. For example, if you try to eliminate Z by taking the second equation from 4 times the first, you will get $4(X + Y + Z) - (3Y + 4Z) = 4W - 2W$, or $4X + Y = 2W$, which is the third equation over again.

The reason is that the problem does not have a unique solution. You could remove the support at B completely and just support the shelf at A and C, with $X = Z = \frac{1}{2}W$ and $Y = 0$. Or you could remove the support at C and just support the shelf at A and B, with $X = \frac{1}{3}W$, $Y = \frac{2}{3}W$ and $Z = 0$. It is easy to check that both these sets of values satisfy the three equations you started with.

A problem like this is said to be **indeterminate**. In practice, if you were to build the shelf, it would bend a little and the supports might not be exactly level; and a small adjustment in the heights would change the proportions of the weight taken by each support.

The best that you can do is to write down some inequalities satisfied by X, Y, and Z. None of these forces can be negative. The equation $\mathcal{M}(A)$ above shows that, since $Z \geqslant 0$, $Y \leqslant \frac{2}{3}W$; and since $Y \geqslant 0$, $Z \leqslant \frac{1}{2}W$. The equation $\mathcal{M}(C)$ shows that, since $Y \geqslant 0$, $X \leqslant \frac{1}{2}W$. Also, from the equation $\mathcal{M}(B)$, $3X = Z + W$; since $Z \geqslant 0$, $X \geqslant \frac{1}{3}W$.

If you have done any linear programming, you will know how to show sets of inequalities like this graphically.

In Fig. 6.23, X, Y and Z can take any set of values represented by points on the line joining $\left(\frac{1}{2}W, 0, \frac{1}{2}W\right)$ and $\left(\frac{1}{3}W, \frac{2}{3}W, 0\right)$. These end points correspond to the cases where the supports at B and C are removed.

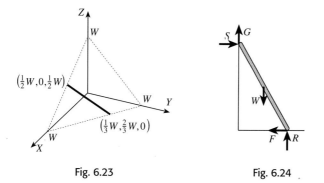

Fig. 6.23   Fig. 6.24

Another example of an indeterminate problem is when you set a ladder up against a rough wall on rough ground. When, as at the beginning of this chapter, both the wall and the ground are smooth, it is impossible for the ladder to rest in equilibrium. But if there is friction at both contacts, then you have four unknowns (R, S, F and G in Fig. 6.24), and you can only write down three independent equations.

You can investigate this further for yourself in Exercise 6B, Question 15.

Exercise 6B

1   A fridge of mass 60 kg and width 80 cm stands on a kitchen floor. The coefficient of friction between the base and the floor is 0.4. A woman tries to push the fridge across the floor. What is the greatest height at which she can apply the force if the fridge is to remain vertical as she pushes?

2   The diagram shows a square picture frame of weight 200 N which has to be pushed down a ramp inclined at 5° to the horizontal. The coefficient of friction between the frame and the ramp is 0.55. A force is applied to the frame parallel to the ramp at the top corner of the frame. This force is gradually increased until the frame moves. Find how large the force is when equilibrium is broken, and whether with this force the frame tilts or slides down the ramp.

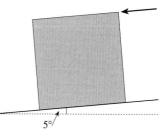

3 A uniformly loaded box of fish is 90 cm long, 15 cm high and weighs 200 N. The coefficient of friction between the box and the ground is $\frac{2}{3}$. A rope is attached to the top of the box at one end and held at 45° to the horizontal. The tension in the rope is increased until the box starts to move along the ground. Find the tension needed to move the box, and show that with this force the box will not lift off the ground.

4 A prism has a cross-section in the form of a rhombus with acute angle 40°. It is placed on a shelf which is originally horizontal, as shown in the diagram. The coefficient of friction between the prism and the shelf is 0.4. The shelf is now gradually rotated about a horizontal axis until equilibrium is broken.

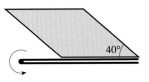

   (a) Find the angle through which the shelf must be rotated before the prism topples, assuming that it has not slid first.

   (b) Find the angle through which the shelf must be rotated before the prism slides, assuming that it has not toppled first.

   Hence determine how equilibrium is broken.

5 A chair weighing 50 newtons stands on a rough floor. Its centre of mass is 30 cm behind the front legs, and 20 cm in front of the back legs. The back of the chair is 1 metre high. If a gradually increasing horizontal force is applied at the top of the back of the chair in a forward direction, the chair slides forwards. If a force of the same magnitude is applied at the same point in the opposite direction, the chair topples. What can you say about the coefficient of friction?

6 An Arctic explorer drags a sledge across a horizontal ice-field by means of a rope attached to his body harness. The rope is 5 metres long, and attached to him at a height of 1.4 metres. The sledge is 3 metres long, and the coefficient of friction between the sledge and the ice is 0.2. Where must the centre of mass of the loaded sledge be if it is not to tip up as it is pulled?

7 A cylindrical tin has radius 6 cm and height 30 cm, and weighs 100 newtons. The tin stands on a table, 40 cm from the edge, which is smooth and rounded. A string is attached to the point of the top rim of the tin closest to the edge of the table; it passes over the edge and holds a bucket at its other end. Water is poured into the bucket until equilibrium is broken.

   (a) How much must the bucket weigh before the tin starts to topple over?

   (b) What can be said about the coefficient of friction between the tin and the table if the tin doesn't slide before it begins to topple?

8 A uniform cubical box of weight W stands on a horizontal floor. The coefficient of friction is μ. To try to pull it along the floor, a force of magnitude P is applied at the centre of one of the top edges, at an angle α above the horizontal, where $0 \leqslant \alpha < \frac{1}{2}\pi$.

   (a) Show that, if the box does not topple, it will slide when $P = \dfrac{\mu W}{\cos\alpha + \mu\sin\alpha}$.

   (b) Show that, if the box does not slide, it will topple when $P = \dfrac{W}{2\cos\alpha}$.

   The value of P is gradually increased from zero. What condition must be satisfied by μ and α if the box begins to slide before it topples?

9 A standard lamp has a square base with edges of length b. Its centre of mass is at a height h above its base. When it is placed on a sloping ramp at an angle α to the horizontal, it is on the point of both sliding down the ramp and toppling. Show that $\tan \alpha = \mu = \dfrac{b}{2h}$.

A force is now applied parallel to the ramp to try to push it up the slope. Show that, if the lamp is to slide rather than topple, the force must be applied below the level of the centre of mass.

10 Forces act on the rectangular plate $ABCD$ as shown. The plate is in equilibrium. Find F and x.

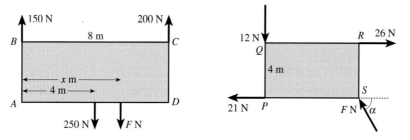

11 Forces act on the plate $PQRS$ as shown above. The distance PQ is 4 metres. Given that the plate is in equilibrium, find

    (a) F,   (b) the angle α,   (c) the distance PS.

12 Forces act on the triangular plate ABO as shown. The coordinates of A and B are $(L, 0)$ and $(0, L)$. If the plate is in equilibrium, find the components of F in the x- and y-directions, and the equation of the line of action of F.

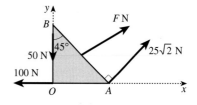

13 Some of the forces which act on a rigid object, and the coordinates of points at which they are applied, are given; the units are newtons and metres. The symbol $\begin{pmatrix} X \\ Y \end{pmatrix}$ denotes a force whose components in the directions of the x- and y-axes are X and Y. Where possible, find another force which, when combined with the given ones, will keep the object in equilibrium. Find also the equation of the line along which this force must act.

(a) $\begin{pmatrix} 2 \\ 0 \end{pmatrix}$ at $(3,2)$, $\begin{pmatrix} 0 \\ 4 \end{pmatrix}$ at $(1,0)$

(b) $\begin{pmatrix} 3 \\ -2 \end{pmatrix}$ at $(0,3)$, $\begin{pmatrix} 1 \\ 3 \end{pmatrix}$ at $(-2,1)$

(c) $\begin{pmatrix} 2 \\ 0 \end{pmatrix}$ at $(7,2)$, $\begin{pmatrix} 1 \\ -3 \end{pmatrix}$ at $(1,0)$, $\begin{pmatrix} -3 \\ 1 \end{pmatrix}$ at $(4,-1)$

(d) $\begin{pmatrix} 5 \\ -3 \end{pmatrix}$ at $(1,2)$, $\begin{pmatrix} -2 \\ 1 \end{pmatrix}$ at $(6,5)$, $\begin{pmatrix} -3 \\ 2 \end{pmatrix}$ at $(0,-1)$

(e) $\begin{pmatrix} 2 \\ 0 \end{pmatrix}$ at $(1,4)$, $\begin{pmatrix} 0 \\ -3 \end{pmatrix}$ at $(5,2)$, $\begin{pmatrix} -2 \\ 3 \end{pmatrix}$ at $(0,0)$

14 A uniform box has a central square cross-section *ABCD* with sides of length 60 cm. It stands on a smooth slope at an angle of 30° to the horizontal, with the side *DC* in contact with the slope and *D* below *C*. Equilibrium is maintained by a horizontal force applied at *A*. If the resultant normal contact force acts at the point *E*, calculate the distance *CE*.

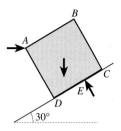

15* This question refers to Fig. 6.24. Consider the special case in which the ladder is in equilibrium with the top at a height of 4 metres above the ground and the foot at a distance of 2 metres from the wall.

   (a) Write down equations of resolving vertically and horizontally, and moments about the top and the foot of the ladder. Show that you cannot solve these to find the four unknowns R, S, F and G.

   (b) Write down an equation of moments about the corner where the ground meets the wall. Does this, combined with your equations in part (a), enable you to find the four unknowns?

   (c) Is it possible to have equilibrium with
      (i) F,   (ii) G
      acting in the direction opposite to that shown in the figure?

   (d) If equilibrium is limiting with F and G acting in the directions shown in the figure, and if the coefficient of friction is the same at both contacts, find the coefficient of friction.

   (e) Show that, if the coefficients of friction at the foot and the top of the ladder are μ_1 and μ_2 respectively, then $\mu_1(\mu_2 + 4) \geqslant 1$.

Miscellaneous exercise 6

1 Forces act on the plate *OABC* as shown. The distance *OC* is 5 metres. Given that the plate is in equilibrium, find the equation of the line of action of the force of magnitude *F* newtons.

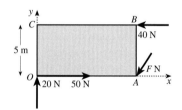

2 A uniform rod *AB*, of length 0.6 m and mass 3.2 kg, is smoothly hinged at *A* to a fixed vertical wall. The rod is held in equilibrium by a horizontal force of magnitude *F* newtons, acting at *B* in the vertical plane containing *AB*. The rod makes an angle of 35° with the wall (see diagram). Find

   (a) the value of *F*,

   (b) the horizontal and vertical components of the force on the rod at *A*, indicating clearly the directions in which these components act.   (OCR)

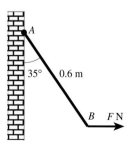

3 A uniform rod AB has mass 1.2 kg and length 50 cm. The end A of the
   rod is pivoted at a fixed point. A light inextensible string has one end
   attached to B and the other end attached to a fixed point C. The point
   C is in the same vertical plane as AB and is such that AB is at right
   angles to BC. The rod is in equilibrium, inclined at 20° to the
   horizontal with B higher than A, as shown. Calculate

   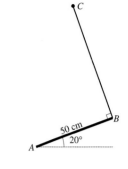

   (a) the tension in the string,

   (b) the horizontal and vertical components of the force acting on
        the rod at A.   (OCR)

4 Two circular pipes are fixed with their axes horizontal and
   parallel to each other. A uniform plank AB, of length 2 m
   and weight 162 N, rests on the pipes, with A higher than B,
   in a vertical plane which is perpendicular to the axes of the
   pipes (see diagram). The plank touches one of the pipes at
   X and the other at Y, where $AX = 60$ cm, $XY = 70$ cm and X
   is higher than Y. The plank makes an angle of 30° with the
   horizontal. Calculate the normal components of the contact
   forces on the plank at X and Y.

   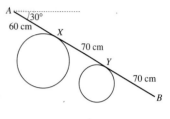

   The coefficient of friction has the same value μ at each contact. Given that the plank is on
   the point of slipping, find μ.   (OCR)

5 A uniform rectangular box stands on a horizontal floor and leans against a
   vertical wall. The diagram shows the vertical cross-section $ABCD$
   containing the centre of mass G of the box. $AD = 2$ m, $AB = 0.5$ m and AD
   makes an angle θ with the horizontal. The weight of the box is 200 N.

   (a) By splitting the weight into components parallel and perpendicular to
        AD, or otherwise, show that the anticlockwise moment of the weight
        about the point D is $(200\cos\theta - 50\sin\theta)$ N m.

   (b) The contact at A between the box and the wall is smooth. Find, in terms of θ, the
        magnitude of the force acting on the box at A.

   (c) The contact at D between the box and the ground is rough, with coefficient of friction
        0.3. Given that the box is about to slip, find the value of θ.   (OCR)

6 A uniform solid cylinder has height 30 cm and radius
   10 cm. The cylinder is held on a rough plane, with its base
   in contact with the plane, as shown in the diagram. The
   plane is inclined at a fixed angle α to the horizontal. The
   cylinder is released. The coefficient of friction between the
   cylinder and the plane is μ. Given that the cylinder
   remains in equilibrium, show that $\tan\alpha \leqslant \frac{2}{3}$ and $\tan\alpha \leqslant \mu$.

   Describe briefly, giving reasons, what, if anything, happens
   when the cylinder is released in each of the following cases:

   (a) $\mu = \frac{1}{3}$ and $\tan\alpha = \frac{1}{2}$,   (b) $\mu = \frac{4}{5}$ and $\tan\alpha = \frac{3}{4}$.   (OCR)

7 A uniform cylinder of radius 0.05 m is held on a rough plane inclined at 15° to the horizontal (see diagram). The coefficient of friction between the plane and the end of the cylinder in contact with it is 0.3. The cylinder is released from rest. Determine whether or not the cylinder remains in equilibrium in each of the following cases:

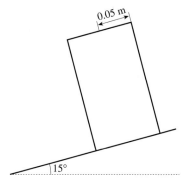

(a) the height of the cylinder is 0.4 m;

(b) the height of the cylinder is 0.35 m.

(If, in either case, the cylinder does not remain in equilibrium, you should state with a reason the way in which the cylinder starts to move.)   (OCR)

8 A ladder is in a vertical plane which is perpendicular to a vertical wall, and leans against the wall. The base of the ladder is on horizontal ground and the angle between the ladder and the ground is 70°. The ladder is in equilibrium with a woman standing on the ladder at a point three-quarters of the way up. By considering a model in which the wall is taken to be smooth, the ladder is a uniform rod of mass 10 kg and the woman is a particle of mass 50 kg,

(a) state the direction of the contact force exerted on the ladder by the wall, and calculate the magnitude of this force,

(b) calculate the horizontal and vertical components of the contact force exerted on the ladder by the ground.

The woman now stands on the ladder at a point lower than three-quarters of the way up. For each of the three quantities calculated in (a) and (b), state which of the following statements applies:

the new value is greater than the old value;

the new value is equal to the old value;

the new value is less than the old value.   (OCR)

9 An L-shaped block has weight W and dimensions as shown in the diagram. The block is at rest on a horizontal table in the position shown. When a horizontal force P is applied to the midpoint of an upper edge, at right angles to the vertical faces, the block topples if the direction of the force is as shown in the first diagram, and slides if the direction is as shown in the second diagram.

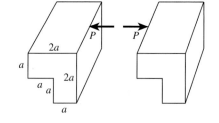

Show that $\frac{1}{12} < \mu < \frac{5}{12}$, where μ is the coefficient of friction between the block and the table.

10 An L-shaped prism has weight W and dimensions as shown. The prism rests in contact with horizontal ground. A force of magnitude T is applied to the point A of the prism in a direction making an angle β with the ground, as shown in the diagram.

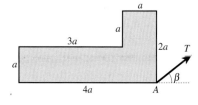

(a) Given that A is on the point of lifting off the ground, show that $T \sin \beta = \frac{23}{40} W$.

(b) Given that the coefficient of friction between the prism and the ground is 0.5, and that A is on the point of moving along the ground, show that $T(\sin \beta + 2 \cos \beta) = W$.

Deduce that, if T is gradually increased from zero, the prism will slide before it starts to lift at A if $\tan \beta < \frac{46}{17}$.

11 A uniform sheet-metal trough of weight W has a cross-section $ABCD$ in which $AB = BC = CD$ and angle $ABC = 150° =$ angle BCD. Initially the trough is placed with AB in contact with the ground, and a small block of weight W is placed on it at the mid-point of AB. Show that the trough can remain at rest in equilibrium in this position.

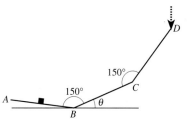

A small downwards force is now applied at D, so that the trough rotates slowly about the edge through B. The figure shows the situation when BC makes an angle θ with the horizontal, where $\theta < 30°$. The coefficient of friction between the block and the trough is 0.4. Determine whether the block starts to slide down AB before the trough falls on its base, or vice versa.

12 The diagram shows a uniform plank of weight W leaning in equilibrium against a vertical wall. The angle between the plank and the horizontal is α. The normal and frictional components of the contact force exerted on the plank by the ground are R and F respectively. The normal and frictional components of the contact force exerted on the plank by the wall are N and S respectively. The coefficient of friction between the ground and the plank is μ.

(a) Show that $W + 2F \tan \alpha = 2R$.

(b) Making the assumption that the wall is smooth, state the value of R in terms of W and show that $F = \dfrac{W}{2 \tan \alpha}$. Deduce that the assumption is false if $\mu < \dfrac{1}{2 \tan \alpha}$.

(c) Making the assumptions instead that the wall is near smooth, and that $S = kN$ where k is small, show that $\dfrac{F}{R} = \dfrac{1}{2 \tan \alpha + k}$. Given that $\tan \alpha = 2$, that $\mu = 10k$ and that the plank is on the point of slipping, find μ.

13 A uniform straight rod AB has length l and weight $2kW$. The rod is in equilibrium, with the end B in contact with a smooth vertical wall and the end A in contact with rough horizontal ground. The rod lies in a vertical plane perpendicular to the wall. The angle between the rod and the ground is θ. A particle of weight W is attached to the rod at the point whose distance from A is xl. The magnitude of the force exerted by the wall on the rod is $\sqrt{3}kW$.

(a) Find, in terms of k and W, the horizontal and vertical components of the force exerted by the ground on the rod.

(b) Find x in terms of k and θ.

Deduce that θ cannot be less than $30°$.   (OCR)

14 The diagram shows a uniform plank of weight W in equilibrium, with its lower end on rough ground and its upper end against a rough fixed plane inclined at $60°$ to the horizontal. The angle between the plank and the horizontal is $30°$. The normal and frictional components of the contact force exerted on the plank by the ground are R and F respectively. The normal and frictional components of the contact force exerted on the plank by the inclined plane are S and G respectively.

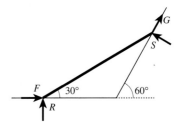

Given that $9G = \sqrt{3}S$,

(a) find F, G, R and S in terms of W,   (b) show that $\dfrac{F}{R} = \tfrac{2}{7}\sqrt{3}$.

15 The diagram shows a cylindrical drum fixed on its side on horizontal ground, and a uniform plank AB, of weight W, resting with the end A on the drum and the end B on the ground. AB is a tangent to the circular cross-section of the drum. The coefficients of friction for the contacts at A and B are each μ, and

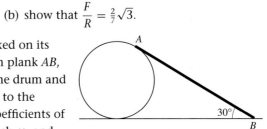

AB is inclined at $30°$ to the ground. The plank is on the point of slipping.

(a) By resolving for the forces on the plank, show that the normal force at A has magnitude $\dfrac{2\mu W}{1+\mu^2}$.

(b) By taking moments about B, show that the normal force at A has magnitude $\tfrac{1}{4}\sqrt{3}W$.

(c) Hence find a quadratic equation satisfied by μ. Solve the quadratic equation and, by considering the normal force at B, find which of the two values of μ applies in this case.   (OCR)

Revision exercise 1

1 A man is sawing through a plank. He exerts a force of 80 newtons on each forward stroke, and 100 newtons on each backward stroke. The length of each stroke is 30 cm. If he completes 25 strokes a minute, what power is he exerting?

2 Two parallel rails are a horizontal distance 2 metres apart. One is slightly higher than the other, so that a girder AB of length 10 metres can be placed horizontally to pass between the rails. The end A projects 1 metre beyond the higher rail, and the end B projects 7 metres beyond the lower rail. The girder is uniform and has weight 9000 newtons.

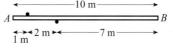

(a) What is the largest weight that can be hung from the girder at any point of its length without disturbing the equilibrium?

(b) If this weight is hung from B, what are the contact forces between the girder and the rails?

3 In the figure the curve AB is a snow slope mounted on a frame used for ski-jumping practice. Skiers start from rest at A, 30 metres above the horizontal ground, and launch themselves into the air from B, 10 metres above the ground, at 10° to the horizontal. C is the point on the ground vertically below B. It is calculated that, if friction, any force exerted by the skier and forces on the skier from the air are neglected, the skier will land at D. Calculate the distance CD.

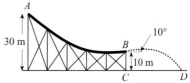

4 A sheet of metal is cut into the T-shape shown in the figure. It is supported on rails at A and B. What can you say about l if the shape can rest vertically and stably in the position shown?

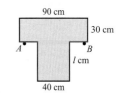

5 A uniform circular cylinder, of radius 6 cm and height 15 cm, is in equilibrium on a fixed inclined plane with one of its ends in contact with the plane.

(a) Given that the cylinder is on the point of toppling, find the angle the plane makes with the horizontal.

The cylinder is now placed on a horizontal board with one of its ends in contact with the board. The board is then tilted so that the angle it makes with the horizontal gradually increases.

(b) Given that the coefficient of friction between the cylinder and the board is $\frac{3}{4}$, determine whether or not the cylinder will slide before it topples, justifying your answer.   (OCR)

6 The power developed by a car's engine in top gear is 40 kW. When travelling at v m s^{-1} the car experiences air resistance of $0.32v^2$ newtons. Neglecting other resistances, calculate the top speed of the car.

If the car has mass 1600 kg, calculate the acceleration of which it is capable when travelling at 40 m s^{-1}.

When climbing a hill the driver finds that, with the engine at full power, the car will not go faster than 30 m s^{-1}. Find the angle that the road makes with the horizontal.

7 A rigid body ABC consists of two uniform rods AB and BC, rigidly joined at B. The lengths of AB and BC are 13 cm and 20 cm respectively, and their weights are 13 N and 20 N respectively. The distance of B from AC is 12 cm. The body hangs in equilibrium, with AC horizontal, from two vertical strings attached at A and C. Find the tension in each string.   (OCR)

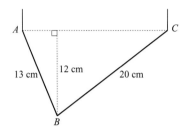

8 A cyclist and his machine have a combined mass of 80 kg. The cyclist ascends a straight hill AB of constant slope, starting from rest at A and reaching a speed of 5 m s^{-1} at B. The level of B is 4 m above the level of A.

(a) Find the gain in kinetic energy and the gain in gravitational potential energy of the cyclist and his machine.

During the ascent the resistance to motion is constant and has magnitude 70 N.

(b) Given that the work done by the cyclist in ascending the hill is 8000 J, find the distance AB.

At B the cyclist is working at 720 watts and starts to move in a straight line along horizontal ground. The resistance to motion has the same magnitude of 70 N as before.

(c) Find the acceleration with which the cyclist starts to move horizontally.   (OCR)

9 The end A of a uniform rod AB, of length 30 cm and weight 13 N, is freely hinged at a fixed point. One end of a light inextensible string of length 72 cm is attached to the end B of the rod. The other end of the string is attached to a fixed point C, which is at the same horizontal level as A. The rod is in equilibrium with the string at right angles to the rod, as shown. Find

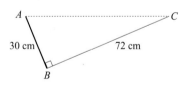

(a) the tension in the string,

(b) the magnitude and direction of the force acting on the rod at A.   (OCR)

10 The student living in room number 6 cuts this shape out of a sheet of cardboard and fixes it to the door with a drawing pin.

(a) How many squares away from the left upright should the pin be placed so that the numeral hangs true?

(b) If the student puts the pin in at the point P, how many degrees out of true will the numeral hang?

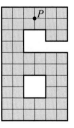

11 A roof slopes at an angle of 30° to the horizontal. The surface is rough and a small object of mass 0.3 kg sliding down the roof experiences a constant frictional force of magnitude 0.5 N. The object slides from rest at the top of the roof for a distance of 12 m to the edge. Air resistance is to be ignored.

(a) Calculate the speed of the object when it leaves the roof.

The object is 4 m above the ground when it leaves the roof.

(b) Calculate the speed at which the object strikes the ground.

(c) Find the direction of motion of the object just before it strikes the ground.   (OCR)

12 A flexible chain of mass m and length l hangs over a smooth horizontal nail with equal lengths on either side. Equilibrium is disturbed by pulling one end of the chain down by a very small amount, so that the chain begins to slip over the nail. Taking the level of the nail as the baseline, find the potential energy of the chain

(a) when it is hanging in equilibrium,

(b) when the last link of the chain has just slipped over the nail.

Hence find the speed with which the chain is moving vertically as the end slips off the nail.

13

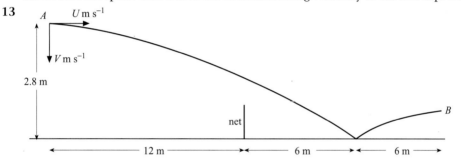

The diagram shows the trajectory of a tennis ball during a serve. The server's racket hits the ball at a point A which is 2.8 metres above the ground, and projects the ball towards the receiver with initial velocity components U m s^{-1} horizontally and V m s^{-1} vertically downwards. The server and the receiver are each at a distance of 12 metres horizontally from the net, and the ball bounces halfway between the net and the receiver. The receiver's racket hits the ball 0.6 seconds after the serve, at the point B. Assume that the ball may be treated as a particle, that air resistance may be neglected, and that the ball's horizontal speed is unaffected by the bounce.

(a) Show that $U = 40$.

(b) Find the value of V, and show that the ball clears the net, which has a height of 0.91 metres, by approximately 0.24 metres.

(c) The point B is 0.75 metres above the ground. Calculate the direction in which the ball is travelling when the receiver's racket hits it at B.

Suppose now that air resistance is taken into account, but that the other assumptions and all the given distances and times remain unchanged. State, with a reason, whether the value of U is larger or smaller than 40.   (OCR)

14 A wire AB 10 metres long is bent into an arc of a circle. It is mounted in a vertical plane so that the tangent at B is horizontal and the tangent at A is at 40° to the horizontal, with the level of B below the level of A. A bead of mass 2 grams is threaded on the wire at A and released. Find its speed when it reaches B

    (a) if the wire is smooth,

    (b) if there is a resistance of constant magnitude 0.004 newtons.

15 A child makes a pile of four cubes on the table, with edges of length 8 cm, 6 cm, 4 cm and 2 cm, as shown in the diagram. Find the height of the centre of mass of the pile above the table

    (a) if the cubes are solid and all made of the same material,

    (b) if the cubes are hollow and made of the same sheet material.

16 A ruler 1 metre long weighs 2 newtons. A boy supports it horizontally using the index fingers of his two hands. His left and right fingers are at the 0 cm and 80 cm marks respectively. He then tries to bring his fingers together slowly, applying horizontal forces of equal magnitude just large enough for one finger to slip. The coefficient of friction between each finger and the ruler is 0.5. Which finger will slip, and what initial force will be needed? What will happen after that?

Suppose now that the coefficient of friction is 0.5 if there is no movement, but that it is only 0.4 when there is movement between the surfaces. Show that in this case the first finger to slip will continue to do so until it reaches the 26 cm mark, and that after that the other finger will start to slip. Up to what mark will the second finger move?

17 The diagram shows a racing dinghy crewed by two people each of weight 800 newtons, sailing straight ahead at constant speed. The wind on the sails is horizontal, and has a sideways component of S newtons and a forward component of F newtons, acting at a height 3.2 metres above sea level. The water exerts a sideways force on the hull and the keel of P newtons, acting 0.8 metres below sea level. To keep the boat on an even keel, the crew place their feet on the deck rail and lean out from the side of the dinghy, so that their weight acts along a line 2 metres from the centre line of the boat. Calculate S.

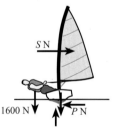

If the resultant wind force is at 65° to the direction of the boat, calculate the combined resistance of the air and the water to the forward motion of the boat.

18 In the game of cricket, a player sometimes has to throw the ball from the edge of the field to another player in the middle of the field as quickly and accurately as possible. The motion of the ball is modelled as that of a particle moving under gravity with constant acceleration, and the two players are 60 metres apart.

    (a) A player throws the ball with a speed of $20\,\mathrm{m\,s^{-1}}$ at an angle of 45° above the horizontal from a height 2 metres above ground level. Show that the ball bounces before it reaches the other player 60 metres away.

(b) A player who can throw the ball with a speed of $25\,\mathrm{m\,s^{-1}}$ throws it with this speed, from a height of 2 metres above ground level, at an angle α above the horizontal. The ball travels without bouncing to the other player 60 metres away who catches it at a height of 1 metre above ground level. Using the cartesian equation of the trajectory, or otherwise, find the two possible values of α, and find the time taken for the throw when the more suitable of the two values for α is used.   (OCR)

19 An earth-moving vehicle runs on two continuous metal tracks. The length of track in contact with the ground is 3 metres, and the outsides of the two tracks are 2 metres apart. The centre of the rectangular patch of ground between the tracks is O. The vehicle is in two parts. The part which includes the tracks and the engine has mass 2 tonnes, and its centre of mass is 0.4 metres above O. The other part, which includes the cabin, the earth-moving mechanism and the load, can have mass up to 3 tonnes; this part can rotate about a vertical axis above O. Its centre of mass may be as much as 2.4 metres above the ground, and 0.5 metres from the axis of rotation.

(a) What can you say about the position of the centre of mass of the whole vehicle including its load?

(b) What is the greatest angle of the slope on which the vehicle should be operated

(i) with the tracks facing up or down the slope,
(ii) with the tracks facing across the slope?

20 A uniform circular hoop, of mass 2 kg and radius 0.5 metres, rests in a vertical plane in contact with a small rough peg A. The point B of the hoop is at the opposite end of the diameter through A. The hoop is held in equilibrium by means of a force of magnitude P newtons acting at B. The line of action of this force lies in the plane of the hoop, and is directed along the tangent to the hoop at B. The line AB makes an angle θ with the downward vertical at A.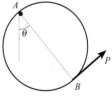

(a) Given that $\theta = 30°$, find the value of P.

(b) Given instead that the coefficient of friction between the hoop and the peg is $\frac{2}{3}$ and that the equilibrium is limiting, find θ.   (OCR)

21 The square $ABCD$ in the diagram is the central cross-section of a cuboidal block of weight W. The block stands on the ground with AD against a vertical wall. The edge through A perpendicular to $ABCD$ is smoothly hinged to the wall. A cable is attached to the block at B, and this is used to raise the block slowly off the ground until AB is vertical. The cable passes over a pulley at the point E above A such that $AE = AB$, and the other end is wound onto a drum powered by a motor. Show that, when AB makes an angle θ with the horizontal, the tension in the cable is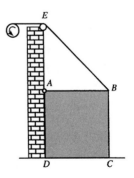

$$\tfrac{1}{2}\sqrt{2}\,W\frac{\sin(45° + \theta)}{\sin(45° + \tfrac{1}{2}\theta)}.$$

Sketch graphs of $\sin(45° + \theta)$ and $\sin\left(45° + \tfrac{1}{2}\theta\right)$ for values of θ from $0°$ to $90°$, and use these to describe how the tension in the cable varies as the block is raised.

7 Impulse and restitution

This chapter is about the impulses which objects exert on each other when they collide, and the relation between the separation speed and the approach speed. When you have completed the chapter, you should

- know the meaning of impulse, and the relation connecting impulse with change in momentum
- be able to calculate the impulse when objects collide
- know Newton's law of impact, and use the coefficient of restitution
- understand the idea of compression and restitution during an impact
- know that imperfectly elastic collisions result in a reduction of the total kinetic energy.

7.1 Impulse

Suppose that a force F acts on an object of mass m for a time t, and that as a result its velocity changes from u to v. It was shown in M1 Section 8.1 that combining the equations $F = ma$ and $v = u + at$ leads to the 'momentum equation'

$$Ft = mv - mu.$$

The name 'momentum' was then given to the quantity

mass × velocity,

so that the expression on the right side of the momentum equation represents the change in the momentum of the object as a result of the action of the force.

The expression Ft on the left side of the momentum equation is called the **impulse** of the force. For example, a force of 50 newtons acting for 6 seconds produces an impulse of 300 newton seconds. The momentum equation can then be summarised as:

> **The impulse–momentum principle** The impulse applied to an object in a given direction is equal to the gain in momentum of the object in that direction.

Example 7.1.1
A tennis player serves the ball with a speed of $50 \, \text{m s}^{-1}$. The mass of the ball is 60 grams. Find the impulse from the racket on the ball.

> The mass of the ball in basic SI units is $0.06 \, \text{kg}$, so the ball gains momentum of $0.06 \times 50 \, \text{N s}$. This results from the impulse it receives from the racket. The impulse from the racket on the ball is therefore $3 \, \text{N s}$.

Example 7.1.2

In cricket a batsman receives a ball travelling at $25\,\text{m s}^{-1}$. He hits it straight back towards the bowler with an impulse of $6\,\text{N s}$. The mass of the ball is $0.15\,\text{kg}$. Find the speed with which the ball leaves the bat.

Because the ball changes direction when it is hit, you have to choose which direction along the line between the wickets is to be taken as the positive direction. Take this to be from the batsman towards the bowler.

The ball is originally travelling in the negative direction, from the bowler towards the batsman, so its momentum is $-0.15 \times 25\,\text{N s}$, which is $-3.75\,\text{N s}$. This momentum is increased by the impulse of $6\,\text{N s}$, so the momentum of the ball after it is hit is $(6 - 3.75)\,\text{N s}$, which is $2.25\,\text{N s}$.

If the speed of the ball is then $v\,\text{m s}^{-1}$, then

$$0.15v = 2.25,$$

which gives $v = 15$.

The ball is hit back towards the bowler with a speed of $15\,\text{m s}^{-1}$.

In both these examples the impulse is the result of a sharp blow which acts for a very short time. Because the time is small, the force of the blow is large. You would need quite an elaborate experiment to determine this time or the magnitude of the force. But often it is simply the size of the impulse that is of interest, rather than the actual force and time.

There are various ways of producing an impulse of this kind: by striking an object with a bat or a boot, by jerking it into motion with a string, by firing it from a gun, in a collision with another object, and so on. But in all these applications the principle is the same, that the impulse is equal to the gain in momentum.

In practice, the force which produces the impulse is often not constant, as suggested by Fig. 7.1, but more like the graph in Fig. 7.2. For example, if you kick a football, the force on the ball is quite small on first contact, but becomes much larger as the force from the boot distorts the surface of the ball around the region of contact.

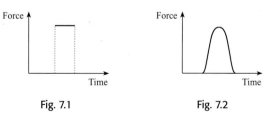

Fig. 7.1   Fig. 7.2

In Fig. 7.1 the impulse Ft is represented by the area under the force–time graph. This representation holds also in Fig. 7.2. When the force is not constant, the impulse is given by an integral $\int_{t_1}^{t_2} F\,\mathrm{d}t$, where t_1 and t_2 are the times at which the action of the force begins and ends. The momentum equation then takes the form

$$\int_{t_1}^{t_2} F\,\mathrm{d}t = mv_2 - mv_1,$$

which is a consequence of integrating the equation $F = m\dfrac{\mathrm{d}v}{\mathrm{d}t}$ with respect to t.

7.2   Impulses in collisions

The impulse–momentum principle can be used to justify the conservation of momentum, which you used in M1 Section 8.2 to calculate the outcome of collisions between moving objects. Calling the objects A and B, the argument runs as follows.

For the object A:

> Impulse of B on A = momentum of A after collision
> $\qquad\qquad\qquad\qquad$ − momentum of A before collision.

For the object B:

> Impulse of A on B = momentum of B after collision
> $\qquad\qquad\qquad\qquad$ − momentum of B before collision.

By Newton's third law, the force from B on A is equal in magnitude and opposite in direction to the force from A on B. It follows that the impulse of B on A and the impulse of A on B have equal magnitude in opposite directions, and therefore the sum of the two impulses is zero. So, if you add the two equations, you get

> 0 = total momentum of A and B after collision
> $\qquad$ − total momentum of A and B before collision.

That is, the total momentum of A and B is the same after the collision as it was before.

If all you want to know is the velocity after the collision of one of the objects, you can get this directly from the conservation of momentum equation without worrying about the impulse. But if you also want to know how hard the collision is, you need to use an impulse–momentum equation as well.

To illustrate this, here is a second look at M1 Example 8.2.2, extended to calculate the impulse when the wagons collide.

Example 7.2.1
Two wagons are moving in the same direction along a horizontal track. The front wagon, of mass 500 kg, is moving at $3\,\mathrm{m\,s^{-1}}$. The rear wagon, of mass 800 kg, is moving at $5\,\mathrm{m\,s^{-1}}$. As a result of the collision the speed of the rear wagon is reduced to $4\,\mathrm{m\,s^{-1}}$. Find the impulse which each wagon exerts on the other.

Denote the speed of the front wagon after the collision by $x \, \text{m s}^{-1}$, and the magnitude of the impulses by $I \, \text{N s}$ (see Fig. 7.3).

Velocities before

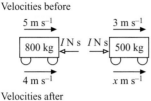

Velocities after

Fig. 7.3

The conservation of the total momentum of the two wagons is expressed by the equation

$$800 \times 5 + 500 \times 3 = 800 \times 4 + 500x,$$

which gives $x = \dfrac{4000 + 1500 - 3200}{500} = \dfrac{2300}{500} = 4.6.$

To find the impulse, you can apply the impulse–momentum equation to either the front or the rear wagon.

Front wagon: $I = 500x - 500 \times 3$,   so $I = 500(x - 3) = 500 \times 1.6 = 800.$
Rear wagon: $-I = 800 \times 4 - 800 \times 5$,   so $I = 800 \times 5 - 800 \times 4 = 800.$

Notice the signs in the equation for the rear wagon. The positive direction has been taken to the right. If it had been taken to the left, the impulse would have been positive and the velocities negative, so that the equation would be $I = 800 \times (-4) - 800 \times (-5)$.

The impulse of each wagon on the other has magnitude $800 \, \text{N s}$.

The method doesn't only apply to collisions. In the next example the impulse is not produced by a contact force but by the jerk from a rope, that is a large tension force acting for a short time. It is often important to calculate this, since if the impulse is too large the rope may break.

Example 7.2.2
A disabled car of mass $1800 \, \text{kg}$ is being towed by a van of mass $1200 \, \text{kg}$. The van driver starts from rest and, as the rope becomes taut, he uses the clutch to disconnect the engine. The van is then travelling at $5 \, \text{m s}^{-1}$. Once the rope becomes taut both vehicles have the same speed. Find the impulse of the tension in the rope.

You have a choice of method. You can either write impulse–momentum equations for each vehicle separately, or you can use the conservation of momentum principle for the two vehicles together. If you choose the second method, the force in the rope is an internal force, and its impulse does not come into the equation.

Denote the common speed after the rope becomes taut by $v \, \text{m s}^{-1}$, and the impulse of the tension by $I \, \text{N s}$. Fig. 7.4 shows the velocities and the impulses.

For the car: $I = 1800v$.

For the van: $-I = 1200v - 1200 \times 5$.

Conservation of momentum:

$1200 \times 5 = 1800v + 1200v$.

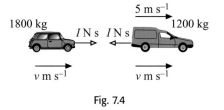

Fig. 7.4

You have three equations, but you only need two of them. In fact, the third equation can be obtained by adding the first two and rearranging the terms.

It is probably simplest to use the third equation to find $v = 2$, and then to substitute this in the first equation to get $I = 3600$.

The impulse from the rope is $3600 \, \text{N s}$.

Exercise 7A

1 A croquet ball of mass 0.45 kg is struck with speed $4 \, \text{m s}^{-1}$. Calculate the magnitude of the impulse of the ball on the mallet head.

2 A stationary table-tennis ball of mass 2.5 g is given a speed of $10 \, \text{m s}^{-1}$. Calculate the impulse required in N s.

3 A stationary tennis ball of mass 0.05 kg is given a speed of $120 \, \text{km h}^{-1}$ by the server. Calculate the impulse on the ball in N s.

   The ball is travelling at $72 \, \text{km h}^{-1}$ when it is struck by the player receiving serve, who reverses its direction of motion and reduces its speed to $60 \, \text{km h}^{-1}$. Calculate the impulse required for the shot in N s.

4 A 0.5 kg stone falls from rest a distance of 40 metres before being brought to rest again by its impact with the ground. Find the magnitude and direction of the impulse of the ground on the stone.

5 A climber of mass 70 kg falls 10 metres before being brought to rest by her inextensible safety rope. Calculate the impulse exerted on the climber by the rope.

6 A collision occurs between two empty trucks, each of mass 600 kg, moving in the same direction along a horizontal track. Initially their speeds are $8 \, \text{m s}^{-1}$ and $5 \, \text{m s}^{-1}$.

   (a) If the trucks become coupled together, calculate their common speed, and the impulse on each truck.

   (b) Given that the trucks remain uncoupled, and that after the collision one has speed $7 \, \text{m s}^{-1}$, calculate the speed of the other truck. State whether it is the front or rear truck which has speed $7 \, \text{m s}^{-1}$, and calculate the impulse on each truck.

7 A stationary car of mass 1000 kg has a bumper which can withstand an impulse of 1000 N s without damage. Calculate the maximum speed at which it can be struck by an 800 kg car, and remain undamaged, if

(a) the heavier car remains stationary,

(b) the cars have a common speed after impact.

8 Three particles A, B and C, each of mass m, lie in the same straight line. A is projected towards B with speed 3u. After the collision between A and B, B subsequently strikes C, after which all three particles have the same velocity. Calculate in terms of m and u the magnitude of the impulses in the collisions between

(a) A and B,   (b) B and C.

9 A collision occurs between particles A and B which are moving in opposite directions in the same straight line. The impulse on each particle in the collision is 2 N s.

(a) Given that A has mass 0.4 kg and initial velocity 3 m s^{-1}, calculate its final velocity.

(b) Given that the velocity of B changes by 2.5 m s^{-1}, calculate the mass of B.

(c) Deduce the maximum value for the initial speed of B.

10 An ornithologist of mass 75 kg is ringing birds which are nesting on a cliff ledge. As a safety precaution she attaches a rope to herself and to a boulder of mass 100 kg on the very rough surface of the cliff top. (If she falls, the boulder will be jerked into motion, but will quickly be brought to rest by friction.) She loses her footing and falls a distance of 10 metres before the rope becomes taut. Find

(a) her speed just before the rope becomes taut,

(b) the impulsive tension in the rope as it becomes taut,

(c) the speed of herself and the boulder just after the rope becomes taut.

7.3   Elasticity in collisions

Here is an experiment for you to try. Take two old tennis balls, pass threads through them and tie a knot at the end. Then tie the other ends to hooks screwed into a shelf, so that the balls can hang from the hooks, just touching each other with the threads vertical, as in Fig. 7.5.

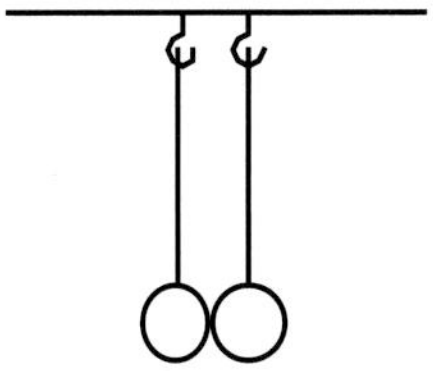

Now pull the balls apart, by the same amount on either side of the vertical line of symmetry, and let go. The balls should meet when the threads are vertical, and then rebound away from each other. Notice how far they rebound, compared with the original separation when you let them go.

Fig. 7.5

Next, repeat the experiment with squash balls, table-tennis balls, or with oranges, apples, or balls made of Plasticene. Do they rebound more, or less, or about the same amount as the tennis balls?

You obviously can't find this out by using conservation of momentum. When the two balls collide, they are moving at equal speeds in opposite directions. Since they also have the same mass, their total momentum is zero. The conservation principle tells you that the total momentum is still zero after the collision, which means that the balls rebound from each other with equal speeds.

But you can't calculate what these speeds are. In fact your experiments will show that the speeds will be different with different materials. They depend on what is called the 'elasticity' of the materials.

To make this more precise, you can introduce some measurement into your experiment. Place a board behind the apparatus, so that you can measure the height of the balls above the level when the threads are vertical (see Fig. 7.6). Record the height h_{bef} of the balls before you let them go, and the height h_{aft} to which they rise on the rebound. Do this with several different values of h_{bef}, and plot a graph of h_{aft} against h_{bef}.

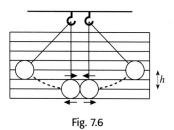

Fig. 7.6

You should find that the points you have plotted lie approximately on a straight line through the origin. Calculate the gradient of this straight line for each of the different materials you have used in your experiment.

The reason for measuring the heights is that you can use them to find the speeds of the balls before and after they collide. In fact, the speed of each ball before the collision is $\sqrt{2gh_{\text{bef}}}$, and the speed after the collision is $\sqrt{2gh_{\text{aft}}}$. (This is shown in Example 3.1.1.) Denoting these by $\text{speed}_{\text{bef}}$ and $\text{speed}_{\text{aft}}$, it follows that

$$\frac{\text{speed}_{\text{aft}}}{\text{speed}_{\text{bef}}} = \sqrt{\frac{2gh_{\text{aft}}}{2gh_{\text{bef}}}} = \sqrt{\frac{h_{\text{aft}}}{h_{\text{bef}}}}.$$

Now $\dfrac{h_{\text{aft}}}{h_{\text{bef}}}$ is the gradient of the $(h_{\text{bef}}, h_{\text{aft}})$ graph, so that $\dfrac{\text{speed}_{\text{aft}}}{\text{speed}_{\text{bef}}}$ is the square root of this gradient.

To complete the experiment, make a list of the materials you have used, and the value of the ratio $\dfrac{\text{speed}_{\text{aft}}}{\text{speed}_{\text{bef}}}$ for each.

7.4   The coefficient of restitution

The collisions in the experiment in the last section are very special, since the masses and speeds of the two objects were equal, and both objects were of the same material. But the results are examples of a more general rule which applies to any collision in which the velocities before and after are along one straight line. This is called **direct impact**.

Fig. 7.7 illustrates a general collision between two objects.

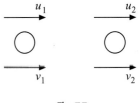

Fig. 7.7

The suffixes 1 and 2 are used for the masses and velocities of the objects on the left and right respectively. The letter u is used for velocities before the collision, and v for velocities after the collision. The positive direction is taken to the right, but velocities can be either positive or negative.

For a collision to occur, u_1 must be greater than u_2. In this case the object on the left is catching up the object on the right at a rate of $u_1 - u_2$. This is called the **approach speed** before the collision.

After the collision v_2 will be greater than v_1, and the object on the right is moving away from the object on the left at a rate of $v_2 - v_1$. This is called the **separation speed**.

In the experiment with the tennis balls, the approach speed is $\text{speed}_{\text{bef}} - (-\text{speed}_{\text{bef}})$, or $2\,\text{speed}_{\text{bef}}$. The separation speed is $\text{speed}_{\text{aft}} - (-\text{speed}_{\text{aft}})$, or $2\,\text{speed}_{\text{aft}}$. So

$$\frac{\text{separation speed}}{\text{approach speed}} = \frac{2\,\text{speed}_{\text{aft}}}{2\,\text{speed}_{\text{bef}}} = \frac{\text{speed}_{\text{aft}}}{\text{speed}_{\text{bef}}}.$$

Now the experiment in the last section shows that this ratio is constant. It therefore supports the general rule which provides a model for the outcome of any collision.

> **Newton's law of impact**   If two objects moving in the same straight line collide, the ratio $\dfrac{\text{separation speed}}{\text{approach speed}}$ is constant.
>
> This value of the constant, called the **coefficient of restitution**, depends on the shape of the objects and the materials they consist of.

The coefficient of restitution is always denoted by the letter e. Its value is between 0 and 1. The value $e = 1$ never occurs in practice, but it is sometimes used in models as a first approximation; the collision is then said to be **perfectly elastic**. If $e = 0$, the collision is **inelastic**.

> Although Newton's law of impact has been discussed in terms of the collision of two spheres, it is often applied to collisions between objects of other shapes.
>
> Some people like to remember the law in the algebraic form
>
> $$v_2 - v_1 = -e(u_2 - u_1).$$

By putting together the conservation of momentum and the law of impact, you can predict the outcome of any collision if the value of e is known.

Example 7.4.1

In a warehouse a package of mass $10\,\text{kg}$ moving at $5\,\text{m\,s}^{-1}$ collides with a stationary box of mass $12\,\text{kg}$. If the coefficient of restitution is 0.1, find the speeds of each after the collision.

The collision is illustrated in Fig. 7.8. Let the speeds of the package and the box after the collision be $x\,\text{m\,s}^{-1}$ and $y\,\text{m\,s}^{-1}$.

The approach speed is $5\,\text{m\,s}^{-1}$, so the separation speed is $0.1 \times 5\,\text{m\,s}^{-1}$, which is $0.5\,\text{m\,s}^{-1}$.

This gives the equation

$$y - x = 0.5.$$

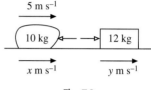

Fig. 7.8

Also, by conservation of momentum,

$$10 \times 5 = 10x + 12y.$$

Substituting $x + 0.5$ for y in the second equation gives $50 = 10x + 12\,(x + 0.5)$, which is $44 = 22x$. So $x = 2$ and $y = 2.5$.

The speeds of the package and the box are $2\,\text{m\,s}^{-1}$ and $2.5\,\text{m\,s}^{-1}$.

Example 7.4.2

A metal ball of mass 70 grams is moving at $4\,\text{m\,s}^{-1}$. It collides with a wooden ball of mass 30 grams, which is moving in the same line in the opposite direction at $6\,\text{m\,s}^{-1}$. The coefficient of restitution is 0.5. Find the speeds of the balls after the collision.

Because the balls are moving in opposite directions, you must be careful about signs. Take the direction of motion of the metal ball to be positive, and denote the velocities of the balls after impact by $x\,\text{m\,s}^{-1}$ and $y\,\text{m\,s}^{-1}$, as in Fig. 7.9.

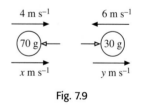

Fig. 7.9

The approach speed is $10\,\text{m\,s}^{-1}$, so the separation speed is $0.5 \times 10\,\text{m\,s}^{-1}$, which is $5\,\text{m\,s}^{-1}$. So $y - x = 5$, or $y = x + 5$.

Since all the masses are in grams, you can work with units of grams and $\text{m\,s}^{-1}$. The unit of momentum would then be millinewton seconds (mN s). The conservation of momentum equation is

$$70 \times 4 + 30 \times (-6) = 70x + 30y.$$

Substituting $x + 5$ for y gives

$$280 - 180 = 70x + 30\,(x + 5),$$

which can be simplified to

$$100x = -50, \text{ giving } x = -0.5.$$

Then $y = (-0.5) + 5 = 4.5$.

Both balls change their directions of motion as a result of the collision. The metal ball rebounds at $0.5\,\text{m\,s}^{-1}$, and the wooden ball at $4.5\,\text{m\,s}^{-1}$.

Example 7.4.3

Three trucks, of masses 800 kg, 600 kg and 400 kg are in line on a track. The 600 kg and 400 kg trucks are stationary, and the 800 kg truck is moving towards them at $10 \, \text{m s}^{-1}$. The coefficient of restitution between the first two trucks is 0.4, and between the second and third trucks is e. What can you say about e if there are more than two collisions? Can there be more than three?

The algebra towards the end of this example gets a little complicated. You have been left to work out some of the details for yourself.

Fig. 7.10 shows the impulses and velocities (in m s^{-1}) at each collision. Notice that on each occasion the speed of the truck not involved in the collision doesn't change.

First collision

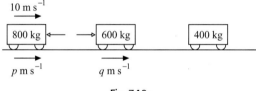

Fig. 7.10a

Conservation of momentum: $800 \times 10 = 800p + 600q$.

Law of impact: $q - p = 0.4 \times 10$.

These equations reduce to $4p + 3q = 40$ and $q - p = 4$, which have solution $p = 4$ and $q = 8$. These values are shown in Fig. 7.10b.

Second collision

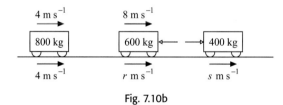

Fig. 7.10b

Conservation of momentum: $600 \times 8 = 600r + 400s$.

Law of impact: $s - r = e \times 8$.

These equations reduce to $3r + 2s = 24$ and $s - r = 8e$, which have solution $r = 1.6(3 - 2e)$ and $s = 4.8(1 + e)$. These values are shown in Fig. 7.10c.

There will be another collision if the 800 kg truck is now moving faster than the 600 kg truck, that is if $p > r$, so $4 > 1.6(3 - 2e)$, which gives $e > 0.25$.

Third collision (if $e > 0.25$)

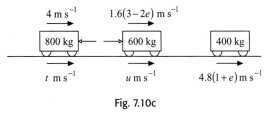

Fig. 7.10c

Conservation of momentum: $800 \times 4 + 600 \times 1.6(3 - 2e) = 800t + 600u.$

Law of impact: $u - t = 0.4 \times (1.6(3 - 2e) - 4).$

To find if there will be yet another collision, you need to know if u can be greater than s. The equations give $u = \frac{1}{1400}(6336 - 2944e)$, and you have already found that $s = 4.8(1 + e)$.

Now since $e > 0.25$,

$$u < \tfrac{1}{1400}(6336 - 2944 \times 0.25) = \frac{5600}{1400} = 4,$$

and $s > 4.8(1 + 0.25) = 6.$

So u is not greater than s, and there are no more collisions.

There will be a third collision if $e > 0.25$, but no more.

7.5   Impacts with a fixed surface

When a ball hits and rebounds from a fixed flat surface, you can still use Newton's law of impact to calculate the speed of the rebound.

If the ball is moving at right angles to the surface, the approach and separation speeds are just the speeds of the ball before and after it hits the surface.

Example 7.5.1
A hockey player practises shooting at goal by standing 12 metres away from a wall and hitting the ball directly towards it. She hits the ball with speed $10 \, \text{m s}^{-1}$, and the coefficient of restitution between the ball and the wall is 0.6. If the resistance from the ground is negligible, find how long it takes for the ball to come back to her.

Since the resistance is negligible, the ball travels at constant speed in each direction. It therefore approaches the wall at $10 \, \text{m s}^{-1}$, and rebounds with a speed of $0.6 \times 10 \, \text{m s}^{-1}$, which is $6 \, \text{m s}^{-1}$.

The time for the ball to travel from the player to the wall and back is therefore $\left(\dfrac{12}{10} + \dfrac{12}{6} \right)$ seconds, which is 3.2 seconds.

Example 7.5.2

A tennis player throws a ball down to the ground with a speed of $4\,\text{m}\,\text{s}^{-1}$ from a height of 1 metre. On the rebound the ball just comes up to the level from which it was thrown. Find the coefficient of restitution.

You can calculate the speeds of the ball just before and after the bounce by using the equation $v^2 = u^2 + 2as$.

In the descent, taking downwards to be positive, $u = 4$, $a = 9.8$ and $s = 1$, so

$$v^2 = 4^2 + 2 \times 9.8 \times 1 = 35.6, \quad \text{giving} \quad v = \sqrt{35.6}.$$

On the rebound, taking upwards to be positive, $v = 0$, $a = -9.8$ and $s = 1$, so

$$0^2 = u^2 + 2 \times (-9.8) \times 1, \quad \text{giving} \quad u = \sqrt{19.6}.$$

The coefficient of restitution is therefore $\dfrac{\sqrt{19.6}}{\sqrt{35.6}} = 0.74$ correct to 2 significant figures.

7.6*   Compression and restitution

The word 'restitution' means restoring something to its original state. Its use as a technical term needs some explanation. You may omit this section if you wish.

High-speed photographs of balls colliding show that during the impact they go out of shape, as illustrated in Fig. 7.11. At the instant of maximum distortion, both balls are moving at the same speed.

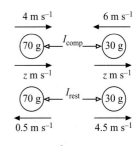

Fig. 7.11

Consider the metal ball and wooden ball in Example 7.4.2. Before and after the collision the total momentum of the balls was $100\,\text{mN}\,\text{s}$. If their common speed at maximum compression was $z\,\text{m}\,\text{s}^{-1}$, conservation of momentum shows that

$$70 \times 4 + 30 \times (-6) = (70 + 30)z, \quad \text{so} \quad z = 1.$$

You can now think of the collision in two stages: a compression stage, and a restitution stage. Split the impulse into two parts, $I_{\text{comp}}\,\text{mN}\,\text{s}$ and $I_{\text{rest}}\,\text{mN}\,\text{s}$, in the two stages. This is illustrated in Fig. 7.12.

Applying the impulse–momentum equation for the wooden ball in each stage,

$$I_{\text{comp}} = 30 \times 1 - 30 \times (-6) = 210 \quad \text{and}$$
$$I_{\text{rest}} = 30 \times 4.5 - 30 \times 1 = 105.$$

Fig. 7.12

So $I_{\text{rest}} = 0.5 I_{\text{comp}}$, which for this example is $I_{\text{rest}} = e I_{\text{comp}}$.

This is true for any collision. You can prove it by algebra, though the details are quite complicated. (See Section 7.8.)

> In a collision between two objects moving in the same line, the impulse during the restitution stage is e times the impulse during the compression stage.

This is the property which accounts for the term 'coefficient of restitution'.

Exercise 7B

1 A block P moving on a horizontal surface with speed $4\,\mathrm{m\,s^{-1}}$ strikes a stationary block Q. After the collision, both blocks move in the same direction with speeds $3\,\mathrm{m\,s^{-1}}$ and $1\,\mathrm{m\,s^{-1}}$. State which block has speed $3\,\mathrm{m\,s^{-1}}$ and calculate the coefficient of restitution.

2 A ball P moving with speed $4\,\mathrm{m\,s^{-1}}$ strikes a ball Q moving in the same straight line in the same direction with speed $1\,\mathrm{m\,s^{-1}}$. After the collision, both balls move in the same direction with speeds $3\,\mathrm{m\,s^{-1}}$ and $2.5\,\mathrm{m\,s^{-1}}$. State which ball has speed $3\,\mathrm{m\,s^{-1}}$ and calculate the coefficient of restitution.

3 A ball A moving with speed $4\,\mathrm{m\,s^{-1}}$ strikes a particle B moving in the same straight line in the opposite direction with speed $1\,\mathrm{m\,s^{-1}}$. After the collision, the balls move with speeds $3\,\mathrm{m\,s^{-1}}$ and $1.5\,\mathrm{m\,s^{-1}}$. Calculate two possible values for the coefficient of restitution.

4 A boy stands 15 metres away from a vertical wall and kicks a ball along the ground towards it. The ball hits the wall 1.5 seconds after it is kicked, and then returns to the boy after a further 2 seconds. The resistance from the ground is negligible. What is the coefficient of restitution between the ball and the wall?

If the mass of the ball is $0.4\,\mathrm{kg}$, find the magnitude of the impulse on the ball from

(a) the boy's boot,   (b) the wall.

5 A ball of mass $0.1\,\mathrm{kg}$ is projected downwards with speed $2\,\mathrm{m\,s^{-1}}$ onto a fixed horizontal surface. It leaves the surface, and just reaches the point from which it was projected, 1.25 metres above the surface. Calculate the coefficient of restitution.

6 A girl releases a ball from rest at a point above a fixed horizontal surface. The ball strikes the surface after t seconds, and the girl catches the ball when it is next stationary, T seconds after its release. Find, in terms of t and T, the speed with which the ball strikes the surface, and the speed with which it rebounds. Calculate the coefficient of restitution in terms of t and T.

7 On a model railway a truck of mass $0.3\,\mathrm{kg}$, moving at $1.2\,\mathrm{m\,s^{-1}}$, collides with a stationary truck of mass $0.5\,\mathrm{kg}$. After the impact the speed of the first truck is reduced to $0.2\,\mathrm{m\,s^{-1}}$. Find the speed with which the other truck starts to move, and the coefficient of restitution.

If instead the $0.5\,\mathrm{kg}$ truck was sent at $1.2\,\mathrm{m\,s^{-1}}$ towards the stationary $0.3\,\mathrm{kg}$ truck, what would be the speeds of the two trucks after the impact?

8 In a game of snooker the white ball, moving at $2\,\mathrm{m\,s^{-1}}$, strikes the pink. The pink ball starts to move with a speed of $1.6\,\mathrm{m\,s^{-1}}$ in the same direction. The balls have the same mass. Find the speed of the white ball after the impact, and the coefficient of restitution.

9 A collision occurs between two identical toy trucks P and Q moving in opposite directions in the same straight line. Before the collision P has speed $3\,\mathrm{m\,s^{-1}}$ and Q has speed $1\,\mathrm{m\,s^{-1}}$. Calculate the speeds of P and Q after the collision, and state if either direction of motion is changed, if the coefficient of restitution is

(a) 0.9,   (b) 0.5,   (c) 0.1.

10 A collision occurs between two spheres P and Q, of masses $0.1\,\mathrm{kg}$ and $0.4\,\mathrm{kg}$ respectively, moving in the same direction in the same straight line. Before the collision P has speed $3\,\mathrm{m\,s^{-1}}$ and Q has speed $1\,\mathrm{m\,s^{-1}}$. Calculate the speeds of P and Q after the collision and state if either direction of motion is changed if the coefficient of restitution is

(a) 0.95,   (b) 0.875,   (c) 0.8.

11 A block P of mass $0.3\,\mathrm{kg}$ moving with speed $3\,\mathrm{m\,s^{-1}}$ strikes a block Q of mass $0.5\,\mathrm{kg}$ moving in the same straight line in the same direction with speed $2\,\mathrm{m\,s^{-1}}$. After the collision, Q has speed $2.5\,\mathrm{m\,s^{-1}}$. Calculate the coefficient of restitution.

12 A child is playing with a toy car of mass $0.8\,\mathrm{kg}$ and a truck of mass $2\,\mathrm{kg}$. He sends the car off across the floor with a speed of $2\,\mathrm{m\,s^{-1}}$, then sends the truck after it with a speed of $3\,\mathrm{m\,s^{-1}}$. The coefficient of restitution is 0.4. Find the speeds of the car and the truck after the collision.

13 A sphere of mass $2\,\mathrm{kg}$ moving at $5\,\mathrm{m\,s^{-1}}$ collides directly with a sphere of mass $3\,\mathrm{kg}$ moving at $1\,\mathrm{m\,s^{-1}}$ in the opposite direction. The coefficient of restitution is $\frac{1}{3}$. Find the speeds of the two spheres after the collision.

14 A sphere of mass m_1 moving with speed u collides with a stationary sphere of mass m_2. The first sphere is brought to rest by the collision. Prove that $m_1 \leqslant m_2$.

15 A disc A of mass 90 grams moving at $5\,\mathrm{m\,s^{-1}}$ collides directly with a disc B of mass 10 grams moving at $3\,\mathrm{m\,s^{-1}}$ in the same direction. Explain why the speed of disc B after the collision can't be

(a) $7\,\mathrm{m\,s^{-1}}$,   (b) $4\,\mathrm{m\,s^{-1}}$.

What is the possible range of speeds of disc B after the collision?

16 A truck of mass $300\,\mathrm{kg}$ travelling at $4\,\mathrm{m\,s^{-1}}$ collides with a second truck travelling at $1\,\mathrm{m\,s^{-1}}$ in the opposite direction. The first truck is brought to rest by the collision. If the coefficient of restitution is 0.4, find the mass of the second truck.

17* A sphere A of mass $0.8\,\mathrm{kg}$ moving with speed $2\,\mathrm{m\,s^{-1}}$ strikes a stationary sphere B of mass $0.2\,\mathrm{kg}$. After the collision, both spheres move in the same direction and B has speed $3\,\mathrm{m\,s^{-1}}$. Calculate

(a) the common speed of the spheres during the collision,

(b) I_{comp} and I_{rest}.

Hence calculate the coefficient of restitution.

18* A ball P of mass $0.5\,\text{kg}$ moving with speed $3.5\,\text{m s}^{-1}$ strikes a stationary ball Q of mass $0.3\,\text{kg}$. After the collision, Q has speed $3\,\text{m s}^{-1}$. Calculate I_{comp} and I_{rest} and hence the coefficient of restitution.

19* A sphere P of mass $1\,\text{kg}$ moving with speed $2\,\text{m s}^{-1}$ strikes a sphere Q of mass $0.2\,\text{kg}$ moving in the opposite direction with speed $6\,\text{m s}^{-1}$. Find the common speed of the two spheres during the collision and calculate I_{comp}. After the collision P has speed $0.4\,\text{m s}^{-1}$. Calculate both possible values for I_{rest} and the corresponding values for the coefficient of restitution.

20 Particles A and B, of masses $0.1\,\text{kg}$ and $0.2\,\text{kg}$ respectively, can move on a smooth horizontal table. Initially A is moving with speed $3\,\text{m s}^{-1}$ directly towards B, which is at rest. The collision between A and B is perfectly elastic. Find the speeds of the particles immediately after the collision.

After the collision B hits and rebounds from a vertical barrier on the table. The barrier is perpendicular to the direction of motion of B, so that B moves in the same straight line throughout. After the rebound from the barrier, B and A are moving with the same speed. Find the magnitude of the impulse exerted by the barrier on B, and the coefficient of restitution.   (OCR)

21 A sphere Q is at rest on a smooth horizontal surface at a distance d from a vertical wall. A sphere P, with the same mass as Q, is moving towards Q with speed u in a straight line which is perpendicular to the wall. The coefficient of restitution between P and Q is e. Calculate the speeds of P and Q after their first collision in terms of u and e. Q strikes the wall in a collision for which the coefficient of restitution is e. Calculate the distance from the wall of Q and P when they again collide.

7.7 Effect of collisions on kinetic energy

In the experiment in Section 7.3, suppose that each ball has mass m and that before the collison each has speed u. You have already noted that the momentum of the balls is $mu + (-mu)$, which is zero. But each ball has kinetic energy $\frac{1}{2}mu^2$, which is positive, so the total kinetic energy of the two balls is $\frac{1}{2}mu^2 + \frac{1}{2}mu^2 = mu^2$. (Remember that kinetic energy is a scalar quantity.)

After the collision each ball has speed eu, where e is the coefficient of restitution. The total kinetic energy of the two balls is therefore $\frac{1}{2}me^2u^2 + \frac{1}{2}me^2u^2 = me^2u^2$.

So, unless the collision is perfectly elastic, the effect of the collision is to reduce the total energy by an amount $mu^2 - me^2u^2 = m(1 - e^2)u^2$.

This result is typical of the effect of a collision on the total kinetic energy. You always get a reduction of total kinetic energy when objects collide, unless $e = 1$.

Example 7.7.1

Find the effect of the collision on the total kinetic energy in

(a) Example 7.4.1,   (b) Example 7.4.2,   (c) Example 7.5.2.

(a) Before the collision only the 10 kg package is moving, with kinetic energy $\frac{1}{2} \times 10 \times 5^2$ J, which is 125 J. After the collision the total kinetic energy is $\left(\frac{1}{2} \times 10 \times 2^2 + \frac{1}{2} \times 12 \times 2.5^2\right)$ J, which is $(20 + 37.5)$ J $= 57.5$ J. There is therefore a loss of energy of amount $(125 - 57.5)$ J $= 67.5$ J.

(b) The masses in kg are 0.07 and 0.03, so the kinetic energy before the collision is $\left(\frac{1}{2} \times 0.07 \times 4^2 + \frac{1}{2} \times 0.03 \times 6^2\right)$ J and the kinetic energy afterwards is $\left(\frac{1}{2} \times 0.07 \times 0.5^2 + \frac{1}{2} \times 0.03 \times 4.5^2\right)$ J. In this case both balls are moving more slowly after the collision than before, and the total loss of kinetic energy is $(1.1 - 0.3125)$ J $= 0.7875$ J.

(c) The speed of the tennis ball is reduced from $\sqrt{35.6}\,\text{m s}^{-1}$ to $\sqrt{19.6}\,\text{m s}^{-1}$ as a result of the collision. If the mass of a tennis ball is taken to be 0.06 kg, the loss of kinetic energy is $\left(\frac{1}{2} \times 0.06 \times \sqrt{35.6}^2 - \frac{1}{2} \times 0.06 \times \sqrt{19.6}^2\right)$ J, which is 0.48 J.

Example 7.7.2

A sphere of mass 8 kg moving at $2\,\text{m s}^{-1}$ collides with another sphere of mass 2 kg moving at $3\,\text{m s}^{-1}$ in the opposite direction (see Fig. 7.13). Find, in terms of the coefficient of restitution e, the loss of kinetic energy resulting from the collision.

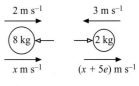

Fig. 7.13

The approach speed is $5\,\text{m s}^{-1}$, so the separation speed is $5e\,\text{m s}^{-1}$. If after the collision the 8 kg sphere is moving at $x\,\text{m s}^{-1}$, the velocity of the 2 kg sphere is $(x + 5e)\,\text{m s}^{-1}$.

The conservation of momentum equation is

$$8 \times 2 + 2 \times (-3) = 8x + 2(x + 5e),$$

which gives $x = 1 - e$ and $x + 5e = 1 + 4e$.

The kinetic energy before the collision is $\left(\frac{1}{2} \times 8 \times 2^2 + \frac{1}{2} \times 2 \times 3^2\right)$ J, which is 25 J. After the collision it is $\left(\frac{1}{2} \times 8 \times (1 - e)^2 + \frac{1}{2} \times 2 \times (1 + 4e)^2\right)$ J, which can be simplified to $(5 + 20e^2)$ J. The loss of energy is therefore $(25 - (5 + 20e^2))$ J, which is $20(1 - e^2)$ J.

Notice again in this example the appearance of the factor $(1 - e^2)$. This always features when you find an algebraic expression for the loss of kinetic energy. The general result is:

If objects of mass m_1 and m_2 collide, the total kinetic energy is reduced by

$$\frac{1}{2}\frac{m_1 m_2}{m_1 + m_2}(1 - e^2)A^2, \text{ where } A \text{ is the approach speed.}$$

It is not worthwhile remembering this formula, but you may like to check it from the answers to Examples 7.7.1 and 7.7.2. A proof is given in the next section.

7.8*   Some general proofs

This chapter has included statements of two general rules, the relation between the impulses during restitution and compression (Section 7.6) and the formula for loss of energy (Section 7.7), but these have only been shown to be true in numerical examples. They can be proved by algebra, but the details are rather tricky; the clue lies in introducing the common velocity of the two objects at maximum distortion, as in Section 7.6.

You may if you wish omit this section and go straight to Exercise 7C.

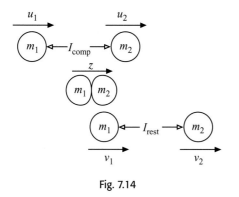

Fig. 7.14

Suppose that two objects of mass m_1 and m_2 are moving with velocities u_1 and u_2 before a collision, and v_1 and v_2 afterwards (see Fig. 7.14). At the instant of maximum distortion both objects are moving with the same velocity, denoted by z. Since the total momentum is conserved right through the collision,

$$m_1 u_1 + m_2 u_2 = m_1 z + m_2 z = m_1 v_1 + m_2 v_2,$$

from which it follows that

$$z = \frac{m_1 u_1 + m_2 u_2}{m_1 + m_2} = \frac{m_1 v_1 + m_2 v_2}{m_1 + m_2}.$$

These expressions may remind you of the formula $\bar{x} = \dfrac{m_1 x_1 + m_2 x_2}{m_1 + m_2}$ for the centre of mass of the two objects. If you differentiate this with respect to the time t, you find that $z = \dfrac{d\bar{x}}{dt}$; that is, z is the velocity of the centre of mass, and this velocity remains constant throughout the collision.

During the period of compression the second object gains velocity $z - u_2$, which can be simplified as

$$z - u_2 = \frac{m_1 u_1 + m_2 u_2}{m_1 + m_2} - u_2 = \frac{(m_1 u_1 + m_2 u_2) - (m_1 u_2 + m_2 u_2)}{m_1 + m_2}$$

$$= \frac{m_1 u_1 - m_1 u_2}{m_1 + m_2} = \frac{m_1}{m_1 + m_2} A,$$

where A denotes the approach speed $u_1 - u_2$.

Similar algebraic calculations (which are left for you to work for yourself) lead to the following mini-theorem.

Mini-theorem If z is the common velocity of the two objects at the instant of maximum distortion, then

$$z - u_2 = \frac{k}{m_2} A, \quad u_1 - z = \frac{k}{m_1} A, \quad v_2 - z = \frac{k}{m_2} S, \quad z - v_1 = \frac{k}{m_1} S,$$

where A is the approach speed, S is the separation speed and $k = \dfrac{m_1 m_2}{m_1 + m_2}$.

These equations can be used to prove the two main results given in this chapter, which can now be stated as theorems. They both use Newton's experimental law of impact, in the form $S = eA$.

Theorem The impulse during the restitution stage is e times the impulse during the compression stage.

Proof During the compression stage the impulse of the first object on the second is

$$I_{\text{comp}} = m_2 z - m_2 u_2 = m_2(z - u_2) = kA,$$

using the mini-theorem.

During the restitution stage the impulse is

$$I_{\text{rest}} = m_2 v_2 - m_2 z = m_2(v_2 - z) = kS.$$

Since $S = eA$, it follows that $I_{\text{rest}} = e I_{\text{comp}}$.

Theorem During the collision the total kinetic energy is reduced by $\frac{1}{2} k(1 - e^2) A^2$.

Proof The loss of kinetic energy is

$$\left(\tfrac{1}{2} m_1 u_1^2 + \tfrac{1}{2} m_2 u_2^2\right) - \left(\tfrac{1}{2} m_1 v_1^2 + \tfrac{1}{2} m_2 v_2^2\right)$$

$$= \tfrac{1}{2} m_1 \left(z + \frac{k}{m_1} A\right)^2 + \tfrac{1}{2} m_2 \left(z - \frac{k}{m_2} A\right)^2 - \tfrac{1}{2} m_1 \left(z - \frac{k}{m_1} S\right)^2 - \tfrac{1}{2} m_2 \left(z + \frac{k}{m_2} S\right)^2,$$

using the mini-theorem. You can check for yourself that if you multiply out the four brackets and simplify the expression, you are left with just

$$\tfrac{1}{2} \frac{k^2}{m_1} A^2 + \tfrac{1}{2} \frac{k^2}{m_2} A^2 - \tfrac{1}{2} \frac{k^2}{m_1} S^2 - \tfrac{1}{2} \frac{k^2}{m_2} S^2 = \tfrac{1}{2} \left(\frac{1}{m_1} + \frac{1}{m_2}\right) k^2 (A^2 - S^2)$$

$$= \tfrac{1}{2} \left(\frac{m_1 + m_2}{m_1 m_2}\right) k^2 (A^2 - e^2 A^2)$$

$$= \tfrac{1}{2} \frac{1}{k} k^2 (1 - e^2) A^2 = \tfrac{1}{2} k(1 - e^2) A^2.$$

It follows from this theorem that there is no loss of kinetic energy if $e = 1$, and that the smaller the value of e, the greater the loss of energy during the collision.

Exercise 7C

1   A truck of mass $400\,\text{kg}$ moves on a smooth horizontal track with speed $3\,\text{m\,s}^{-1}$. It strikes an identical stationary truck and the coefficient of restitution is 0.2. Calculate the kinetic energy of the moving truck before the collision, and of each truck after the collision.

2   An unloaded railway wagon A, of mass $800\,\text{kg}$, and a loaded wagon B, of mass $3000\,\text{kg}$, are free to move on a straight horizontal track. Wagon A is travelling at a speed of $8\,\text{m\,s}^{-1}$ when it runs into B, which is stationary, causing B to start to move with a speed of $2\,\text{m\,s}^{-1}$. Calculate

   (a) the speed of A immediately after the impact,

   (b) the loss of kinetic energy due to the impact.   (OCR)

3   Two marbles, one blue and the other red, have the same radius. Each marble has the same mass 5 grams. The marbles are moving directly towards each other on a smooth horizontal table. Just before they collide the blue marble has speed $0.5\,\text{m\,s}^{-1}$ and the red marble has speed $0.3\,\text{m\,s}^{-1}$. Immediately after the collision the red marble has speed $0.3\,\text{m\,s}^{-1}$.

   (a) Find the speed of the blue marble immediately after the collision.

   (b) Find, in joules, the loss of kinetic energy in the collision.   (OCR)

4* A collision occurs between two discs A, of mass $0.4\,\text{kg}$, and B, of mass $0.8\,\text{kg}$, moving in the same direction with speeds $6\,\text{m\,s}^{-1}$ and $2\,\text{m\,s}^{-1}$ respectively. Given that the coefficient of restitution is 0.5, calculate the energy change of each disc in the compression and restitution phases of the collision.

Miscellaneous exercise 7

1   A golfer strikes a stationary ball of mass 46 g and gives it an initial speed of $15\,\text{m\,s}^{-1}$. Calculate the magnitude of the impulse on the ball.   (OCR)

2   A tennis ball is dropped from rest at a height of 2.5 metres onto a fixed horizontal surface. The ball rebounds to a height of 1.4 metres. Modelling the ball as a particle, and neglecting air resistance, find the coefficient of restitution between the ball and the surface.   (OCR)

3   A footballer kicks a stationary ball of mass $0.4\,\text{kg}$ and gives it an impulse of $6\,\text{N\,s}$. Calculate the initial speed of the ball, and state one assumption made.   (OCR)

4   Two identical particles are moving in the same straight line. Immediately before they collide, they are moving with speeds $1\,\text{m\,s}^{-1}$ and $2\,\text{m\,s}^{-1}$ in the same direction. Given that the coefficient of restitution is 0.8, calculate the speeds of the two particles after the collision.   (OCR)

5   Two particles A and B, each of mass $0.2\,\text{kg}$, move in the same direction along the same straight line with speeds $5\,\text{m\,s}^{-1}$ and $3\,\text{m\,s}^{-1}$ respectively. They collide and, in the collision, each receives an impulse of magnitude $0.3\,\text{N\,s}$. Show that the speed of A immediately after the collision is $3.5\,\text{m\,s}^{-1}$ and calculate the speed of B. Hence calculate the coefficient of restitution.   (OCR)

6 Two particles A and B, moving in the same direction, collide and combine to form a single particle. State the coefficient of restitution for the collision. The mass of A is 0.2 kg and the mass of B is 0.3 kg. Immediately before the collision, A has speed 5 m s^{-1} and B has speed 4 m s^{-1}. Calculate

   (a) the speed of the single particle immediately after the collision,

   (b) the magnitude of the impulse on A.   (OCR)

7 A particle P of mass 1 kg, moving with speed 6 m s^{-1}, makes a direct impact with a stationary particle Q of mass 0.5 kg. The collision between P and Q is perfectly elastic. Calculate

   (a) the speed of Q immediately after the collision,

   (b) the magnitude of the impulse on Q in the collision.   (OCR)

8 A collision occurs between two particles P and Q moving in opposite directions along the same straight line. Immediately before the collision P and Q have speeds 3 m s^{-1} and 7 m s^{-1} respectively. Immediately after the collision Q has speed 9 m s^{-1}. The coefficient of restitution is 0.8.

   (a) Calculate the speed of P immediately after the collision.

   (b) Calculate the ratio of the masses of the particles.   (OCR)

9 The diagram shows two smooth balls P and Q of equal diameter. The balls have masses 0.6 kg and 0.5 kg respectively, and are free to move on a smooth horizontal table. A smooth vertical wall is situated at one edge of the table. The ball P is projected towards the wall in a direction at right angles to it. Before reaching the wall, P collides directly with the ball Q, which is stationary. Immediately after the collision P continues to move in the same direction as before, with speed 0.75 m s^{-1}, and Q starts to move with speed 2.1 m s^{-1}. Calculate the speed of projection of P.

   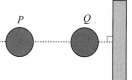

   Q subsequently strikes the wall, losing 0.62 joules of energy in the impact. Calculate the speed with which Q rebounds from the wall.   (OCR)

10 A particle of mass 0.3 kg is dropped from rest from a height of 2.5 metres onto a smooth horizontal plane. The coefficient of restitution between the plane and the particle is 0.8.

   (a) Find the speed with which the particle hits the plane.

   (b) Determine the time taken until the particle strikes the plane.

   (c) Find the speed with which the particle leaves the plane and the impulse imparted to the particle by the plane.

   (d) Determine the height above the plane to which the particle first rises.

   Assume now that you are to repeat the calculations for an environment where the acceleration due to gravity is considerably more than on Earth. State for each of (a), (b), (c) and (d) whether your answers would be now greater than, less than, or the same as before.   (OCR, adapted)

11 The diagram shows two uniform spherical balls of the same radius, which are at rest on a smooth horizontal table and touch each other. Ball A has mass $4m$ and ball B has mass m. An impulse of magnitude I is applied to A along the line of centres and, as a result, A moves with initial speed U and B moves with initial speed $2U$. Find I, in terms of m and U, and find also the magnitude of the impulse acting on A due to B.

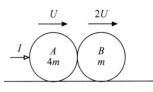

Show that the total kinetic energy of A and B after the impulse acts is $\frac{2}{3}IU$.

Ball B strikes a vertical barrier and returns along its initial path with the same speed as before. After the balls collide the total kinetic energy is $\frac{4}{5}mU^2$. Find, in terms of U, the speed of each ball after this collision. (OCR)

12 Two particles P and Q, of masses m and $2m$ respectively, moving in the same straight line, but in opposite directions, on a smooth horizontal table, with speeds $3u$ and u respectively, collide. Given that Q receives an impulse of magnitude $5mu$ from P at the collision, find the velocities of the particles after the collision and show that there is a loss in energy of $\frac{5}{4}mu^2$ due to the collision. (OCR)

13 A smooth groove in the shape of a circle has been cut in a horizontal surface. Identical beads P and Q are placed in the groove at opposite ends of a diameter. P is projected horizontally along the groove with speed u. Calculate the speeds of the beads after P strikes Q in terms of u and e, where e is the coefficient of restitution.

A second collision occurs after Q has completed 2 circuits. Prove that $e = \frac{1}{3}$.

Calculate the speeds of P and Q immediately after the second collision.

8 Motion round a circle

This chapter deals with the connection between force, velocity and acceleration for an object modelled as a particle moving round a circular path. When you have completed it, you should

- know the meaning of angular speed
- know the equation connecting tangential speed and angular speed
- know how to calculate the acceleration in circular motion with constant speed
- be able to solve problems in two and three dimensions involving objects moving round a circular path with constant speed.

8.1 Two practical examples

Fast trains from London to Cambridge travel for some distance along a straight track at constant speed. As a passenger you are hardly aware of how fast the train is moving. By Newton's first law, the forces from the seat supporting you are the same as they are when the train is stationary.

As the train approaches Hitchin (see Fig. 8.1), you become conscious that it is slowing down. If you are facing backwards, the force from the back of the seat increases, so that you decelerate at the same rate as the train. Once the speed has dropped sufficiently for the train to negotiate the bend ahead, this force reverts to its previous value.

The next force that you experience is a sideways force, and then you know that the train has left the main line and has started to round the bend on the Cambridge line. This force lasts as long as the bend continues.

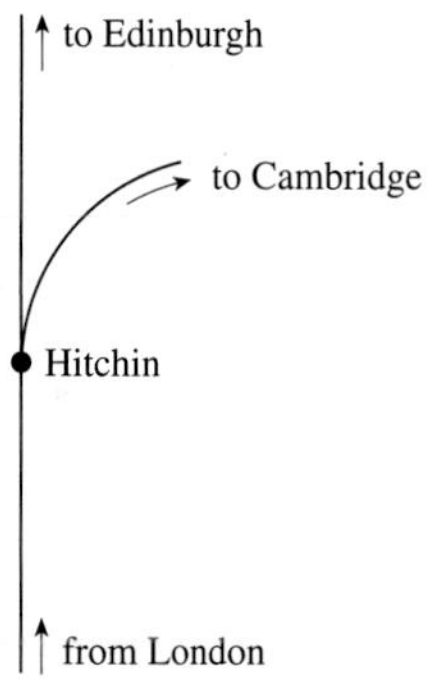

Fig. 8.1

Where there is force, there must be acceleration. An object moving in a curved path has an acceleration directed inwards along the normal to the curve. If the path is circular, this normal is along the radius, that is towards the centre of the circle.

You may think it surprising that an object can be accelerating if its speed is constant. But although the speed stays the same, the velocity is changing. Force is needed to change the direction of the velocity.

It was similar reasoning that led Newton to his theory of gravitational attraction. He observed that the Moon goes round the Earth in a nearly circular path. If there were no force, then the Moon should simply move in a straight line. Since in fact it moves in a circle, there must be a force on the Moon directed along the radius, that is towards the Earth. This force produces an acceleration, called the gravitational acceleration.

The next step is to find how to calculate this acceleration. This is the subject of the next three sections.

8.2 Angular speed

For a particle moving along a straight line, speed is calculated as the rate at which the distance is changing. You can measure the speed of a particle moving in a circle in the same way. But often it is more convenient to measure the speed by finding the rate at which the radius is turning.

Fig. 8.2 shows a particle P moving at constant speed v round a circle with centre O and radius r. At any instant it is moving in the direction of the tangent to the circle, so its speed is sometimes called the **tangential speed**.

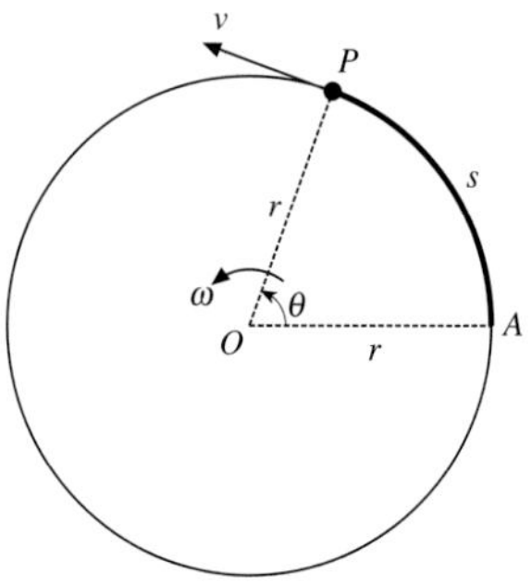

Fig. 8.2

Suppose that, at a time t after the particle passes a point A on the circle, it has moved a distance s, and that angle AOP is θ radians. Then the speed of the particle is $\dfrac{s}{t}$, and $s = r\theta$. So the speed is $\dfrac{r\theta}{t}$, which can be rearranged as $r \times \dfrac{\theta}{t}$.

The quantity $\dfrac{\theta}{t}$ which appears in this expression is called the **angular speed** of the particle about O. It is usually denoted by the greek letter ω (omega). In a diagram angular speed is shown by an arrow with a curved shaft and the same head as the velocity arrow, as in Fig. 8.2.

The tangential speed of the particle can then be expressed in terms of r and ω.

> A particle moving round a circle of radius r with angular speed ω has tangential speed v given by $v = r\omega$.

In SI units, with r in metres and v in $\mathrm{m\,s^{-1}}$, ω is in $\mathrm{rad\,s^{-1}}$. If it is more convenient, other units of distance and time can be used, provided that they are consistent. But it is essential that the unit for angular speed is always radians per unit time.

If the speed of the particle round the circle is not constant, the definition of angular speed can be generalised as the rate of increase of the angle θ with respect to time, measured by the derivative $\dfrac{\mathrm{d}\theta}{\mathrm{d}t}$. But in this chapter all the examples are about objects moving with constant angular speed.

Example 8.2.1
A car's tachometer records the engine speed as 3000 revolutions per minute. What is this in $\mathrm{rad\,s^{-1}}$?

Engine speeds are often quoted in revolutions per minute, but calculations are usually carried out in SI units, with time in seconds. If the engine makes 3000 revolutions in a minute, it makes $3000 \div 60$ revolutions in each second. So the engine speed is 50 revolutions per second.

Each revolution is 2π radians, and the engine makes 50 revolutions in each second. The angular speed is therefore $50 \times 2\pi \ \mathrm{rad\,s^{-1}}$. This is $314 \ \mathrm{rad\,s^{-1}}$, correct to 3 significant figures.

Example 8.2.2

Taking the orbit of the Earth round the Sun to be a circle of radius 1.495×10^{11} metres, calculate the speed at which the Earth is moving.

The Earth completes the orbit in a year, which is approximately $365\frac{1}{4}$ days taking leap years into account. This is $365.25 \times 24 \times 60 \times 60$ seconds, or about 3.155×10^7 seconds. So the equation $\omega = \dfrac{\theta}{t}$ gives the angular speed of the Earth about the Sun as

$$\frac{2\pi}{3.155 \times 10^7} \text{ rad s}^{-1} = 1.991\ldots \times 10^{-7} \text{ rad s}^{-1}.$$

Using the equation $v = r\omega$, the tangential speed of the Earth is

$$(1.495 \times 10^{11}) \times (1.991\ldots \times 10^{-7}) \text{ m s}^{-1} \approx 29\,766 \text{ m s}^{-1}.$$

The speed of the Earth round the Sun is just under $30\,000 \text{ m s}^{-1}$.

Example 8.2.3

The pilot of an aircraft flying at 800 km per hour on a bearing of 250° receives orders to change course to 210°. The manoeuvre is completed in 20 seconds. Calculate the radius of the turn.

The direction of flight changes by 40° in 20 seconds, or 2° in each second. The radius from the centre of the circle is always at right angles to the direction of flight, so this radius rotates at 2° per second. Since 1° is $\frac{1}{180}\pi$ radians, the angular speed is $\frac{1}{90}\pi$ rad s^{-1}.

The speed of the aircraft in km s^{-1} is $\dfrac{800}{60 \times 60}$, which is more simply written as $\frac{2}{9}$. So, using the equation $v = r\omega$,

$$r = \frac{v}{\omega} = \frac{\frac{2}{9}}{\frac{1}{90}\pi} = \frac{20}{\pi} = 6.37, \quad \text{correct to 3 significant figures.}$$

Since the unit of v is km s^{-1}, the unit of r is km.

The radius of the turn is 6.37 km, correct to 3 significant figures.

Exercise 8A

1 A particle moves in a circle of radius 2 metres with speed 3 m s^{-1}. Calculate its angular speed.

2 A cyclist completes a circuit of a circular track in 14 seconds. Calculate her angular speed in rad s^{-1}.

3 A model train moves round a circular track of diameter 1 metre in 3.7 seconds. Calculate the angular and tangential speeds of the train.

4 A metre is approximately one ten-millionth of the distance from the north pole to the equator. Assuming that the Earth is a sphere and that its axis of rotation is stationary, calculate the speed of a building on the equator in m s^{-1}.

5 The tangential speed of an object moving round a circle is given as 8 m s^{-1} or 4 rad s^{-1}. Calculate the radius of its path.

6 An athlete runs round the semicircular end of the track in 12 seconds at a speed of $7\,\mathrm{m\,s^{-1}}$. Calculate his angular speed, and the radius of the semicircle.

7 An aircraft changes its direction of motion from bearing 330° to bearing 120° in 4 seconds. Calculate two possible angular speeds for its turn.

8 An old gramophone record of diameter 30 cm rotates at 78 revolutions per minute. Calculate its angular speed in $\mathrm{rad\,s^{-1}}$, and the speed of the rim of the record in $\mathrm{m\,s^{-1}}$.

9 A train travelling at $180\,\mathrm{km\,h^{-1}}$ moves round a circle of radius 600 metres. Calculate the angular speed of the train in $\mathrm{rad\,s^{-1}}$.

10 A Catherine-wheel spins 15 times each second. Calculate the distance in centimetres from the axis of rotation of a point moving with speed $2\,\mathrm{m\,s^{-1}}$.

11 A flight simulator is modelled as a light rigid rod OA, of length 12 metres, with a particle of mass 75 kg attached to the end A. The rod rotates in a horizontal plane, about a fixed axis through O, with angular speed $\omega\,\mathrm{rad\,s^{-1}}$. Given that the kinetic energy of the particle is 14 000 J, find ω.   (OCR)

8.3 Calculating the acceleration

Knowing r and ω, or r and v, completely determines the motion of a particle moving in a circle at constant speed. So it must be possible to find a formula for the acceleration in terms of either of these pairs of quantities. In this section the results will just be stated; a proof is given in the next section.

In terms of r and ω, the acceleration of the particle towards the centre of the circle is $r\omega^2$. Since ω can be written as $\dfrac{v}{r}$, this formula can also be written as $r \times \left(\dfrac{v}{r}\right)^2$, which is $\dfrac{v^2}{r}$. It is worth knowing the result in both forms, since it is sometimes more convenient to use angular speed and sometimes tangential speed.

> A particle moving round a circular path of radius r with constant angular speed ω and tangential speed v has acceleration of magnitude $r\omega^2$, or $\dfrac{v^2}{r}$, directed towards the centre of the circle.

The unit of acceleration given by these formulae depends on the units chosen for distance and time. If SI units are used for r and v, and if ω is in $\mathrm{rad\,s^{-1}}$, the acceleration is in $\mathrm{m\,s^{-2}}$.

Example 8.3.1
Astronauts are trained to withstand the effects of high acceleration in a centrifugal machine. They sit or lie in cabins at the end of long metal arms, which rotate them about a vertical axis in a horizontal circle. If the radius of the circle is 12 metres, and the acceleration to be experienced is $10g$, how long should it take for the arms to make one revolution?

An acceleration of $10g$ is $98\,\mathrm{m\,s^{-2}}$. So, using the formula $r\omega^2$ for acceleration, the angular speed ω must satisfy the equation $12\omega^2 = 98$, which gives $\omega = \sqrt{\frac{98}{12}}$.

The time in seconds for a complete rotation takes $\dfrac{2\pi}{\omega}$, which is $2\pi\sqrt{\frac{12}{98}}$, or about 2.20. The arm must make one revolution in about 2.2 seconds.

Example 8.3.2
A handbook of astronomical data states that the Moon describes an approximately circular path of radius $3.844 \times 10^8\,\mathrm{m}$ in 27.32 days. Compare the acceleration of the Moon towards the centre of the Earth with the acceleration due to gravity at the Earth's surface.

The Moon makes one revolution round the Earth in 27.32 days, which is $27.32 \times 24 \times 60 \times 60$ seconds, or $2.36 \times 10^6\,\mathrm{s}$. The angular speed is therefore $\dfrac{2\pi}{2.36 \times 10^6}\,\mathrm{rad\,s^{-1}}$, which is about $2.66 \times 10^{-6}\,\mathrm{rad\,s^{-1}}$.

Using the formula $r\omega^2$, the acceleration of the Moon towards the Earth is therefore

$$(3.844 \times 10^8) \times (2.66 \times 10^{-6})^2\,\mathrm{m\,s^{-2}} \approx 0.002\,72\,\mathrm{m\,s^{-2}}.$$

Comparing this with g, which is approximately $9.8\,\mathrm{m\,s^{-2}}$, the acceleration of the Moon is about $\frac{1}{3600}g$.

This calculation forms the basis of Newton's law of gravitation. The radius of the Moon's orbit is about 60 times the radius of the Earth, and the acceleration of gravity at Moon distance is about $\dfrac{1}{60^2}$ of the acceleration on the Earth's surface. This suggests that the acceleration due to gravity is proportional to the inverse square of the distance from the Earth.

Example 8.3.3
A smooth circular table of radius 1.2 metres has a raised rim. A ball-bearing of mass 50 grams runs round the rim of the table, making one circuit every 4 seconds. Find the magnitude of the contact force on the ball-bearing from the rim.

The ball-bearing rotates through 2π radians about the centre of the table in 4 seconds, an angular speed of $\frac{1}{2}\pi\,\mathrm{rad\,s^{-1}}$. The acceleration of the ball-bearing towards the centre is therefore $1.2 \times \left(\frac{1}{2}\pi\right)^2\,\mathrm{m\,s^{-2}}$, which is $0.3\pi^2\,\mathrm{m\,s^{-2}}$.

The mass of the ball-bearing is 0.05 kg, so the force needed to produce the acceleration is $0.05 \times 0.3\pi^2\,\mathrm{N} = 0.148\,\mathrm{N}$, correct to 3 significant figures.

Example 8.3.4
A racing cyclist rounds a circle of radius 30 metres at a speed of $15\,\mathrm{m\,s^{-1}}$. What must be the coefficient of friction between the tyres and the track for this to be possible?

The $\dfrac{v^2}{r}$ form of the acceleration formula shows that the cyclist requires an acceleration towards the centre of $\dfrac{15^2}{30}\,\mathrm{m\,s^{-2}}$, which is $7.5\,\mathrm{m\,s^{-2}}$.

Fig. 8.3 shows the forces on the cyclist.

The force which produces the acceleration is the friction between the tyres and the track. The mass of the cyclist with his machine is not given, so denote it by M kg. Then the friction force is $7.5M$ newtons.

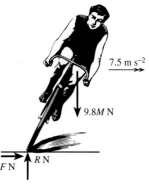

The normal contact force from the ground is equal to the weight, which is $9.8M$ newtons.

So if the tyres are not to slip, the coefficient of friction must not be less than $\dfrac{7.5M}{9.8M}$, which is 0.765, correct to 3 significant figures.

Fig. 8.3

8.4*   Proof of the acceleration formula

You can if you wish omit this section and go straight to Exercise 8B.

When a particle moves along a straight line, the velocity is the derivative of the displacement with respect to time, and the acceleration is the derivative of the velocity. The equations for the motion of a projectile in Chapter 1 show that, if displacement, velocity and acceleration are regarded as vectors, the same relation holds for motion in two dimensions with constant acceleration. That is,

- the relation of the acceleration to the velocity is the same as the relation of the velocity to the displacement.

This principle is the basis from which the acceleration in circular motion can be found.

Fig. 8.4 shows a particle P moving round a circle centre O with angular speed ω. The displacement vector $\overrightarrow{OP}$ is denoted by $\mathbf{r}$, and the velocity vector $\mathbf{v}$ is perpendicular to $\mathbf{r}$.

Fig. 8.5 shows the relation between the velocity and acceleration vectors in a similar way. To do this, the velocity vector has its tail anchored at a point C, so that the displacement $\overrightarrow{CQ}$ represents the velocity. Since the velocity has constant magnitude, the point Q moves round a circle.

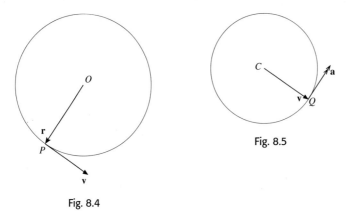

Fig. 8.5

Fig. 8.4

Now the direction of $\overrightarrow{CQ}$ is always $\frac{1}{2}\pi$ radians in advance of the direction of $\overrightarrow{OP}$, so the angular speed of Q about C is also ω.

This has two consequences. First, since the direction of $\mathbf{v}$ is $\frac{1}{2}\pi$ radians in advance of $\mathbf{r}$, and the direction of $\mathbf{a}$ is $\frac{1}{2}\pi$ radians ahead of $\mathbf{v}$, it follows that $\mathbf{a}$ is π radians ahead of $\mathbf{r}$. That is, the direction of the acceleration of the particle is towards O.

Secondly, since the magnitude of $\mathbf{v}$ is $r\omega$, that is ω times the magnitude of $\mathbf{r}$, the magnitude of $\mathbf{a}$ is ω times the magnitude of $\mathbf{v}$, that is $(r\omega)\omega$, or $r\omega^2$. This completes the proof of the result stated in Section 8.3.

Exercise 8B

1 A small coin is placed flat on a record turntable. The coin is at a distance $10\,\text{cm}$ from the axis of the turntable. The turntable is rotating at a constant speed of 33 revolutions per minute, and the coin is not moving on the turntable.

(a) Show that the angular speed of the turntable is $3.46\,\text{rad}\,\text{s}^{-1}$, correct to 3 significant figures.

(b) Find, in $\text{m}\,\text{s}^{-1}$, the speed of the coin.

(c) Find the acceleration of the coin, giving its magnitude in $\text{m}\,\text{s}^{-2}$ and stating its direction. (OCR)

2 A particle P of mass $0.3\,\text{kg}$ is attached to one end of a light inextensible string of length 0.6 metres. The other end of the string is attached to a fixed point O on a smooth horizontal surface. P moves in a circular path on the surface with speed $4\,\text{m}\,\text{s}^{-1}$. Calculate the tension in the string.

Given that the tension in the string cannot exceed $30\,\text{N}$, find the maximum speed of P in $\text{m}\,\text{s}^{-1}$, and the angular speed in $\text{rad}\,\text{s}^{-1}$.

3 A particle P of mass $0.4\,\text{kg}$ moves on a horizontal circle, centre O. The speed of the particle is $3\,\text{m}\,\text{s}^{-1}$ and the force on P directed towards O is $15\,\text{N}$. Calculate the distance OP.

4 A microwave oven has a horizontal circular turntable of radius 0.16 metres. A small object is placed on the turntable, near to its edge. The coefficient of friction between the object and the turntable is 0.02. The object is on the point of slipping when the turntable is rotating with constant angular speed $\omega\,\text{rad}\,\text{s}^{-1}$. Calculate ω. (OCR)

5 A radial force of $20\,\text{N}$ is required to maintain a particle moving in a horizontal circle of diameter 1.8 metres with speed $4.8\,\text{m}\,\text{s}^{-1}$. Calculate the mass of the particle.

6 An object of mass $0.2\,\text{kg}$ is placed on a horizontal turntable at a distance of $15\,\text{cm}$ from the axis of rotation. When the turntable has angular speed $5\,\text{rad}\,\text{s}^{-1}$, friction between the object and turntable is limiting. Calculate the coefficient of friction.

7 A centrifuge consists of a hollow cylinder of diameter 0.8 metres rotating about a vertical axis with angular speed $500\,\text{rad}\,\text{s}^{-1}$. Calculate the magnitude of the contact force between the cylinder and an object of mass $0.7\,\text{kg}$ on the inner surface of the centrifuge.

8 A light rod of length 1.2 metres is freely pivoted at one end to a fixed point O on a smooth horizontal surface. Particles P and Q, each of mass 0.3 kg, are attached to the mid-point and the free end of the rod respectively. The rod rotates in a horizontal circle at constant angular speed. Given that the tension in the rod between P and Q is 18 N, calculate the force on the rod at O.

9 A railway engine travels at a constant speed of v m s^{-1} on a curved track. The curve is an arc of a horizontal circle of radius 550 metres. The magnitude of the acceleration of the engine is 0.22 m s^{-2}. Making a suitable modelling assumption, which should be stated, calculate v.

The mass of the engine is 45 000 kg. Calculate the magnitude of the resultant horizontal force on the engine.   (OCR)

10 Two particles P and Q, of masses M and m respectively, are attached to opposite ends of a light rod of length a. The system is set rotating on a smooth horizontal surface, with the particles moving in concentric circles, centre O, about an axis perpendicular to the rod and the table. If $OP = R$, explain why $MR = m(a - R)$. Hence express R in terms of M, m and a. If the particles rotate about O with angular speed ω, show that the tension in the rod is $\dfrac{Mma\omega^2}{M + m}$.

11 The acceleration due to gravity at a distance r metres from the centre of the Earth is $\dfrac{k}{r^2}$ m s^{-2}, where k is a constant. Estimate the height of a geostationary satellite with an orbit above the Earth's equator, given that the radius of the Earth is 6400 km. (A geostationary satellite is one which moves so that it is always above the same point on the Earth's surface. Its angular speed about the Earth's axis is therefore the same as the angular speed of a point on the equator.)

12 The Earth may be modelled as a uniform sphere of radius 6400 km, rotating on an axis passing through the north and south poles. Calculate the acceleration towards the centre of the Earth of an object placed at the equator.

Objects are released from points just above the Earth's surface at the north pole and the equator. Which will fall to the Earth with the greater acceleration, and by how much?

8.5 Three-dimensional problems

If an airliner has to change course, then the pilot banks the aircraft so that the wings are at an angle to the horizontal (see Fig. 8.6).

The reason for this is to enable the lift force, which in level flight acts vertically and balances the weight, to act at an angle to the vertical. In this way the force can perform two functions at the same time: its vertical component balances the weight, and its horizontal component provides the required acceleration towards the centre of the circular path which the pilot wants to follow.

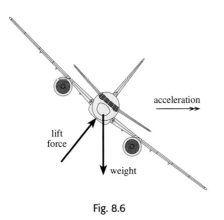

Fig. 8.6

You can use this principle in a number of applications, in which the supporting force may take the form of the tension in a string or the contact force from a surface. The examples in this section show how the principle of resolving can be applied to objects which move in a horizontal circle.

Example 8.5.1

One end of a string of length l is tied to a hook, and a particle of mass m is attached to the other end. With the string taut and making an angle α with the downward vertical, the particle is set in motion so that it rotates in a horizontal circle about the vertical line through the hook. Find the period of one revolution of the particle round the circle.

There are just two forces on the particle, its weight mg and the tension T in the string (see Fig. 8.7). Suppose that the angular speed of the particle is ω. The radius of the circle is $l \sin \alpha$, so the acceleration of the particle is $(l \sin \alpha) \omega^2$. You can now resolve horizontally and vertically to obtain equations connecting the various quantities.

$$\mathcal{R}(\rightarrow) \qquad T \cos \left(\tfrac{1}{2} \pi - \alpha \right) = m (l \sin \alpha) \omega^2,$$
$$\mathcal{R}(\uparrow) \qquad T \cos \alpha - mg = 0.$$

Since $\cos \left(\tfrac{1}{2} \pi - \alpha \right) = \sin \alpha$, the first equation reduces to

$$T = ml\omega^2.$$

Substituting this expression for T in the second equation gives

$$ml\omega^2 \cos \alpha = mg, \quad \text{so} \quad \omega = \sqrt{\frac{g}{l \cos \alpha}}.$$

The time for the particle to describe one revolution of 2π radians is $\dfrac{2\pi}{\omega}$, which is

equal to $2\pi \sqrt{\dfrac{l \cos \alpha}{g}}$.

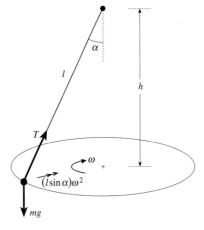

Fig. 8.7

The apparatus in Example 8.5.1 is called a **conical pendulum**, because the string describes the surface of a cone as it rotates.

It is interesting to note that $l \cos \alpha$ is just the depth h of the circular path below the hook, so that the period of one revolution can be written as $2\pi \sqrt{\dfrac{h}{g}}$. This expression is independent of l and of α, and also of m. This means that if you have a number of particles (not necessarily of the same mass) attached to strings of different lengths, all moving in circular paths at the same depth below the hook, they will all take the same time to make a complete revolution.

Example 8.5.2

A bob-sleigh with its two-person team has a total mass of 200 kg. On one stretch of the course the team rounds a horizontal bend of radius 25 metres at a speed of $35 \, \mathrm{m \, s}^{-1}$ They bank the sleigh so that it rounds the bend with no sideways frictional force. Calculate the acceleration of the sleigh as a multiple of g, and find the angle to the horizontal at which the sleigh is banked.

The acceleration towards the centre of the bend is $\dfrac{35^2}{25} \, \mathrm{m \, s}^{-2}$, which is $49 \, \mathrm{m \, s}^{-2}$, or $5 \times 9.8 \, \mathrm{m \, s}^{-2}$. So the acceleration of the sleigh as it rounds the bend is $5g$.

Fig. 8.8 shows the forces on the sleigh as it rounds the bend. Since there is no sideways frictional force, the acceleration towards the centre of the bend is provided entirely by the resolved part of the normal contact force of R newtons.

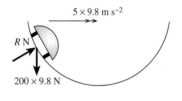

Fig. 8.8

If the angle at which the sleigh is banked is α,

$\mathcal{R}(\uparrow) \quad R \cos \alpha - 200 \times 9.8 = 0$, and
$\mathcal{R}(\rightarrow) \quad R \sin \alpha = 200 \times 5 \times 9.8$.

This gives

$$\begin{aligned}
\tan \alpha &= \frac{R \sin \alpha}{R \cos \alpha} \\
&= \frac{200 \times 5 \times 9.8}{200 \times 9.8} = 5, \text{ so } \alpha \approx 78.7°.
\end{aligned}$$

The sleigh is banked at an angle of about $79°$ to the horizontal.

Exercise 8C

1 A particle is attached to one end of a light inextensible string of length 1.6 metres. The other end of the string is attached to a fixed point. The particle moves, at constant speed, in a horizontal circle, with the string inclined at 55° to the vertical. Calculate the speed of the particle.   (OCR)

2 In a simple model of a 'rotating swing', a particle of mass 30 kg is attached to one end of a light inextensible rope of length 2 metres. The other end is attached to a fixed point O. The particle moves in a horizontal circle at a constant angular speed of 3 rad s^{-1}. The rope is inclined at a constant angle θ to the vertical. Find θ.   (OCR)

3 One end of a light inextensible string of length 0.6 metres is attached to a fixed point A, 0.3 metres above a smooth horizontal surface. The other end of the string is attached to a particle P of mass 0.4 kg. The particle moves with constant speed in a horizontal circle, with the string taut, and making an angle θ with the vertical.

  (a) Show that, when $\theta = 70°$, the particle is not in contact with the surface, and calculate the tension in the string and the angular speed of P.

  (b) When $\theta = 60°$, the contact force between the particle and the surface is zero, and the angular speed of P is $\omega \text{ rad s}^{-1}$. Calculate the tension in the string and the value of ω.

  (c) With $\theta = 60°$, P moves with angular speed 2 rad s^{-1}. Calculate the tension in the string, and the contact force between the particle and the surface.

4 A particle P of mass m kg moves on the smooth inner surface of a fixed hollow hemisphere with centre O, radius a metres and axis vertical. The particle moves in a horizontal circle with centre C and radius r metres, and CP rotates with angular speed $\omega \text{ rad s}^{-1}$. The distance OC is h metres (see diagram). Show that $\omega^2 = \dfrac{g}{h}$, and express the magnitude of the normal contact force between P and the surface in terms of m, g, a and h.   (OCR)

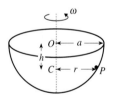

5 A car is travelling around a circular bend on a road banked at an angle α to the horizontal. The car may be modelled as a particle moving in a horizontal circle of radius 120 m. When the car is moving at a constant speed of 20 m s^{-1} there is no frictional force up or down the slope. Find the angle α, giving your answer in degrees correct to 1 decimal place.   (OCR)

6 A vertical post is fixed in the ground. A tennis ball, of mass 0.05 kg, is attached to the top of the post by a string. To control the height of the ball a second string, of the same length as the first, joins the ball to the post at ground level. The ball is moving, with constant speed 5 m s^{-1}, in a horizontal circle of radius 1.2 metres. Each string is taut and inclined at a constant angle of 55° to the vertical, as shown in the diagram. The modelling assumptions made are that both strings are light and inextensible, and that there is no air resistance. Find the tensions in the strings, giving your answers in newtons, correct to 2 decimal places.   (OCR)

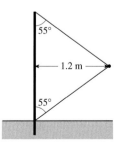

7 A small smooth ring R, of mass 0.4 kg, is threaded on a light inextensible string. The ends are attached to two fixed points A and B, where A is vertically above B. The system rotates about AB. The ring R moves with constant speed in a horizontal circle of radius 0.4 metres. Angle ARB is $90°$ and angle BAR is $35°$ (see diagram).

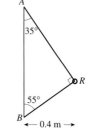

(a) Find the tension in the string.

(b) Find the speed of the ring.   (OCR)

8 An aircraft of mass 2 tonnes flies at $540\,\text{km h}^{-1}$ in a horizontal circular arc to change its direction of motion from bearing $320°$ to bearing $046°$. This manoeuvre is executed in 30 seconds, with the aircraft banked at an angle α to the horizontal. Calculate two values of α and the corresponding values of the lift force perpendicular to the surface of the aircraft's wings.

9 A model aircraft of mass 0.5 kg is attached to one end of a light inextensible string of length 12.5 metres. The other end of the string is attached to a fixed point O. The aircraft travels, with constant speed $24\,\text{m s}^{-1}$, in a horizontal circular path at a height of 3.5 metres above the level of O. It may be assumed that there is no horizontal force on the aircraft due to the air, but that there is a vertical lift force of magnitude V newtons. Calculate the tension in the string and the value of V.   (OCR)

Miscellaneous exercise 8

1 The moon Io orbits the planet Jupiter every 1.528×10^5 seconds. The orbit is approximately circular and of mean radius 4.22×10^8 metres. (Model the motion of Io relative to Jupiter as circular with constant speed.) Calculate

(a) the speed with which Io orbits Jupiter,

(b) the magnitude of the acceleration of Io as it orbits Jupiter.   (OCR)

2 Fighter pilots may experience large accelerations in flight if their planes have to make sudden manoeuvres at high speed. To produce a large acceleration for training purposes a simulator is used. This consists of a horizontal structure OA of length 10 metres with a 'cockpit' at the end A in which the pilot sits. The structure is made to rotate about a vertical axis through O with constant angular speed $\omega\,\text{rad s}^{-1}$ (see the first diagram). Given that the acceleration experienced by the pilot at A has magnitude $5g$, calculate ω.

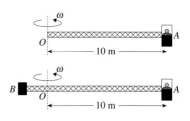

To avoid excessive strain on the mechanism at O, the structure is extended to B, where a counterweight is attached as shown in the second diagram. The mass at B is such that, when the system is rotating, the forces towards O acting on the mass at B and on the pilot at A have equal magnitudes. Show that, when the system is at rest, the weight of the mass at B and the weight of the pilot at A have equal moments about O.   (OCR)

3 The acceleration due to gravity at a point P at a distance r metres from O, the centre of the Earth, is directly proportional to $\dfrac{1}{r^2}$. Assuming the Earth to be a sphere of radius R metres, and the acceleration due to gravity on the Earth's surface to be g m s^{-2}, explain why the acceleration due to gravity at a distance r from the centre of the Earth can be expressed as $\dfrac{gR^2}{r^2}$ m s^{-2}.

A satellite is assumed to move in a circle, whose centre is the centre of the Earth, at a constant speed of 7.5×10^3 m s^{-1}. Taking $g = 9.8$ m s^{-2} and $R = 6.37 \times 10^6$ metres, find the radius of the circle in which the satellite travels. (OCR)

4 A car is moving at a constant speed of v m s^{-1} round a curve which is part of a horizontal circle of radius 50 metres. The acceleration of the car is 3.38 m s^{-2}. Calculate the value of v.

The car has a mass of 900 kg. Calculate the magnitude of the horizontal force acting on the car perpendicular to its direction of motion and suggest the physical cause of this force. (OCR)

5 A horizontal, rough turntable rotates at a constant angular speed of ω radians per second about a vertical axis. A particle of mass 0.1 kg is placed on the turntable at a distance of 0.08 metres from the axis, and does not slip. The coefficient of friction between the turntable and the particle is $\frac{1}{2}$. Find the maximum possible value of ω. (OCR)

6 A car is travelling at a constant speed round a bend that may be modelled as an arc of a circle, with centre O, on a rough horizontal road.

(a) Draw a diagram showing O and the forces acting on the car perpendicular to its direction of motion. Include on your diagram the axis about which the car is turning.

The car is travelling at 6 m s^{-1} and the radius of the car's path is 20 metres.

(b) Calculate the acceleration of the car and state the direction of that acceleration.

(c) Calculate the minimum value of the coefficient of friction, between the car and the road, necessary for the car not to slip outwards. (OCR)

7 A centrifuge consists of a cylindrical drum of radius 0.6 metres. The drum rotates with constant angular speed 5 rad s^{-1} about its axis of symmetry which is vertical. A small block of mass 0.1 kg is at rest relative to the drum on its inner vertical surface. The coefficient of friction between the block and the drum is 0.8. Show that this is sufficient to ensure that the block does not slip.

Given that the drum rotates with a new constant angular speed ω and that the block is about to slip, find the value of ω. (OCR)

8 A particle P is attached to one end of a light inextensible string of length 2 metres. The other end of the string is attached to a fixed point O. The particle moves in a horizontal circle with constant speed v m s^{-1}, with the string taut and inclined at a constant angle of 20° to the vertical. Find v, giving your answer correct to 3 significant figures. (OCR)

9 A conical pendulum consists of a particle attached to the end of a light inextensible string of length 0.8 metres. The particle moves in a horizontal circle, and the system rotates at a constant angular speed of $4\,\mathrm{rad\,s^{-1}}$. Find the angle that the string makes with the vertical.   (OCR)

10 A bend in a horizontal road has a radius of 200 metres. To improve safety, it is decided to bank the road surface at an angle α to the horizontal. It is required that a vehicle can remain stationary on the road when the surface is icy, and the coefficient of friction is 0.052. Calculate the greatest permissible value of α, and the corresponding greatest safe speed, in $\mathrm{km\,h^{-1}}$, of a vehicle when the road surface is icy.

11 A particle P, of mass m, moves at constant speed in a horizontal circle on the inside surface of a smooth hemispherical bowl. The radius of the circle is r and its centre is at C. The contact force acting on the particle has magnitude R and direction making an angle θ with the upward vertical through P, as shown in the diagram.

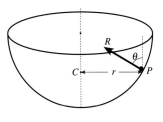

(a) Find R in terms of m, g and θ.

(b) Show that $\omega^2 r = g\tan\theta$, where ω is the angular speed of the radius CP.

The bowl has radius a, and C is at a height $\tfrac{1}{2}a$ above the lowest point of the bowl. Express ω in terms of a and g.

A second particle Q, also of mass m, moves at constant speed on the inside surface of the bowl in a horizontal circle with centre D. The height of D above the lowest point of the bowl is $\tfrac{1}{5}a$. Find the speed of Q in terms of the speed of P.   (OCR)

12 A particle P, of mass m, is moving in a horizontal circle with uniform angular speed ω on the smooth, internal surface of an inverted cone of semi-vertical angle $30°$, whose axis is vertical. The particle is attached to a fixed point O, vertically above the vertex of the cone, by a light inelastic string of length $2l$ which makes an angle of $30°$ to the vertical, as shown in the diagram.

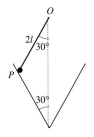

(a) Show that the tension in the string has magnitude $m(\sqrt{3}g - l\omega^2)$.

(b) Find the greatest value of ω which would enable the motion, as described, to be possible. Explain why this value of ω is a maximum and not a minimum.   (OCR)

13 A smooth ring R of mass 0.3 kg is free to slide along a light inextensible string. The ends of the string are attached to fixed points A and B where A is a distance 2.1 metres vertically above B. The ring is moving in a horizontal circle about AB with the string taut. Angle ARB is a right angle, and angle BAR is θ, where $\sin\theta = \tfrac{3}{5}$, as shown in the diagram.

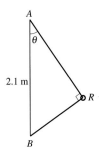

(a) Find the tension in the string.

(b) Find the speed of the ring.   (OCR)

14 One end of a light inextensible string, of length a, is attached to a fixed point A. To the
    other end is attached a particle P, of mass m. The particle moves, with the string taut, on a
    smooth horizontal table, and describes a horizontal circle with centre O, where O is
    vertically below A. The line OP has constant angular speed ω, and the string makes an
    angle of $60°$ with OA. Show that $\omega^2 \leqslant \dfrac{2g}{a}$, and for the case when $\omega^2 = \dfrac{g}{a}$ find, in terms of
    m and g, the tension in the string.

    The string is unfastened from A and the free end passed through a small hole O in the
    table and attached to a particle Q, of mass $2m$. The particle P lies on the smooth
    horizontal table and particle Q hangs below the table. The system is set in motion so that
    P moves in a circle, on the table, with OP having constant angular speed 2Ω and Q moves
    in a horizontal circle with OQ having constant angular speed Ω. Show that the radius of
    the circle described by P is $\frac{1}{3}a$, and find, in terms of m, a and Ω, the tension in the string.
    (OCR)

15 A particle P of mass m kg moves on the smooth inner surface
    of a fixed hollow container whose shape is obtained by
    rotating the curve $y = x^2$ about its vertical axis of symmetry,
    where the units on both axes are metres. The particle moves in
    a horizontal circle with centre C and radius r metres, and CP
    rotates with constant angular speed ω rad s^{-1}, as in the
    diagram. By considering $\dfrac{\mathrm{d}y}{\mathrm{d}x}$, show that the angle θ between
    the normal contact force on P and the horizontal is given by
    $\tan \theta = \dfrac{1}{2r}$, and hence show that $\omega^2 = 2g$.   (OCR)

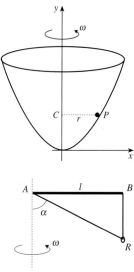

16 The diagram shows a straight rod AB of length l rotating in a
    horizontal plane about the end A. A light inextensible string of
    length k, where $k > l$, is attached to A and B, and carries on it a
    small ring R of mass m, which is free to slide on the string. When
    the constant angular speed of AB is ω, R remains vertically
    below B, and AR makes an acute angle α with the vertical.

    (a) Show that $\tan \frac{1}{2}\alpha = \dfrac{\omega^2 l}{g}$.

    (b) Deduce that $\omega < \sqrt{\dfrac{g}{l}}$ for this motion to occur.

    (c) Show that $k = \dfrac{g}{\omega^2}$.

    The string is now detached from the rod, and the rod is removed. One end of the string is
    fixed at a point O, and the ring R is attached to the other end of the string. The ring is set
    rotating about a vertical axis through O with the string straight, and making a constant
    acute angle θ with the vertical. Show that the new angular speed of R about the vertical
    through O is greater than ω for all values of θ.   (OCR)

9 Geometrical methods

Conditions for the equilibrium of rigid objects can also be expressed in geometrical form. When you have completed this chapter, you should

- know the parallelogram rule for combining forces on a rigid object
- know and be able to apply the conditions for equilibrium of a rigid object acted on by three non-parallel forces
- be able to use geometrical methods to solve problems involving friction, including those in which equilibrium may be broken by either sliding or toppling.

9.1 The parallelogram rule

A narrow boat 20 metres long is being manoeuvred into a mooring by a river bank. Ropes are attached to the boat at the bow and the stern, and these are held by two children on the bank. The girl with the bow rope exerts a force of 40 newtons at an angle 50° to the direction in which the boat is pointing; the boy with the stern rope exerts a force of 30 newtons at right angles to the boat. (See Fig. 9.1.)

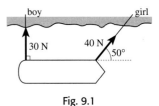

Fig. 9.1

Suppose that only one person was available. Where would the rope have to be attached, and what force should be exerted, to produce the same effect on the boat as the two children?

If the boat could be modelled as a particle, you would use the triangle rule to combine the two forces, as in Fig. 9.2.

Fig. 9.2

You can calculate that this gives a force of 65.9 newtons at 67° to the direction of the boat.

But this boat can't adequately be modelled as a particle. Where the rope is attached makes a lot of difference to how the boat behaves. So the triangle law by itself is not enough.

In Fig. 9.3 the lines of the two ropes are produced backwards to meet at a point X. Since the lines of action of both forces pass through X, the forces have no moment about X. It follows that a single force with the same effect must also have no moment about X, so that its line of action has to pass through X.

So if you draw a line through X at an angle of 67°, a force of 65.9 newtons along this line has the same effect as the original two forces. If this line cuts the side of the boat at Y, as in Fig. 9.3, then the single rope should be attached at Y. You can calculate that Y is 10.1 metres from the stern of the boat.

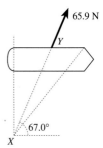

Fig. 9.3

The two parts of this calculation can be amalgamated by replacing the triangle law for combining forces by a parallelogram law, as in Fig. 9.4. Instead of drawing a triangle with the tail of the second arrow at the head of the first, you can draw a parallelogram with the tails of both arrows at X. An arrow along the diagonal with its tail at X then represents the resultant force on the boat in magnitude, direction and line of action.

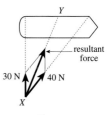

Fig. 9.4

> **The parallelogram rule for combining forces**   If two forces **P** and **Q**, acting along lines which intersect at X, are represented by arrows on some scale with their tails at X which define a parallelogram, and the arrow representing **R** is the diagonal with its tail at X, then the single force **R** has exactly the same effect on a rigid object as the two forces **P** and **Q** acting together.

Example 9.1.1

A triangular plate ABC is placed on a smooth horizontal surface. The length BC is 2 m, and the angles at B and C are $50°$ and $70°$ respectively. Horizontal forces of 30 N and 20 N are applied to the plate at B and C, in the directions of AB and AC respectively, as shown in Fig. 9.5. Find what single force would have the same effect on the plate as these two given forces acting together, and at what point along BC it should be applied.

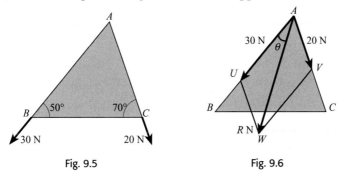

Fig. 9.5   Fig. 9.6

Since the lines of action of both forces pass through A, their resultant also passes through A. It can be found as the diagonal AW of the parallelogram of forces in Fig. 9.6, whose sides AU and AV represent the forces of 30 N and 20 N on some scale. Suppose that the resultant has magnitude R N, and that its direction makes an angle θ with AU.

The cosine and sine rules applied to triangle AUW can be used to calculate R and θ.

Since angle BAC is $180° - (50° + 70°) = 60°$, angle AUW is $120°$. So

$$R^2 = 30^2 + 20^2 - 2 \times 30 \times 20 \times \cos 120°$$
$$= 900 + 400 - 1200 \times \left(-\tfrac{1}{2}\right)$$
$$= 1900,$$

and $\dfrac{\sin \theta}{20} = \dfrac{\sin 120°}{R}$.

These equations give $R = \sqrt{1900} = 43.58\ldots$ and $\theta = 23.41\ldots$.

The position of the point X on BC at which the resultant should be applied can now be found by using the sine rule in triangle ABX to calculate the distance BX (see Fig. 9.7). Since angle BXA is $180° - (50° + \theta) = (130° - \theta)$,

$$\frac{BX}{\sin\theta} = \frac{AB}{\sin(130° - \theta)}.$$

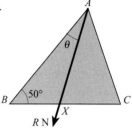

Fig. 9.7

You don't yet know the length AB, but it is given that BC has length 2 m, so AB can be found by using the sine rule in triangle ABC, as

$$\frac{AB}{\sin 70°} = \frac{2}{\sin 60°}.$$

So AB has length $2.170\ldots$ m, and then $BX = 0.8997\ldots$ m, which is 0.900 m correct to 3 significant figures.

The resultant force is 43.6 N at an angle 23.4° to AB, applied at a point X in BC such that $BX = 0.900$ m.

Exercise 9A

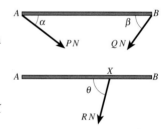

1 AB is a girder 10 metres long. Cables are attached to it at A and B, making angles of α and β with the girder, and tension forces of PN and QN are applied, as shown in the figure. The effect on the girder is the same as that of a single force RN at an angle θ to the girder applied at a point X. By drawing and measurement, find the values of R and θ and the distance AX in the following cases.

(a) $P = 700$, $Q = 1000$, $\alpha = 90°$, $\beta = 60°$

(b) $P = 1000$, $Q = 1200$, $\alpha = 45°$, $\beta = 65°$

(c) $P = 800$, $Q = 1400$, $\alpha = 140°$, $\beta = 160°$

2 With the notation of Question 1, use a parallelogram of forces to calculate the values of R and θ and the distance AX in the following cases.

(a) $P = 1000$, $Q = 500$, $\alpha = 180°$, $\beta = 45°$

(b) $P = 1000$, $Q = 1000$, $\alpha = 130°$, $\beta = 30°$

(c) $P = 1500$, $Q = 1000$, $\alpha = 155°$, $\beta = 115°$

(d) $P = 1000$, $Q = 2000$, $\alpha = 80°$, $\beta = 50°$

3 $ABCD$ is a rectangular table with $AB = 3$ metres and $BC = 2$ metres. Two people push the table with forces of equal magnitude. One pushes at A in the direction of the edge AB, and the other pushes at a point X of DC, in such a way that the resultant force acts through the centre of the table at an angle of 30° to AB. Find the distance DX.

4 Two boys stand at the ends of a diameter *AB* of a circular table. They both push the table with forces of 50 newtons along the tangents at *A* and *B* to try to spin the table clockwise. A third boy, standing at a point *C* halfway round the circumference from *A* to *B*, tries to stop the spin by pushing with a force of 100 newtons anticlockwise. By finding the resultant of two of the forces, and then combining this with the third force, find the magnitude and the line of action of the combined effect of all three forces.

9.2 Three forces in equilibrium

Similar arguments can be used when there are just three forces acting on a rigid object in equilibrium. If these forces are not all parallel, let the lines of action of two of them meet at *X*. Then the moments of these two forces about *X* are 0. Since the moments of all three forces about *X* have to balance, the moment of the third force about *X* must also be 0. This means that the line of action of the third force also goes through *X*.

So if three non-parallel forces are in equilibrium, their lines of action all pass through the same point. They are then said to be 'concurrent'.

Now the conditions for the object to be in equilibrium can be expressed by resolving in two directions and taking moments about one point. You already know that, for a particle acted on by three forces, the resolving equations are equivalent to the triangle of forces rule. (See M1 Section 10.2.) This applies equally well for the forces on a rigid object.

These two ideas can be put together to give conditions for three forces on a rigid object to be in equilibrium, provided that they are not parallel.

> A rigid object acted on by just three non-parallel forces is in equilibrium if
> * the forces can be represented in a triangle of forces, and
> * the lines of action of the forces are concurrent.

You can use this instead of the algebraic methods described in Chapter 6. It is not so general, because it only applies when there are just three forces and these are not parallel. But in this case it often produces more efficient solutions.

Example 9.2.1

A boy is designing a go-kart and wants to know where its centre of mass is. He finds that his kart will rest horizontally with the brakes off if the rear wheels are on a 15° slope and the front wheels on a 22° slope. What does this tell him about the centre of mass?

There are only three forces on the kart, its weight and the contact forces on the front and rear wheels. The lines of action must be concurrent, so the centre of mass *G* lies on a vertical line through the point where the lines of the two contact forces meet (see Fig. 9.8).

Suppose that this line cuts the line joining the axles at a distance a in front of the rear wheels and b behind the front wheels. The contact forces make angles of 75° and 68° with the horizontal, so their lines of action intersect at a point whose height above the axles can be expressed either as $a \tan 75°$ or $b \tan 68°$. Therefore

$$a \tan 75° = b \tan 68°, \text{ so } \frac{a}{b} = \frac{\tan 68°}{\tan 75°} \approx 0.66, \text{ or about}$$

two-thirds.

So if the distance between the axles is d, the centre of mass is on a vertical line about $\frac{2}{5}d$ in front of the rear axle.

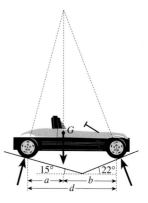

Fig. 9.8

Notice that in this example you don't want to find the contact forces, so the concurrency condition tells you all you need to know.

Example 9.2.2

A window of weight 200 newtons is hinged along its top edge. Its centre of mass is at its geometrical centre. It is kept open at 40° to the vertical by the thrust from a light strut perpendicular to the window and attached to the wall. Calculate the thrust in the strut and the force exerted on the window by the hinge.

When you use algebraic methods it is often best to represent a hinge force by its components in two perpendicular directions. But to use the geometrical conditions you want to reduce the number of forces to three. Two of these are the weight and the thrust in the strut, so you must treat the hinge force as a single force acting at an angle.

In Fig. 9.9 H is the hinge, G the centre of mass of the window, ML the strut and N the point where the vertical through G meets ML, which is the mid-point of ML. The thrust in the strut is T newtons, and the force $\mathbf{R}$ from the hinge is R newtons. The length HL is not given, so denote it by d.

By the concurrency condition, the line of action of the force $\mathbf{R}$ passes through N. You can easily calculate that $ML = d \tan 40°$, so $NL = \frac{1}{2}d \tan 40°$. So if angle $NHL = \theta$,

$$\begin{aligned}
\tan \theta &= \frac{NL}{HL} \\
&= \frac{\frac{1}{2}d \tan 40°}{d} \\
&= \tfrac{1}{2} \tan 40°,
\end{aligned}$$

which gives $\theta = 22.7\ldots°$. Therefore $\mathbf{R}$ makes an angle of $40° - 22.7\ldots° = 17.2\ldots°$ with the vertical.

Fig. 9.9

You now know all the angles in the triangle of forces, which is drawn in Fig. 9.10. By the sine rule,

$$\frac{T}{\sin 17.2...°} = \frac{R}{\sin 50°} = \frac{200}{\sin 112.7...°},$$

so that $T = 64.3$ and $R = 166.1$, correct to 1 decimal place.

The thrust in the strut is about 64 newtons and the force from the hinge is about 166 newtons at 17° to the vertical.

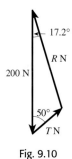

Fig. 9.10

In this example it is interesting to notice that in Fig. 9.9 the triangle HMN has sides parallel to the three forces, so this triangle is similar to the triangle of forces.

Another way of completing the solution would then be to find the lengths MN, NH and HM, and to observe that T, R and 200 are proportional to these lengths. This does not make the calculation any easier, but it would be a good method to use if you were solving the problem by scale drawing.

Exercise 9B

Use the geometrical method described in Section 9.2 to work the problems in this exercise.

1 A uniform rod XY, of length 1 metre and mass 4 kg, is smoothly hinged at X to a vertical wall. The rod is kept in equilibrium, making an angle of 30° with the upward vertical, by a string attached to the rod at Y and to a hook in the wall at the same level as Y. Find the force on the rod from the hinge at X, and the tension in the string.

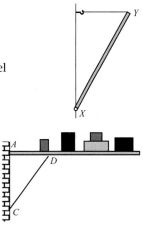

2 A loaded shelf AB is hinged to a wall at A. It is kept in a horizontal position by a light strut CD which supports it at a point D, where $AD = 12$ cm. The other end C of the strut is pinned to the wall, 16 cm below A. The total weight of the shelf and its load is 200 newtons, and its centre of mass is 30 cm horizontally from A. Find the direction and the magnitude of the force on the hinge at A.

3 Two panes of glass are laid on a table, touching each other along one edge. The opposite edges are then raised so that the panes are fixed at angles of 30° and 15° to the horizontal. A non-uniform beam AB, of length 2.5 metres, rests horizontally with one end on each pane and at right angles to the common edge. The end A is in contact with the steeper pane. Making the assumption that the contacts are smooth, find the distance of the centre of mass of the beam from A.

4 A uniform rod PQ has mass 3 kg and length 60 cm. The end P is pivoted at a fixed point and the end Q is attached to one end of a string. The other end of the string is attached to a fixed point R, which is in the same vertical plane as PQ. Angle PQR is a right angle, and PQ is inclined at 15° to the horizontal. Find the force exerted on the rod by the pivot at P

   (a) if Q is higher than P,   (b) if P is higher than Q.

5 A uniform banner is suspended from a horizontal rail AB of length 6 metres. The total weight of 500 newtons is supported by chains attached to hooks P and Q in the roof of a hall and to points X and Y of the rail, where $AX = 2$ metres and $YB = 1$ metre. The hook P is 4 metres directly above A. Find the distance between the hooks, and the tension in the chains.

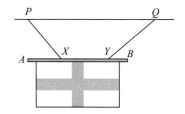

6 A uniform rod of weight 80 newtons is suspended from the ceiling by strings attached to its ends. The rod is in equilibrium at an angle of 10° to the horizontal, and the string attached to the lower end is at an angle of 40° to the vertical. Find the angle which the other string makes with the vertical.

   Find also the tension in the two strings.

7 Two smooth rails are set up in a vertical plane making angles of 20° and 70° with the horizontal. A uniform rod, with a ring at each end, is supported in equilibrium with one ring on each rail. Find the angle which the rod makes with the horizontal.

8 In Question 7, suppose that the rails are set up at 20° and 40° to the horizontal. Use the sine rule twice to show that the angle θ made by the rod with the horizontal then satisfies the equation $\dfrac{\sin(70° - \theta)}{\sin 20°} = \dfrac{\sin(50° + \theta)}{\sin 40°}$, and hence find θ.

9.3* Problems involving friction

You may omit this section if you wish.

It was shown in M1 Section 10.4 that, when a particle is in contact with a rough surface, you can combine the normal force and the friction as a single contact force. This is useful when there are two other forces acting; the total number of forces can then be reduced to three, so that a triangle of forces can be used.

The method is even more powerful when the forces act on a rigid object, since the concurrency rule can often be used to find the angle which the total contact force makes with the normal. This angle cannot be greater than λ, the angle of friction, defined as $\lambda = \tan^{-1} \mu$.

Example 9.3.1
A uniform rod of length l has a ring at one end which can slide along a rough horizontal rail. The coefficient of friction between the ring and the rail is μ. The other end of the rod is attached to the end of the rail by a cord, which is also of length l. What is the smallest angle which the rod can make with the horizontal?

Fig. 9.11 shows the three forces on the rod: its weight, the tension in the cord and the total contact force between the ring and the rail. Let the rod make an angle θ with the horizontal, and let α be the angle which the contact force makes with the vertical. Since the rod and the cord have the same length, the cord also makes an angle θ with the horizontal.

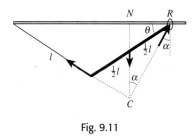

Fig. 9.11

The lines of action of the forces must be concurrent, at the point labelled C. In the figure R is the ring, and the line of action of the weight meets the rail at N. Then

$$RN = \tfrac{1}{2}l\cos\theta \quad \text{and} \quad CN = \tfrac{3}{2}l\sin\theta, \quad \text{so} \quad \tan\alpha = \frac{RN}{CN} = \tfrac{1}{3}\cot\theta.$$

If the ring is not to slide, $\tan\alpha$ must be less than or equal to μ, so that $\tfrac{1}{3}\cot\theta \leqslant \mu$. Therefore $\theta \geqslant \cot^{-1} 3\mu$.

The smallest angle which the rod can make with the horizontal is $\cot^{-1} 3\mu$.

You can often use the method to find whether, as an applied force is increased, equilibrium is broken by sliding or toppling. For example, Fig. 9.12 shows again the box being pushed across the floor, which was discussed in Section 6.2, but now the separate normal and friction forces have been replaced by a total contact force.

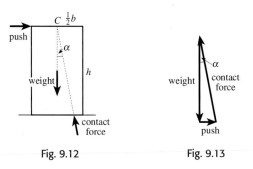

Fig. 9.12   Fig. 9.13

There are three forces, so you can draw a triangle of forces as in Fig. 9.13. You can see from this diagram that, as the push is gradually increased, the angle α between the contact force and the vertical gets bigger.

You also know from Fig. 9.12 that, so long as the box is in equilibrium, the line of action of the contact force has to go through C, the middle of the top of the box. So, as α gets bigger, one of two things can happen. Either α reaches the value λ, in which case the box starts to slide; or the point of the base at which the contact force acts reaches the bottom right corner, so that the box starts to topple.

The condition for sliding is therefore that $\tan\alpha = \mu$, and the condition for toppling that $\tan\alpha = \dfrac{b}{2h}$. So, if you push hard enough, equilibrium is broken by sliding if $\mu < \dfrac{b}{2h}$, and by toppling if $\mu > \dfrac{b}{2h}$.

Example 9.3.2

In a forest, after trees have been felled and trimmed, the trunks are towed to a central collection point. A cable is attached to the narrow end of each trunk, and the tension is then increased by a winch on the towing truck. One such trunk is 10 metres long, and its centre of mass is 6 metres from the end to which the cable is attached. The coefficient of friction of the trunk with the ground is 0.6. What angle should the cable make with the horizontal if the trunk is to be lifted clear of the ground rather than dragged along?

This is the problem solved in Example 6.2.3 by taking moments and resolving. Fig. 9.14 shows the three forces with the normal force and the friction replaced by a total contact force at an angle θ to the vertical. From the triangle of forces (Fig. 9.15), if α remains constant, θ increases as T is increased.

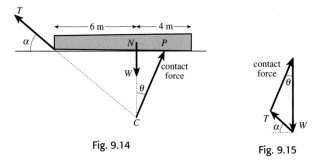

Fig. 9.14   Fig. 9.15

If C is the point where the lines of action concur, and N the point of the tree trunk on the ground below the centre of mass, then $CN = 6\tan\alpha$ metres. So if the contact force acts at P, $NP = 6\tan\alpha\tan\theta$ so long as the trunk is in equilibrium.

Equilibrium can be broken by sliding if $\tan\theta$ reaches the value 0.6, and by toppling if P reaches the end of the trunk, that is if $6\tan\alpha\tan\theta = 4$. So the narrow end will be lifted off the ground if $6 \times 0.6\tan\alpha > 4$, that is if $\alpha > \tan^{-1}\dfrac{4}{3.6}$, or $\alpha > 48.0°$, correct to 3 significant figures.

To lift the trunk clear of the ground before it starts to drag, the cable should make an angle of at least 48° with the horizontal.

You can see from an example like this that the geometrical approach may not only lead to simpler mathematics, but also gives more insight into what happens as the force is increased. So although the limitation to three forces means that you can't always use geometrical methods, they are worth trying when you have a problem to which they can be applied.

Exercise 9C*

You should use a geometrical method to work the problems in this exercise. Questions 4 to 7 are taken from Chapter 6.

1 A uniform ladder has one end on rough horizontal ground and leans at the other end against a vertical window. It rests in equilibrium at 60° to the horizontal. The contact with the window is so smooth that no reliance can be placed on the friction force there. Find the smallest acceptable coefficient of friction between the ladder and the ground.
A painter, whose mass is four times that of the ladder, now climbs up to the window. Find the smallest acceptable coefficient of friction if the ladder is still not to slip.

2 A uniform ladder is placed on rough horizontal ground, and rests over the top of a vertical wall in such a way that one-quarter of its length projects above the wall. The contact between the ladder and the top of the wall is assumed to be smooth. The ladder rests in equilibrium at 60° to the horizontal. Find the least acceptable coefficient of friction between the ladder and the ground.

3 A uniform beam has length 4 metres. One end rests on horizontal ground, and the beam is in equilibrium at 10° to the horizontal, propped against a smooth marble slab of height 0.4 metres, as shown in the diagram. Find the least possible coefficient of friction between the beam and the ground.

4 In a stretching exercise two men, of the same height and weight, stand toe-to-toe, each grasping the other's wrists. Both lean backwards, so that their arms are stretched, and both keep their bodies straight. One of the men is modelled as a rod having one end A in contact with the ground, which is horizontal. The weight of 800 N acts through the point 100 cm from A. The rod is kept at an angle of 66° to the horizontal by a horizontal force of magnitude P newtons applied at the point which is 150 cm from A, as shown in the diagram. Find P.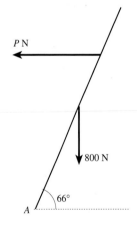

Given that the men are on the point of slipping and that their feet do not touch each other, use the model to estimate the coefficient of friction between the men's shoes and the floor.

5 An Arctic explorer drags a sledge across a horizontal ice-field by means of a rope attached to his body harness. The rope is 5 metres long, and attached to him at a height of 1.4 metres. The sledge is 3 metres long, and the coefficient of friction between the sledge and the ice is 0.2. Where must the centre of mass of the loaded sledge be if it is not to tip up as it is pulled?

6   A cylindrical tin has radius 6 cm and height 30 cm, and weighs 100 newtons. The tin stands on a table, 40 cm from the edge, which is smooth and rounded. A string is attached to the point of the top rim of the tin closest to the edge of the table; it passes over the edge and holds a bucket at its other end. Water is poured into the bucket until equilibrium is broken.

   (a) How much must the bucket weigh before the tin starts to topple over?

   (b) What can be said about the coefficient of friction between the tin and the table if the tin doesn't slide before it begins to topple?

7   A standard lamp has a square base with edges of length b. Its centre of mass is at a height h above its base. When it is placed on a sloping ramp at an angle α to the horizontal, it is on the point of both sliding down the ramp and toppling. Show that $\tan\alpha = \mu = \dfrac{b}{2h}$.

   A force is now applied parallel to the ramp to try to push it up the slope. Show that, if the lamp is to slide rather than topple, the force must be applied below the level of the centre of mass.

Miscellaneous exercise 9

You should use a geometrical method to work the problems in this exercise.

1   A uniform rectangular window of weight 100 N is hinged along its top edge. When closed the window fits into a vertical frame 2 metres high. The window is kept open at 10° to the vertical by a strut which is attached to the centres of the bottom edges of the window and the frame. Find the direction and the magnitude of the force on the window from the hinge. Find also the thrust in the strut.

2   Forces $\mathbf{P}$ and $\mathbf{Q}$, of magnitudes 10 N and 8 N respectively, act along lines AB and AC which are at 50° to each other. Find the magnitude of the resultant, and the angle that it makes with AB.

   If AB and AC each have length 1 m, and the resultant cuts the line BC at X, find the distance BX.

3   A uniform rod BC of length 4 m and weight 20 N hangs in equilibrium from a hook A by strings AB and AC of length 5 m and 3 m respectively. Find the angle that the rod makes with the horizontal, and the tensions in the strings.

4   A rod XY of length 2 m is attached to a fixed point O by two strings OX and OY, of length 2 m and 1.2 m respectively. The rod hangs in equilibrium at 30° to the horizontal. How far from X is the centre of mass of the rod?

5   $ABCD$ is a square table of side 3 metres. Ed and Flo push it together. Ed pushes at A in the direction of the edge AB with a force of 60 newtons. Flo pushes at the midpoint of the edge CD perpendicular to that edge with a force of 80 newtons. Where would one person have to push it, and with what force, to produce the same total effect as Ed and Flo?

6 A tree trunk is to be moved by a resultant force through its centre of mass at 55° to its length. It is pulled by cables from two tractors, with the same tension in each cable. The cable from one tractor is attached at a point 5 metres from the centre of mass, and this pulls at 70° to the trunk. Where should the other cable be attached, and at what angle to the trunk should this be pulled?

7 Two parallel horizontal rails are 25 cm apart, at the same level. A uniform box with rectangular cross-section 34 cm × 22 cm is balanced on the rails at an angle of θ to the horizontal. If the contact of the faces of the box with the rails is smooth, show that for the box to rest in equilibrium

$$\frac{25\cos\theta - 17}{25\sin\theta - 11} = \tan\theta.$$

Deduce that $25\cos 2\theta = 17\cos\theta - 11\sin\theta$, and use a numerical method to estimate the value of θ.

8* An athlete is training in the gym. In one exercise he stands upright with his chest pressed against a horizontal rail at shoulder level. He grasps the rail and then leans back with his body straight until his arms are fully stretched. Estimates of his physical measurements are:

Height of shoulders above the floor	150 cm
Height of centre of mass above the floor	120 cm
Length of outstretched arms	60 cm

Use a simplified model to estimate the least possible coefficient of friction between his feet and the floor if he is not to slip while doing this exercise.

9* For the situation of Miscellaneous exercise 6 Question 5 part (c), obtain the equation $\cos\theta - 0.25\sin\theta = 0.6\sin\theta$, and hence calculate θ.

10 For the situation in Miscellaneous exercise 6 Question 8, show that the ratio of the horizontal and vertical components of the contact force at the ground is equal to $\frac{17}{24}\tan 20°$.

11* For the situation in Miscellaneous exercise 6 Question 10, show that the centre of mass of the prism is a horizontal distance $1.7a$ from A. Hence obtain the condition $\tan\beta < \frac{46}{17}$ for the prism to slide before it starts to lift.

12* For the situation in Miscellaneous exercise 6 Question 15, use the sine rule twice to show that the angle of friction λ at the two contacts satisfies the equation

$$\frac{\sin(30° - \lambda)}{\cos\lambda} = \frac{\sin\lambda}{\sin(60° - \lambda)}.$$

Use the identity $\cos(A - B) - \cos(A + B) \equiv 2\sin A\sin B$ to deduce that $\sin 2\lambda = \frac{1}{2}\cos 30°$, and hence find the value of μ.

10 Centres of mass of special shapes

In Chapter 5 all the objects are made up from components whose centres of mass are at their geometrical centres. In this chapter the ideas are extended to various shapes which do not have a geometrical centre. When you have completed the chapter, you should

- know formulae for locating the centre of mass of objects modelled as wires, laminas, solids or shells of various standard shapes
- be able to find the centre of mass of objects made up of components with these shapes
- be able to find the centre of mass of objects formed by removing parts from an object whose centre of mass you already know.

At this stage it is not possible to give reasons for many of the results stated. For the shapes considered in this chapter, and many others, finding the centre of mass involves methods using integration. These are explained in module M4.

10.1 Uniform wire shapes

By a 'wire' is meant an object which can be modelled by a curve having no thickness. A uniform wire has constant mass per unit length.

You already know how to find the centre of mass of a wire bent into straight sections, such as the triangle in Example 5.2.2. Another important shape is a circular arc.

Fig. 10.1 shows a wire AB bent into the shape of an arc of a circle of radius r, centre O. The centre of mass G is obviously on the radius which bisects the angle AOB, so it is convenient to call the angle AOB 2α, so angle $AOG = \alpha$. Then, *if the angle α is measured in radians*, it can be shown that

$$OG = \frac{r \sin \alpha}{\alpha}.$$

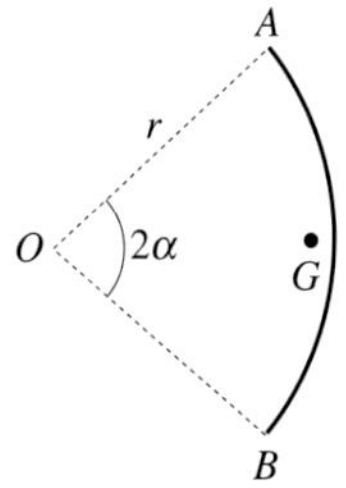

An important special case is when the wire is bent into a semicircle. Then angle $AOB = \pi$, so $\alpha = \frac{1}{2}\pi$ and $\sin \alpha = 1$, giving

$$OG = \frac{2r}{\pi}.$$

Fig. 10.1

Although the general formula can't be proved at this stage, here are two arguments which suggest that it is reasonable. (For a third argument, see Exercise 10A Question 12.)

- It was shown in C4 Section 1.2 that if $0 < \theta < \frac{1}{2}\pi$, $\cos\theta < \dfrac{\sin\theta}{\theta} < 1$. It is easy to see that this in fact holds if $0 < \theta < \pi$. Writing θ as α and multiplying by r, this gives $r\cos\alpha < OG < r$. So, as you would expect, the formula gives a position for G which always lies inside the 'bow' formed by the arc AB and the chord AB.

- If you put together two arcs like Fig. 10.1, with centres of mass G_1 and G_2, as in Fig. 10.2, then you get an arc making an angle 4α at O.

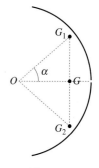

Its centre of mass must be at G, the midpoint of G_1G_2. The distance OG is therefore $OG_1 \cos\alpha$, so

$$OG = \frac{r \sin\alpha \cos\alpha}{\alpha}$$
$$= \frac{r \times 2\sin\alpha \cos\alpha}{2\alpha} = \frac{r\sin 2\alpha}{2\alpha}.$$

This is what you would expect from the formula, replacing α by 2α.

Fig. 10.2

Example 10.1.1

A letter D is formed by bending a uniform wire into the shape of a semicircle and its diameter. If this hangs freely from its top left corner, what will be the angle between the upright and the vertical?

Denote the radius of the semicircle by r, and suppose that the wire has mass k per unit length. O is the centre of the semicircle, G is the centre of mass of the letter D and $OG = \bar{x}$. Then the data are summarised in Table 10.3.

	Diameter	Semicircle	Whole figure
Mass	$2rk$	πrk	$(2+\pi)rk$
Distance from O	0	$\dfrac{2r}{\pi}$	$\bar{x}$

Table 10.3

The usual formula gives

$$\bar{x} = \frac{2rk \times 0 + \pi rk \times \left(\dfrac{2r}{\pi}\right)}{(2+\pi)rk} = \frac{2r^2 k}{(2+\pi)rk} = \frac{2r}{2+\pi}.$$

Fig. 10.4 shows the letter hung from the top left corner, with the vertical joining that corner to the centre of mass. The upright makes an angle θ with the vertical, where $\tan\theta = \dfrac{\bar{x}}{r} = \dfrac{2}{2+\pi}$, which gives $\theta = 21.3°$, correct to 1 decimal place.

The upright makes an angle of 21.3° with the vertical.

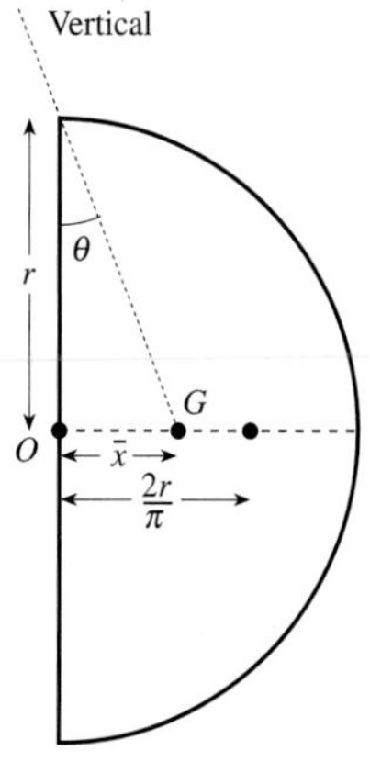

Fig. 10.4

10.2 Uniform lamina shapes

By a 'lamina' is meant an object which can be modelled by a plane region with no thickness. A uniform lamina has constant mass per unit area.

You already know that if a uniform lamina has a point of central symmetry then that point is the centre of mass.

A triangle doesn't have a centre of symmetry. One way to find its centre of mass is to cut it into a large number of narrow strips parallel to one side, as in Fig. 10.5.

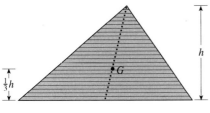

Fig. 10.5

To a close approximation the centre of mass of each strip lies on the median, that is the line which joins the midpoint of that side to the opposite vertex. So the centre of mass of the triangular lamina lies somewhere on this line.

You can use this argument for each of the three sides in turn. It follows that the centre of mass is at the point where the three medians meet, which is called the centroid of the triangle. (See C4 Example 4.5.2, where it is proved that, if the vertices have position vectors $\mathbf{a}$, $\mathbf{b}$ and $\mathbf{c}$, then the medians meet at the point G with position vector $\frac{1}{3}(\mathbf{a} + \mathbf{b} + \mathbf{c})$.) An important property of the centroid is that, along each median, it lies one-third of the way from the midpoint of the side to the vertex. So if the triangle has height h, the centre of mass G is $\frac{1}{3}h$ above the base.

Example 10.2.1

Fig. 10.6 shows a uniform plate OAB in the shape of an isosceles triangle. The plate is free to rotate in a vertical plane about a hinge at O, and it is supported with its line of symmetry at $40°$ to the horizontal by a force of $10\,\text{N}$ at A in the direction of the edge AB. Find the mass of the plate.

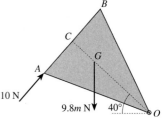

Fig. 10.6

Let the mass of the plate be m kg, so that the weight is $9.8\,m$ N. This acts along a vertical line through the centre of mass G of the plate.

If C is the midpoint of AB, OC is a median of the triangle, and $OG = \frac{2}{3}OC$. So the perpendicular distance from O to the line of action of the weight is $\frac{2}{3}OC \cos 40°$.

$\mathcal{M}(O) \qquad 9.8m \times \frac{2}{3}OC \cos 40° = 10 \times OC.$

So $\quad m = \dfrac{10}{9.8 \times \frac{2}{3} \cos 40°} = 1.998\ldots$.

The mass of the plate is $2.00\,\text{kg}$, correct to 3 significant figures.

Example 10.2.2

A uniform trapezium-shaped lamina has its vertices at the origin O and at the points A (8, 6), B (28, 6) and C (30, 0). Find the coordinates $(\bar{x}, \bar{y})$ of its centre of mass. (See Fig. 10.7.)

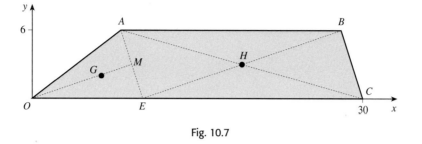

Fig. 10.7

If E is the point (10,0), think of the trapezium as made up of the triangle OEA and the parallelogram $ECBA$. Their areas (in appropriate units) are $\frac{1}{2} \times 10 \times 6 = 30$ and $20 \times 6 = 120$. Suppose that the mass of a unit area of the lamina is k.

The centre of mass of the triangle is at G, two-thirds of the way along the median OM, where M is the midpoint of AE. M has coordinates $\left(\frac{1}{2}(8 + 10), \frac{1}{2}(6 + 0)\right)$ which is (9, 3), so G has coordinates (6, 2).

The parallelogram has point symmetry about the point H where its diagonals intersect; for every point P inside the parallelogram, there is another point Q inside the parallelogram such that H is the mid-point of PQ. The centre of mass of the parallelogram is therefore at H, whose coordinates are (19, 3).

The data are summarised in Table 10.8.

	Triangle	Parallelogram	Trapezium
Mass	30k	120k	150k
x-coordinate	6	19	$\bar{x}$
y-coordinate	2	3	$\bar{y}$

Table 10.8

The usual equations give

$$\bar{x} = \frac{30k \times 6 + 120k \times 19}{150k} = 16.4, \quad \bar{y} = \frac{30k \times 2 + 120k \times 3}{150k} = 2.8.$$

The centre of mass of the trapezium is at the point (16.4, 2.8).

Another lamina shape with no centre of symmetry is a sector of a circle, shown as OAB in Fig. 10.9.

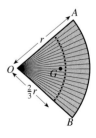

Its centre of mass can also be located by cutting into a large number of pieces, but this time along radii. Each piece is then very nearly a triangle, with its centre of mass $\frac{2}{3}r$ from O to a very close approximation. These centres of mass lie on a circular arc of radius $\frac{2}{3}r$. So if G is the centre of mass

Fig. 10.9

of the sector, the formula in Section 10.1 gives

$$OG = \frac{2r \sin \alpha}{3\alpha},$$

where the angle AOB is 2α radians.

An important special case is the semicircular lamina, for which $\alpha = \frac{1}{2}\pi$. The formula then gives

$$OG = \frac{4r}{3\pi}.$$

Example 10.2.3

A uniform metal plate, in the shape of a sector OAB of a circle centre O, is free to rotate about a horizontal axis through A and B. What can you say about the angle AOB if the plate can swing like a pendulum with O below AB?

Denote the radius of the circle by r, the angle AOB by 2α radians, and the centre of mass of the plate by G (see Fig. 10.10).

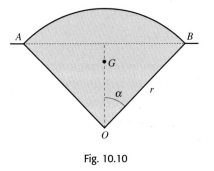

Fig. 10.10

For the plate to swing like a pendulum with O below AB, the centre of mass must be below AB. Then, if the plate is displaced from the vertical position by a small angle, the moment of the weight will act so as to restore the plate to the vertical. The condition for this to occur is that OG is less than the distance from O to AB, so

$$\frac{2r \sin \alpha}{3\alpha} < r \cos \alpha.$$

Dividing both sides by r and using $\dfrac{\sin \alpha}{\cos \alpha} = \tan \alpha$, this inequality can be rearranged as

$$\tan \alpha < \tfrac{3}{2}\alpha.$$

This cannot be solved exactly, but you can use graphs or a numerical method to find an approximate solution. Fig. 10.11 shows the graphs of $y = \tan x$ and $y = \frac{3}{2}x$, which intersect where $x \approx 0.967$. You can see that $\tan \alpha < \frac{3}{2}\alpha$ if α is less than this value.

So the plate will swing with O below AB if angle AOB is less than 2×0.967 radians, which is about $111°$.

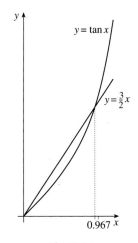

Fig. 10.11

Exercise 10A

1 A uniform triangular plate ABC has mass 60 kg. The triangle ABC is right-angled at B and $AB = 2$ m. The plate is vertical and rests on two supports at A and B, with AB horizontal (see diagram).

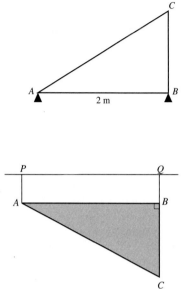

(a) State the horizontal distance of the centre of mass of the plate from A.

(b) Find the magnitudes of the forces on the supports at A and B.   (OCR)

2 The uniform triangular lamina ABC has weight 30 N and is right-angled at B; $AB = 30$ cm and $BC = 15$ cm. The lamina is suspended by vertical light strings PA and QB, and hangs in equilibrium in a vertical plane with AB horizontal and BC vertical (see diagram). Find the tensions in the strings.

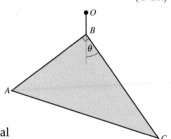

The string QB is now cut, and the lamina settles in equilibrium supported only by the string PA. What angle does AB make with the vertical?   (OCR)

3 A uniform lamina has the shape of an equilateral triangle with sides of length 6.9 cm. Find, by drawing or calculation, the distance of the centre of mass of the lamina from one of its sides.   (OCR)

4 A uniform triangular lamina ABC is in equilibrium, suspended from a fixed point O by a light inelastic string attached to the point B of the lamina, as shown in the diagram. $AB = 45$ cm, $BC = 60$ cm and angle $ABC = 90°$. Calculate the angle θ between BC and the downward vertical.   (OCR)

5 A kite is constructed of a thin uniform sheet. It is symmetrical about its longer diagonal, whose length is 1.2 metres, and the diagonals cross 0.45 metres from one end of it. Find the distance of the centre of mass from the point where the diagonals cross.

6 A quadrilateral has vertices at the points with coordinates $(0, 0)$, $(12, 0)$, $(9, 12)$ and $(0, 9)$. Find the coordinates of the centre of mass of a uniform lamina bounded by this quadrilateral.

7 A mirror glass has the shape of a rectangle, of width w and height h, surmounted by a semicircle of diameter w. Show that the height of the centre of mass above the base of the rectangle is $\dfrac{12h^2 + 3\pi hw + 2w^2}{24h + 3\pi w}$.

8 A trough has a cross-section in the form of a trapezium. Its base has length 1 metre, and the sides slope out at 45° to the horizontal. The trough is filled with feed to a depth of x metres. Find the value of x given that the centre of mass of the contents of the trough is $\frac{1}{2}$ metre above the base.

9 A strip light is shaped into the outline of a crescent with pointed corners at A and B, 2 metres apart. The convex edge of the crescent is a semicircle; the concave edge is one-sixth of a circle of radius 2 metres. Find the distance of the centre of mass of the crescent from the line AB.

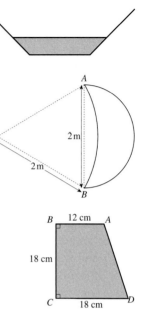

10 A trapezium-shaped block of uniform thickness has the corners of one of its faces labelled A, B, C and D, as shown in the diagram. Angles ABC and BCD are right angles. The block stands on a plane which is inclined at an angle α to the horizontal. In which of the following configurations P, Q and R is the block on the point of toppling when $\tan\alpha$ is

(a) $\frac{11}{24}$,   (b) $\frac{19}{21}$,   (c) $\frac{24}{19}$?

P AB coincides with a line of greatest slope with B above A.

Q BC coincides with a line of greatest slope with C above B.

R CD coincides with a line of greatest slope with D above C.

11 A structure made from uniform wire consists of the arc AB of a circle of radius 10 cm, which subtends an angle of 110° at its centre, together with the chord AB. The structure is suspended freely from A, as shown in the diagram. Find the angle θ which the chord AB makes with the downward vertical.

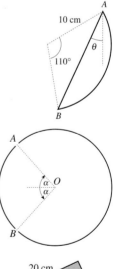

12 The diagram shows a uniform circular wire of radius r whose centre is O. It is cut at A and B into two parts, where angle $AOB = 2\alpha$. If its mass per unit length is k, write down the mass of each part and the distance of its centre of mass from O.

Use the formula $\bar{x} = \dfrac{m_1x_1 + m_2x_2}{m_1 + m_2}$ to verify that the centre of mass of the two parts together is at O.

13 A uniform lamina is made up of two rectangular parts, each 10 cm × 20 cm, and a part in the form of a circular sector with centre at O, radius 10 cm and angle 130°, as shown in the diagram. The centre of mass of the lamina is at G. Find the distance OG.

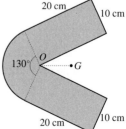

10.3   Uniform solid shapes

A uniform solid has constant mass per unit volume.

Fig. 10.12 shows a solid hemisphere with centre O and radius r. Since this is a solid of revolution (see C3 Chapter 11), its centre of mass G lies on the axis of rotation. It can be proved that $OG = \frac{3}{8}r$.

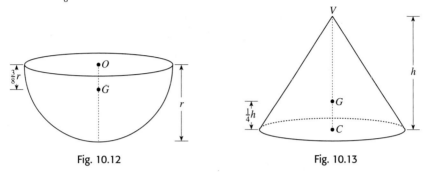

Fig. 10.12   Fig. 10.13

Fig. 10.13 shows a circular cone, with its vertex V at a height h above the centre of the base. Its centre of mass lies on the axis of rotation at a height $\frac{1}{4}h$ above the base.

The result for the cone can be generalised to any uniform solid cone or pyramid. If C is the centre of mass of the base, considered as a lamina, and if the vertex is V, then the centre of mass lies one-quarter of the way up the line joining C to V.

Example 10.3.1

Two containers, one in the shape of a hemisphere and the other in the shape of a circular cone with its vertex downwards, are fixed side-by-side with their circular rims at the same level, as shown in Fig. 10.14. The containers have the same volume, and their rims have the same radius r. The hemisphere is filled with liquid. If this liquid is siphoned into the cone, show that the centre of mass of the liquid drops, and find by how much.

The volume of the hemisphere is $\frac{1}{2}\left(\frac{4}{3}\pi r^3\right) = \frac{2}{3}\pi r^3$.
If the height of the cone is h, the volume of the cone is $\frac{1}{3}\pi r^2 h$. Since the volumes are equal,

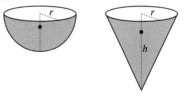

$$\tfrac{1}{3}\pi r^2 h = \tfrac{2}{3}\pi r^3,$$

which gives $h = 2r$.

Fig. 10.14

The centre of mass of the liquid in the hemispherical container is $\frac{3}{8}r$ below the level of the rim. When the liquid is transferred to the cone, the centre of mass is $\frac{1}{4}h$ below the rim. Since $h = 2r$, $\frac{1}{4}h = \frac{1}{2}r$.

So the centre of mass of the liquid drops by $\frac{1}{2}r - \frac{3}{8}r$, which is $\frac{1}{8}r$.

Example 10.3.2

Fig. 10.15 shows a toy made of a solid cone, of height h and base radius r, and a solid hemisphere of radius r, glued together across their flat surfaces. The toy stands on a rough horizontal floor with the vertex of the cone pointing upwards. If it is given a small knock sideways, what will happen?

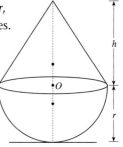

Fig. 10.15

In the figure O is the centre of the circle common to the cone and the hemisphere. Let $\bar{y}$ be the height of the centre of mass above O. Suppose that the toy is made of material of mass k per unit volume. The data are in Table 10.16.

	Cone	Hemisphere	Whole toy
Mass	$\frac{1}{3}\pi r^2 h k$	$\frac{2}{3}\pi r^3 k$	$\frac{1}{3}\pi r^2 (h+2r)k$
Height above O	$\frac{1}{4}h$	$-\frac{3}{8}r$	$\bar{y}$

Table 10.16

This gives

$$\bar{y} = \frac{\frac{1}{12}\pi r^2 h^2 k - \frac{1}{4}\pi r^4 k}{\frac{1}{3}\pi r^2 (h+2r)k} = \frac{\frac{1}{4}(h^2 - 3r^2)}{(h+2r)}.$$

What happens after the toy is knocked depends on whether $\bar{y} > 0$ or $\bar{y} < 0$. Fig. 10.17 shows the situation $\bar{y} > 0$, so that the centre of mass is above O. Then the weight of the toy has a clockwise moment about the point of contact of the toy and the floor, so the toy will fall over further.

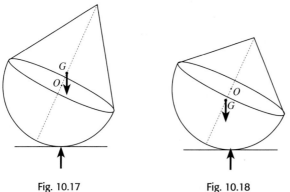

Fig. 10.17   Fig. 10.18

If $\bar{y} < 0$, as in Fig. 10.18, the weight has an anticlockwise moment, which returns the toy to its vertical position.

So if $h > \sqrt{3}r$, the toy will fall over; if $h < \sqrt{3}r$, it will stay upright.

In this example the vertical position of the toy is always a position of equilibrium. If a small knock makes it fall over further, the equilibrium is called **unstable**; if it returns towards the equilibrium position, the equilibrium is **stable**.

10.4   Uniform shell shapes

By a 'shell' is meant an object which can be modelled by a curved surface having no thickness. For example, the peel of an orange or the Earth's crust could be modelled as a spherical shell. A uniform shell has constant mass per unit area.

The centre of mass of any shell which is a surface of revolution has its centre of mass on the axis of rotation. For a hemispherical shell with centre O and radius r, the centre of mass is $\frac{1}{2}r$ from O (see Fig. 10.19).

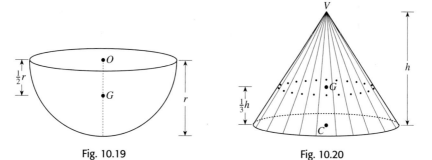

Fig. 10.19   Fig. 10.20

By a conical shell is meant simply the curved surface, not including the base. Like the circular sector in Fig. 10.9, this can be cut up into a large number of near-triangular strips, each of which would have its centre of mass $\frac{1}{3}h$ above the base, as illustrated in Fig. 10.20. All these centres of mass would lie on a circle. It follows that the centre of mass of the complete conical shell is $\frac{1}{3}h$ above the base.

Example 10.4.1
Fig. 10.21 shows a lantern made of glass of uniform thickness. It is formed by joining together a conical shell of height 6 cm, a cylindrical shell of height 10 cm and a hemisphere, all of radius 8 cm. Find the depth of the centre of mass of the lantern below the vertex V of the cone.

Let the mass of the glass be k kg for each cm^2 of its surface area.

The area of a conical surface is given by the formula $\pi r l$, where l is the slant height. In this case the slant height is $\sqrt{6^2 + 8^2}$ cm $= 10$ cm, so the surface area is $\pi \times 8 \times 10$ cm^2. The area of the cylindrical surface is $2\pi \times 8 \times 10$ cm^2, and the area of the hemisphere is $2\pi \times 8^2$ cm^2.

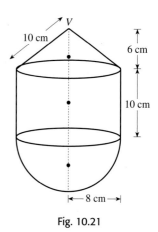

Fig. 10.21

Using the results for a conical shell and a hemispherical shell given above, the centre of mass of the cone is $\frac{1}{3} \times 6$ cm above its base, and the centre of mass of the hemisphere is $\frac{1}{2} \times 8$ cm below its centre. The centre of mass of the cylinder is at its geometrical centre.

The data are summarised in Table 10.22.

	Cone	Cylinder	Hemisphere	Whole lantern
Mass (kg)	$80\pi k$	$160\pi k$	$128\pi k$	$368\pi k$
Depth below V (cm)	4	11	20	$\bar{d}$

Table 10.22

The distance of the centre of mass below V, in cm, is therefore

$$\bar{d} = \frac{80\pi k \times 4 + 160\pi k \times 11 + 128\pi k \times 20}{80\pi k + 160\pi k + 128\pi k} \approx 12.6.$$

The centre of mass of the lantern is about 12.6 cm below V.

10.5*   Finding centres of mass by subtraction

Sometimes an object is formed not by putting several parts together, but by removing bits from an object which was originally whole. The examples in this section show how to find the centre of mass in such cases. You may omit this section if you wish.

Example 10.5.1

A mechanism includes a uniform circular metal plate of radius 10 cm, with two circular holes cut out of it. The design specification describes these by marking two diameters as coordinate axes on the plate. One hole has radius 2 cm with its centre at (6, 0), the other has radius 4 cm with its centre at (−2, 5). Find the centre of mass of the plate with holes in it, shown in Fig. 10.23.

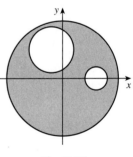

Fig. 10.23

If the mass of the metal is k kg per cm², the original plate had mass $100\pi k$ kg, and the metal removed from the holes had mass $4\pi k$ kg and $16\pi k$ kg. The metal that remains therefore has mass $80\pi k$ kg.

You can argue that if you put the metal back in the two holes, then the three parts would make up the complete circular plate that you started with. This could be shown by the data table in Table 10.24.

Mass (kg)	$80\pi k$	$4\pi k$	$16\pi k$	$100\pi k$
x-coordinate (cm)	$\bar{x}$	6	−2	0
y-coordinate (cm)	$\bar{y}$	0	5	0

Table 10.24

From this you can make up the equations (cancelling the common factor πk)

$$80\bar{x} + 4 \times 6 + 16 \times (-2) = 100 \times 0 \quad \text{and} \quad 80\bar{y} + 4 \times 0 + 16 \times 5 = 100 \times 0.$$

These give $\bar{x} = \dfrac{8}{80} = 0.1$ and $\bar{y} = -1$.

The centre of mass of the plate with holes in it is at $(0.1, -1)$.

Example 10.5.2

In Fig. 10.25, OAB is a quadrant of a circle made of plywood. The triangle OAB is sawn off and discarded, to leave a segment bounded by the line AB and the arc AB. The line AB has length 2 metres. Find the distance of the centre of mass G of the segment from the line AB.

You can make an equation by expressing the fact that the triangle and the segment together make up the quadrant OAB.

If M is the midpoint of AB, the distance OM is 1 m so the triangle OAB has area $1\,\text{m}^2$ and its centre of mass is $\frac{2}{3}$ m from O.

The circle has radius $\sqrt{2}$ m, so the original quadrant has area $\frac{1}{4}\pi \times (\sqrt{2})^2\,\text{m}^2$, which is $\frac{1}{2}\pi\,\text{m}^2$. The distance of its centre of mass from O is given by the formula $\dfrac{2r\sin\alpha}{3\alpha}$ with $\alpha = \frac{1}{4}\pi$, so this is

$\dfrac{2\sqrt{2} \times \dfrac{1}{\sqrt{2}}}{3 \times \frac{1}{4}\pi}$, which can be simplified to give $\dfrac{8}{3\pi}$ m.

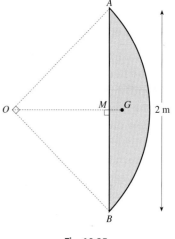

Fig. 10.25

Suppose that the plywood has mass k per unit area.
Denote OG by $\bar{x}$ metres. Then the data can be summarised as in Table 10.26.

	Triangle	Segment	Quadrant
Mass (kg)	k	$\left(\frac{1}{2}\pi - 1\right)k$	$\frac{1}{2}\pi k$
Distance from O (m)	$\frac{2}{3}$	$\bar{x}$	$\dfrac{8}{3\pi}$

Table 10.26

So $\bar{x}$ can be found from the equation

$$\tfrac{2}{3}k + \left(\tfrac{1}{2}\pi - 1\right)k\bar{x} = \tfrac{1}{2}\pi k \times \dfrac{8}{3\pi}, \quad \text{giving} \quad \bar{x} = \dfrac{\frac{2}{3}}{\frac{1}{2}\pi - 1} \approx 1.168.$$

G is about 1.168 metres from O, which is 0.168 metres from AB.

Exercise 10B

1 A wizard has a hat in the shape of a conical shell, with base radius 10 cm and height 60 cm. There is a small hole in the rim, which the wizard uses to hang his hat from a hook in the ceiling. If the hat hangs in equilibrium, how far is the point of the hat below the level of the hook?

2 A uniform solid cone has base radius 8 cm and height 40 cm. It is placed on a very rough inclined plane. What is the largest angle the plane can make with the horizontal if the cone is not to topple over?

3 A hemispherical bowl of radius 12 cm and mass 2 kg is filled with ice cream of mass 3 kg. It stands on a table. Find the height above the table of the centre of mass of the bowl with its contents.

4 The diagram shows a hat consisting of a hemispherical shell of radius 10 cm with a brim of outside radius 15 cm. It is made of material of uniform thickness. Find the distance of the centre of mass of the hat from the plane of the brim.

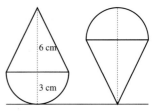

5 A uniform solid consists of a cylindrical part of radius r and length l, and a hemispherical part of radius r. One end of the cylinder is in contact with the plane face of the hemisphere, and there is no overlap. The solid is held on a horizontal surface, with a generator AB of the cylinder in contact with the horizontal surface, as shown in the diagram. The solid is then released. Determine whether the cylindrical part continues to be in contact with the horizontal surface, or whether the solid rolls so that the hemisphere is in contact with the horizontal surface, when

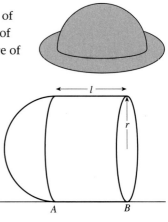

   (a) $l = r$,   (b) $l = \frac{1}{2}r$.

6* A uniform square of cardboard has sides of length 20 cm. A square hole is punched in it, with its centre 4 cm from one side and 3 cm from an adjacent side. The sides of the hole have length 4 cm. Find the position of the centre of mass of the card that remains. Does the answer depend on the angle at which the hole is punched?

7* A uniform solid cone, of radius 10 cm and height 16 cm, has a cylindrical hole of radius 5 cm bored into its base to a depth of 6 cm. The axis of the hole coincides with the axis of the cone. The cone is freely suspended from a point of the circumference of the base of the cone, as shown in the diagram. Find α, the acute angle that the axis makes with the vertical.

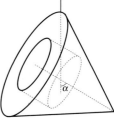

8 A closed container consists of a hemispherical shell of mass 0.04 kg and radius 3 cm, and a conical shell of mass 0.045 kg, radius 3 cm and height 6 cm. The shells are joined so that their axes of symmetry coincide, as shown in both figures. The container holds 18π cm^3 of fine dry sand of density 2.3 kg per 1000 cm^3. The container is held with its axis vertical, firstly with the conical part uppermost as in the first figure, then with the hemispherical part uppermost, as in the second figure. Show that the sand just occupies the hemispherical part in the first case, and just occupies the conical part in the second case.

   Find, in each case, the height of the centre of mass of the container (with sand), above its lowest point.

9* The wing of a hang-glider is a uniform lamina, formed by removing from a square of side l a quadrant of a circle of radius l, with its centre at one corner of the square. Find the distance of the centre of mass of the wing from the opposite corner.

10 A road cone consists of a 45 cm × 45 cm square base of height 5 cm, and a conical shell of radius 15 cm and height 75 cm. The base has a circular hole through it, of radius 15 cm, to facilitate stacking. The base is made of rubber of density 1 kg per 1000 cm³ and the conical shell has mass 0.5 kg. The cone is held with an edge of the base in contact with a horizontal surface, and with the axis of the shell making an angle α with the horizontal, as shown in the diagram. The cone is now released. Find the angle β such that the cone assumes the upright position if $\alpha > \beta$ and the cone topples if $\alpha < \beta$.

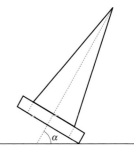

11* A 16 cm × 6 cm rectangular hole is cut in a uniform circular lamina of radius 12 cm. One of the 16 cm sides of the rectangle, labelled AB, coincides with a diameter of the circle, and the midpoint of AB coincides with O, the centre of the circle. The lamina is freely suspended from a point at the end of the diameter containing AB, as shown in the diagram. Find the angle θ between this diameter and the downward vertical.   (OCR)

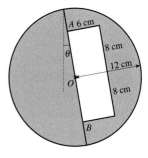

Miscellaneous exercise 10

1 A uniform lamina $ABCD$ is in the form of the trapezium shown in the diagram. The sides AD and BC are parallel, and each is at right angles to AB. The centre of mass of the lamina lies on CE, where $AE = 10$ cm and $ED = L$ cm. Find the value of L.   (OCR)

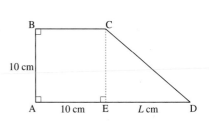

2 A uniform hollow hemisphere has mass 0.6 kg and diameter 0.2 m. A uniform hollow cylinder has mass 1.4 kg, length 0.3 m and diameter 0.2 m. The hemisphere is attached to the cylinder, with the circumference of its base coinciding with one end of the cylinder (see the first diagram).

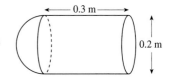

(a) Show that the distance of the centre of mass of the combined object from its open end is 0.21 m.

(b) The combined object is placed on an inclined plane (see the second diagram). The surface of the plane is rough enough to prevent slipping. Given that the object is about to topple, calculate the angle which the plane makes with the horizontal.   (OCR)

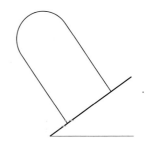

3 A right-angled triangular prism has weight W. The sides
   containing the right angle have lengths $3a$ and b. The
   prism is at rest with its edges of length $3a$ in contact with
   a horizontal table. When a horizontal force of magnitude
   P is applied to the midpoint of the uppermost edge, at
   right angles to the vertical face, the prism topples if the
   direction of the force is as shown in the first diagram and
   slides if the direction is as shown in the second diagram.
   Show that $\dfrac{a}{b} < \mu < \dfrac{2a}{b}$, where μ is the coefficient of friction
   between the prism and the table.

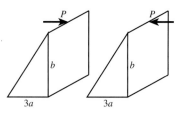

4 Triangle ABC is the cross-section through the centre of mass G
   of a uniform triangular prism. $AB = BC = 3a$ and the angle
   ABC is a right angle. Write down the perpendicular distance
   of G from BC.

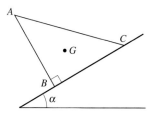

   The prism rests in equilibrium on an inclined plane which is
   sufficiently rough to prevent sliding. The edges of the prism
   perpendicular to ABC are horizontal, and BC coincides with a
   line of greatest slope of the plane.

   (a) The plane is inclined at an angle α to the horizontal, and B
       is below C as shown in the first diagram. Show that
       $\tan \alpha \leqslant 1$.

   (b) The plane is inclined at an angle β to the horizontal, and C
       is below B as shown in the second diagram. Given that the
       prism is on the point of toppling, find the value of
       $\tan \beta$.   (OCR)

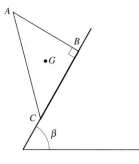

5 A conical shell has weight W and slant height equal to
   4 times the radius of its rim. The shell rests with its surface
   in contact with horizontal ground. A force of magnitude T
   is applied to the shell's vertex O in a direction making an
   angle β with the ground, as shown in the diagram.

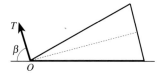

   (a) Given that O is on the point of leaving the ground, show that $T \sin \beta = \frac{3}{8} W$.

   (b) Given that the coefficient of friction between the shell's surface and the ground is 0.4,
       and that O is on the point of moving along the ground, show that
       $T(5 \cos \beta + 2 \sin \beta) = 2W$.

   Deduce that if T is gradually increased from zero the shell will start to lift at O before sliding
   if $\tan \beta > \frac{3}{2}$.

6 Repeat Question 5 when the force of magnitude T is
   applied at the point P of the rim which is in contact
   with the ground (as shown in the diagram) showing
   that $T \sin \beta = \frac{5}{8} W$ when P is on the point of leaving
   the ground, $T(5 \cos \beta + 2 \sin \beta) = 2W$ as before in
   part (b), and $\tan \beta > \frac{25}{6}$ in the final part.

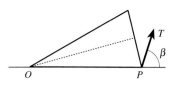

7   A vessel consists of a base, two ends and two sides, all of the same uniform material, arranged as shown in the diagram. The base is a $12\,\text{cm} \times 5\,\text{cm}$ rectangle, and the ends are $8\,\text{cm} \times 5\,\text{cm}$ and $10\,\text{cm} \times 5\,\text{cm}$ rectangles. Each of the sides is in the form of a trapezium $ABCD$ in which $AB = 12\,\text{cm}$, $BC = 10\,\text{cm}$, $CD = 18\,\text{cm}$ and $DA = 8\,\text{cm}$, and which is right-angled at A and at D. Show that the centre of mass of the vessel is about $7.52\,\text{cm}$ from the end containing DA. Deduce that the vessel can stand on its base without toppling.

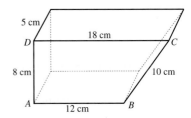

8   A vessel consists of a base, two ends and two sides, arranged as shown in the diagram. The base is a $6\,\text{cm} \times 4\,\text{cm}$ rectangle, and the ends are $5\,\text{cm} \times 4\,\text{cm}$ and $13\,\text{cm} \times 4\,\text{cm}$ rectangles. Each of the sides is in the form of a trapezium $ABCD$ in which $AB = 6\,\text{cm}$, $BC = 13\,\text{cm}$, $CD = 18\,\text{cm}$ and $DA = 5\,\text{cm}$, and which is right-angled at A and at D. The base is sufficiently heavy for the vessel to be capable of standing on its base when empty, without toppling. Water is poured slowly into the vessel. Assuming the weight of the vessel can be ignored, show that the vessel topples when the depth of water reaches d cm, where $d^2 = 18.75$.

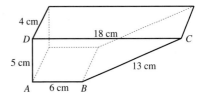

9   A uniform lamina of weight W has the shape of a semicircle with diameter AB. The point A is pivoted at a fixed point. The lamina is kept in equilibrium, with AB vertical, by a force of magnitude P acting horizontally with a line of action passing through the centre of the semicircle.

Find the magnitude and direction of the force exerted by the pivot on the lamina at A.

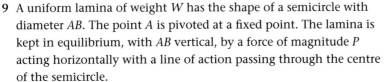

10 A uniform wire, in the shape of a semicircle, is at rest on a smooth horizontal table with its diameter making an angle α with the horizontal $\left(0 < \alpha < \tan^{-1} \frac{1}{2}\pi\right)$. The wire is held in this position by a force of magnitude P acting vertically upwards at the uppermost point of the wire. The force exerted by the table on the hemisphere is R (see diagram).

Show that $\dfrac{R}{P} = \dfrac{\pi}{2\tan\alpha} - 1$.

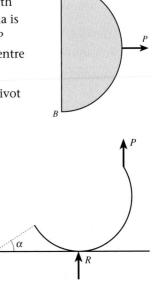

11 A light vase has a 12 cm × 12 cm square cross-section and
height 30 cm. The vase is placed on a plane inclined at
$\tan^{-1} \frac{1}{2}$ to the horizontal, with two parallel edges of its base
coinciding with lines of greatest slope of the plane. Water
is poured slowly into the vase. Determine whether the vase
topples without first overflowing or whether it overflows
without toppling.

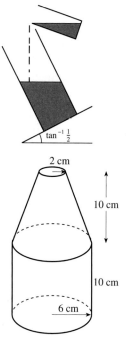

12* A uniform solid consisting of two parts, a circular cylinder of
radius 6 cm and height 10 cm and a cone frustum of end radii
6 cm and 2 cm and height 10 cm, is arranged as shown in the
diagram. Find the distance of the centre of mass of the solid
from its base.

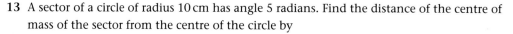

13 A sector of a circle of radius 10 cm has angle 5 radians. Find the distance of the centre of
mass of the sector from the centre of the circle by

(a) direct application of the relevant formula in Section 10.2,

(b)* treating the sector as a circle from which the corresponding minor sector has been
removed.

14* A uniform rectangular lamina, L cm × 10 cm, has a
circular hole in it of radius 4 cm. The centre of the
hole lies on the line midway between the sides of
length L cm, and the line midway between the sides
of length 10 cm is a tangent to the circular boundary
of the hole. When suspended freely from a corner as
shown in the diagram, the sides of length L cm make
an angle of 25° with the vertical. Find L.

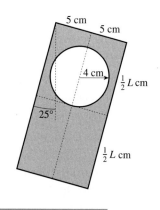

11 Strategies for solving problems

This chapter is about choosing the method to use when you have a problem to solve. When you have completed it, you should

- be able to judge which methods are appropriate in a particular problem, and the relative advantages of using various methods.

You may regard this chapter as an optional part of the course. The aim is to help you to take a systematic approach to the solution of problems in mechanics. There are three independent sections, each dealing with problems of a particular type: equilibrium problems, problems involving motion, and problems that can be solved using ideas of momentum and energy. There is no essentially new mechanics in the chapter, but the examples have been chosen to bring out the advantages and disadvantages of different methods. For this reason, you will find some of the examples and exercises more challenging than those in other chapters of the book.

11.1 Equilibrium problems

When you have a problem involving an object in equilibrium, the first decision is whether to use an algebraic method (equations of moments or resolving or both) or a geometrical method (concurrence and triangle of forces). Sometimes this is just a matter of personal preference, but some problems are more approachable by one method or the other.

Geometrical methods are generally only useful when there are just two or three forces. If two forces are in equilibrium, they have equal magnitude and act along the same line. If three forces are in equilibrium, their lines of action are either concurrent or parallel, and they may be represented in a vector triangle of forces. However, if there are more than three forces it may be worth combining pairs of forces to reduce the total number; for example, replacing a normal contact force and a frictional force by a total contact force, or replacing two weights by a single weight at the centre of mass.

If you are using an algebraic method, you have a wide choice of possible directions to resolve in, and of points to take moments about. A good choice may lead to an equation involving only one or two of the unknowns, which can improve the efficiency of the solution.

If an object is supported by a hinge, you won't know either the magnitude or the direction of the force it exerts. Usually, if you are using a geometrical method, it is best to treat it as a single force; but with an algebraic method it is often better to replace the single force by its components in two perpendicular directions.

These points are illustrated in the examples that follow.

Example 11.1.1

A uniform ladder of weight W and length l rests at 20° to the vertical, with one end on horizontal ground and the other end against a vertical wall. A tie-bar has one end fixed at the corner C where the wall meets the ground; the other end is fixed to the ladder so that the tie-bar is perpendicular to the ladder. If there are no frictional forces, find the tension in the bar.

There are four forces on the ladder (Fig. 11.1), and there is no good reason to combine any pair of them, so a geometrical method isn't suitable.

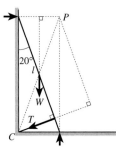

Only the tension T and the weight W are of interest, so it is a good idea to write an equation which doesn't bring in either of the normal contact forces. You can do this by taking moments about the point P where the lines of action of these two forces meet.

Fig. 11.1

The ladder is described as 'uniform', which means that its centre of mass is at its midpoint. The distance from P to the line of action of W is therefore $\frac{1}{2}l\sin 20°$.

The wall, the ground and the lines of the two normal forces form a rectangle whose diagonals are CP and the ladder. Therefore CP has length l and makes an angle of 20° with the vertical. So the angle between CP and the tie-bar is $90° - 2 \times 20° = 50°$, and the perpendicular distance from P to the line of action of T is $l\sin 50°$.

$$\mathcal{M}(P) \qquad W \times \tfrac{1}{2}l\sin 20° = T \times l\sin 50°,$$

so $\quad T = \dfrac{W\sin 20°}{2\sin 50°} = 0.223W$, correct to 3 significant figures.

Example 11.1.2

A uniform ladder AB is set up against a wall. The coefficient of friction μ is the same for both contacts, where $\mu < 1$. Prove that, if equilibrium is limiting, the ladder makes an angle $2\tan^{-1}\mu$ with the vertical.

There are five forces on the ladder: its weight, and normal and frictional forces at A and B. But if you combine both pairs of normal and friction forces as single contact forces, the number of forces is reduced to three. Denote $\tan^{-1}\mu$ by λ, the angle of friction.

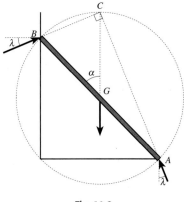

In Fig. 11.2, since friction is limiting, the contact force at A makes an angle λ with the vertical and the contact force at B makes an angle λ with the horizontal, so the two contact forces are at right angles to each other. Let their lines of action meet in C.

Fig. 11.2

The only other force is the weight of the ladder, so C must be directly above G, the centre of mass of the ladder. Also the ladder is uniform, so that G is the midpoint of AB.

The solution can be completed by a geometrical argument. A circle with centre G and diameter AB passes through C, so that triangle GCA is isosceles. Let angle $BGC = \alpha$. Then, since angle $GCA = \lambda$, it follows that $\alpha = 2\lambda$, which is $2\tan^{-1}\mu$.

Example 11.1.3

A uniform roll of carpet of length l and weight W is lying on the floor. It is raised to the vertical by applying a force at one end which is always at right angles to the roll.

(a) Find the ratio of the frictional force to the normal contact force when the roll makes an angle θ with the floor.

(b) How large must the coefficient of friction be if the roll is not to slip on the floor while it is being raised?

Part (a)

Algebraic method 1   Fig. 11.3 shows the situation when the carpet roll makes an angle θ with the floor, being raised by a force P at right angles to its length. The normal force and the friction at the end on the floor are R and F.

The simplest equation of moments to write is about the end of the roll in contact with the floor.

$$\mathcal{M}(\text{end on floor}) \quad Pl = W(\tfrac{1}{2}l\cos\theta),$$

which gives $P = \tfrac{1}{2}W\cos\theta$.

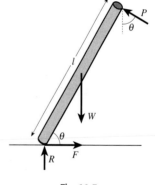

Fig. 11.3

Since this equation doesn't involve either R or F, you will need two resolving equations to find them. Note that, since the roll makes an angle θ with the horizontal, the force P makes an angle θ with the vertical.

$\mathcal{R}(\rightarrow)$ $\qquad\qquad F = P\sin\theta.$
$\mathcal{R}(\uparrow)$ $\qquad R + P\cos\theta = W.$

From these you can find $F = \tfrac{1}{2}W\sin\theta\cos\theta$ and $R = W(1 - \tfrac{1}{2}\cos^2\theta)$, so

$$\frac{F}{R} = \frac{\sin\theta\cos\theta}{2 - \cos^2\theta}.$$

Algebraic method 2   The drawback of Method 1 is that, by taking moments about the end of the roll on the floor, the equation doesn't involve either R or F, which are the two forces whose ratio you want to find. To get $\dfrac{F}{R}$ directly, you could take moments about the point X where the lines of action of the forces P and W intersect.

Then, with the notation of Fig. 11.4,

$$\mathcal{M}(X) \quad F \times XN = R \times XM.$$

The downside of this method is that, although XM is easily found as

$$XM = NO = \tfrac{1}{2}l\cos\theta,$$

it is not so easy to find XN. For this you need the two right-angled triangles GQX and ONG:

$$XN = XG + GN$$
$$= \tfrac{1}{2}l\cosec\theta + \tfrac{1}{2}l\sin\theta = \tfrac{1}{2}l(\cosec\theta + \sin\theta).$$

So $\dfrac{F}{R} = \dfrac{XM}{XN} = \dfrac{\tfrac{1}{2}l\cos\theta}{\tfrac{1}{2}l(\cosec\theta + \sin\theta)} = \dfrac{\cos\theta}{\cosec\theta + \sin\theta}.$

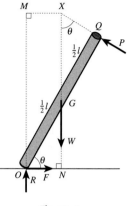

Fig. 11.4

Geometrical method 1   Combine the friction and the normal contact force into a resultant contact force C at an angle α to the vertical, as in Fig. 11.5.

Then, since $\tan\alpha = \dfrac{F}{R}$, the required ratio can be found from the geometry of Fig. 11.5. The solution uses the principle that the lines of action of P, W and C are concurrent.

With this method it is simpler to work with ϕ, the angle between the roll and the vertical, rather than with θ. There are two right-angled triangles in the figure, OQX and GQX, with a common side QX which can be found as either $OQ\tan\beta$ or as $GQ\tan\phi$. Since $OQ = l$ and $GQ = \tfrac{1}{2}l$,

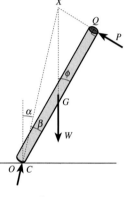

Fig. 11.5

$$l\tan\beta = \tfrac{1}{2}l\tan\phi, \quad \text{so} \quad \tan\beta = \tfrac{1}{2}\tan\phi.$$

Now you want to find $\tan\alpha$, and clearly $\alpha = \phi - \beta$. So

$$\tan\alpha = \tan(\phi - \beta) = \frac{\tan\phi - \tan\beta}{1 + \tan\phi\tan\beta} = \frac{\tan\phi - \tfrac{1}{2}\tan\phi}{1 + \tfrac{1}{2}\tan^2\phi} = \frac{\tfrac{1}{2}\tan\phi}{1 + \tfrac{1}{2}\tan^2\phi}.$$

To get the answer in terms of θ, note that $\phi = \tfrac{1}{2}\pi - \theta$, so $\tan\phi = \dfrac{1}{\tan\theta}$. This gives

$$\tan\alpha = \frac{\dfrac{1}{2\tan\theta}}{1 + \dfrac{1}{2\tan^2\theta}}.$$

Multiplying both numerator and denominator by $2\tan^2\theta$,

$$\frac{F}{R} = \tan\alpha = \frac{\tan\theta}{2\tan^2\theta + 1}.$$

Geometrical method 2 You could also use coordinates to find the angle α. Taking ON and OM in Fig. 11.4 as x- and y-axes, Q has coordinates $(l\cos\theta, l\sin\theta)$, and QX has gradient $-\dfrac{1}{\tan\theta}$, so QX has equation $x\cos\theta + y\sin\theta = l$. Also GX has equation $x = \frac{1}{2}l\cos\theta$, so the coordinates of X are $\left(\frac{1}{2}l\cos\theta, \dfrac{\frac{1}{2}l(2-\cos^2\theta)}{\sin\theta}\right)$. Then, from Fig. 11.5, $\tan\alpha = \dfrac{x}{y} = \dfrac{\sin\theta\cos\theta}{2-\cos^2\theta}$.

Part (b)

The various methods in part (a) give three apparently different expressions for $\dfrac{F}{R}$.

It is an interesting exercise in trigonometry to show that they are in fact the same. For a quick check, use a graphic calculator to show graphs of the three functions. You will see from your graphs that the ratio starts with the value 0 when $\theta = 0$, rises to a maximum and then falls back to 0 when $\theta = \frac{1}{2}\pi$. If the roll is not to slip as it is raised, the coefficient of friction must be greater than or equal to the maximum value.

The obvious way to find the maximum is to use calculus. For this you need to use the derivatives of various trigonometric functions and the rule for differentiating the quotient of two functions (see C3 Chapter 10 and C4 Chapter 1). It is left to you to check that the maximum occurs when $\tan\theta = \frac{1}{2}\sqrt{2}$, and that the maximum value is $\frac{1}{4}\sqrt{2}$.

You can, however, get the answer more quickly by using an algebraic method. If the ratio $\dfrac{F}{R}$ is denoted by r, then the first geometric method in part (a) gives $r = \dfrac{\tan\theta}{2\tan^2\theta + 1}$, which can be written as $2r\tan^2\theta - \tan\theta + r = 0$.

This is a quadratic equation whose solutions give the values of $\tan\theta$ for which r takes a particular value. For this equation to have roots, the discriminant '$b^2 - 4ac$' must be positive or zero. That is $1 - 4(2r)r \geqslant 0$, which gives $r \leqslant \sqrt{\frac{1}{8}} = \frac{1}{4}\sqrt{2}$.

So the ratio $\dfrac{F}{R}$ is never greater than $\frac{1}{4}\sqrt{2}$, which means that if $\mu \geqslant \frac{1}{4}\sqrt{2}$ the roll of carpet will not slip as it is raised to the vertical position.

Exercise 11A

Try to solve each question of this exercise by more than one method.

1 A uniform rigid rod AB has length $2\,\text{m}$ and weight $60\,\text{N}$. The rod is smoothly hinged at its end A to a vertical wall. The rod is held at an angle of $60°$ downward from the wall by a force of magnitude $F\,\text{N}$ acting at B. The force acts at an angle θ upwards from the horizontal, as shown in the diagram. Show that $F\cos(60° - \theta)$ is approximately $26\,\text{N}$. Find the magnitude and direction of the force exerted by the wall on the rod at A when

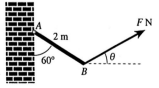

(a) $\theta = 30°$, (b) $\theta = 60°$, (c) $\theta = 90°$.

2 A uniform beam AB has length 4 m and mass 80 kg. A string is attached to the midpoint M of AB and passes over a small pulley P at the top of a wall. The beam is in equilibrium with A in contact with the wall at a point 4 m below P, as shown in the diagram. The string is taut with the part PM at right angles to AB. Find

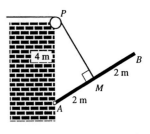

(a) the tension in the string,

(b) the magnitude and direction of the force exerted by the wall on the beam at A.

3 The diagram shows a uniform rod AB, of mass 2 kg and length 0.8 metres, which rests with its end A against a rough vertical wall and makes an angle of 60° with the vertical. It is maintained in this position by means of a string connecting B to a point C of the wall vertically above A. The angle between the string and the rod is 20°. Find the tension in the string, and the smallest possible coefficient of friction between the rod and the wall.   (OCR)

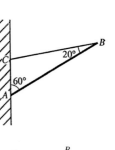

4 $ABCD$ is the central cross-section of a uniform rectangular box, with $AB = 90$ cm and $BC = 100$ cm. The face which includes DC rests against a step 14 cm above ground level, and the edge through D rests on the ground, 48 cm from the step. The contact with the step is smooth, and the contact with the ground is rough with coefficient of friction μ. If the box is on the point of slipping, find μ.

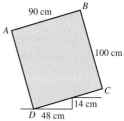

5 A uniform rod is in equilibrium at an angle θ to the vertical, with its lower end on the ground and its upper end resting against a small peg. The coefficient of friction μ is the same at both contacts. Prove that, if equilibrium is limiting, $\sin 2\theta = \dfrac{4\mu}{1 + \mu^2}$.

6 The diagram shows a uniform triangular lamina ABC of weight W newtons. The lamina is right-angled at B, with $AB = 0.6$ m and $BC = 0.8$ m, and rests in a vertical plane with AB in contact with a rough horizontal table. A force of magnitude P newtons is applied at C, in the plane of the lamina and at right angles to AC. Given that the lamina is in equilibrium and on the point of turning about A, find P in terms of W, and the least possible value of the coefficient of friction between the lamina and the table.   (OCR)

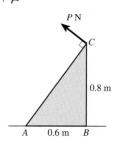

11.2   Problems involving motion

The choice between algebraic and geometrical methods doesn't only occur in equilibrium problems. It also arises in problems which involve motion.

It was shown in M1 Section 9.1 that, if the sides of a vector force diagram are projected on a line in any direction, the relation between the projections is equivalent to an equation of resolving in that direction. The same reasoning can be applied to any vector relation.

For example, in Section 1.1 the displacement–time equation for a projectile was written in the vector form $\mathbf{r} = \mathbf{u}t + \frac{1}{2}\mathbf{g}t^2$. This is illustrated in Fig. 11.6.

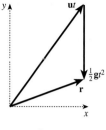

If you project the sides of this triangle on the x-axis and on the y-axis, you get the usual equations for the horizontal and vertical motion. But you can also project the sides in other directions, and this sometimes produces a neater solution to a problem.

Fig. 11.6

Example 11.2.1
Part of a golf course is on a hill which slopes at an angle α to the horizontal. The ball is hit straight up the hill with speed u at an angle θ to the horizontal.

(a) How far up the hill does it first land?

(b) For different values of θ, what is the greatest distance up the hill that the ball can be hit?

Part (a)

Method 1   Fig. 11.7 shows a triangle OAB, which corresponds to the triangle in Fig. 11.6 applied to the flight of the golf ball.

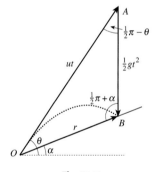

Fig. 11.7

If t is the time that the ball is in the air, the sides of the triangle are $OA = ut$, $AB = \frac{1}{2}gt^2$ and $OB = r$. The angles at O, A and B are $\theta - \alpha$, $\frac{1}{2}\pi - \theta$ and $\frac{1}{2}\pi + \alpha$. The sine rule then gives

$$\frac{r}{\sin\left(\frac{1}{2}\pi - \theta\right)} = \frac{ut}{\sin\left(\frac{1}{2}\pi + \alpha\right)} = \frac{\frac{1}{2}gt^2}{\sin(\theta - \alpha)},$$

or more simply

$$\frac{r}{\cos\theta} = \frac{ut}{\cos\alpha} = \frac{\frac{1}{2}gt^2}{\sin(\theta - \alpha)}.$$

From the first equality, $t = \dfrac{r\cos\alpha}{u\cos\theta}$; and from the second, $t = \dfrac{2u\sin(\theta - \alpha)}{g\cos\alpha}$.

So $\dfrac{r\cos\alpha}{u\cos\theta} = \dfrac{2u\sin(\theta - \alpha)}{g\cos\alpha}$, which gives

$$r = \frac{2u^2\sin(\theta - \alpha)\cos\theta}{g\cos^2\alpha}.$$

Method 2   The simplest way to find the time that the ball is in the air is to resolve the velocity and acceleration vectors perpendicular to the slope, as shown in Fig. 11.8.

The resolved part of the initial velocity is $u \cos\left(\frac{1}{2}\pi - (\theta - \alpha)\right)$, which can be written more simply as $u \sin(\theta - \alpha)$. The resolved part of the acceleration g is $-g \cos\alpha$. So, if z is the perpendicular distance of the ball from the slope at time t,

$$z = u \sin(\theta - \alpha)t - \tfrac{1}{2}(g \cos\alpha)t^2.$$

The ball lands when $z = 0$, and this gives

$$t = \frac{2u \sin(\theta - \alpha)}{g \cos\alpha}.$$

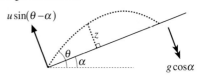

Fig. 11.8

Now resolve horizontally. The acceleration has no resolved part in this direction, and the velocity and displacement have resolved parts $u \cos\theta$ and $r \cos\alpha$. So $r \cos\alpha = (u \cos\theta)t$, which again gives

$$r = \frac{2u^2 \sin(\theta - \alpha) \cos\theta}{g \cos^2\alpha}.$$

Method 3   Another approach is to use the standard cartesian equation for the trajectory (see Section 1.3(iv)). The point where the ball lands has coordinates $(r \cos\alpha, r \sin\alpha)$, and these must satisfy the equation. Therefore

$$r \sin\alpha = r \cos\alpha \tan\theta - \frac{g(r \cos\alpha)^2}{2u^2 \cos^2\theta}.$$

Cancelling the common factor r and rearranging,

$$\frac{gr \cos^2\alpha}{2u^2 \cos\theta} = \cos\theta(\tan\theta \cos\alpha - \sin\alpha).$$

The right side is $\sin\theta \cos\alpha - \cos\theta \sin\alpha = \sin(\theta - \alpha)$, so finally

$$r = \frac{2u^2 \sin(\theta - \alpha) \cos\theta}{g \cos^2\alpha}.$$

Part (b)
The formula for r can be written as the product of two parts,

$$r = \frac{u^2}{g \cos^2\alpha} \times 2 \sin(\theta - \alpha) \cos\theta.$$

Only the second factor involves θ, and you can use the identity

$$2 \sin A \cos B \equiv \sin(A + B) + \sin(A - B)$$

(see C3 Section 6.3, Example 6.3.4) to write this as

$$2 \sin(\theta - \alpha) \cos\theta = \sin(2\theta - \alpha) + \sin(-\alpha) = \sin(2\theta - \alpha) - \sin\alpha.$$

Now only the term $\sin(2\theta - \alpha)$ involves θ, and the greatest value of this is 1. So

$$r_{max} = \frac{u^2}{g \cos^2\alpha} \times (1 - \sin\alpha).$$

This can be simplified by writing $\cos^2 \alpha$ as $1 - \sin^2 \alpha = (1 - \sin \alpha)(1 + \sin \alpha)$. You can then cancel the factor $1 - \sin \alpha$ to get

$$r_{max} = \frac{u^2}{g(1 + \sin \alpha)}.$$

Another equation which should properly be expressed as a vector relationship is Newton's second law of motion, $\mathbf{F} = m\mathbf{a}$. In this complete form, the equation states not just that the magnitude of the force is equal to the magnitude of the acceleration, but also that the force and the acceleration are in the same direction. The symbol $\mathbf{F}$ here stands for the resultant of all the forces acting on the object.

Example 11.2.2

Cars race round a track which includes a horizontal circular arc of radius r. This stretch of the track is banked at an angle α to the horizontal, so that a car driven round the track at a constant speed v experiences no sideways frictional force.

(a) Find an equation connecting v, r, g and α.

(b) If the coefficient of friction is μ, what is the fastest speed at which a car can go round this stretch of the track without skidding?

Part (a)
Method 1 In this example the force which both supports the weight and provides the acceleration is the normal contact force N from the road (see Fig. 11.9).

The acceleration is $\dfrac{v^2}{r}$, so for a car of mass m,

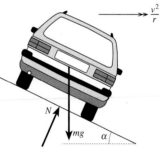

$$\mathcal{R}(\rightarrow) \qquad N \sin \alpha = m\frac{v^2}{r},$$

$$\mathcal{R}(\uparrow) \qquad N \cos \alpha - mg = 0.$$

Substituting $N = \dfrac{mg}{\cos \alpha}$ in the first equation,

cancelling m and using $\dfrac{\sin \alpha}{\cos \alpha} = \tan \alpha$,

$$v^2 = rg \tan \alpha.$$

Fig. 11.9

Method 2 Because the acceleration is in a horizontal direction, the resultant of the two forces mg and N must be horizontal. It follows that the force diagram for finding the resultant of mg and N has the form of Fig. 11.10.

The resultant therefore has magnitude $mg \tan \alpha$, and Newton's second law takes the form

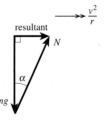

$$mg \tan \alpha = m\frac{v^2}{r},$$

Fig. 11.10

which gives

$$v^2 = rg \tan \alpha.$$

Part (b)

Fig. 11.11 shows a car driven at a speed V, where V is greater than v, so that a frictional force F is needed to keep the car on the circular path.

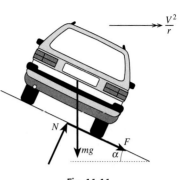

Here are three possible ways of proceeding.

Method 1   Resolve horizontally and vertically, as in part (a).

$$\mathcal{R}(\rightarrow) \qquad N \sin \alpha + F \cos \alpha = m \frac{V^2}{r},$$

$$\mathcal{R}(\uparrow) \qquad N \cos \alpha - F \sin \alpha - mg = 0.$$

Fig. 11.11

These are simultaneous equations for N and F, which can be solved in the usual way. Multiplying the first equation by $\sin \alpha$, the second by $\cos \alpha$ and adding gives

$$(N \sin \alpha + F \cos \alpha) \sin \alpha + (N \cos \alpha - F \sin \alpha) \cos \alpha = \frac{mV^2}{r} \sin \alpha + mg \cos \alpha.$$

Using $\sin^2 \alpha + \cos^2 \alpha = 1$, the left side of this equation is just N, so

$$N = \frac{mV^2}{r} \sin \alpha + mg \cos \alpha.$$

Similarly, multiplying the first by $\cos \alpha$, the second by $\sin \alpha$ and subtracting leads to

$$F = \frac{mV^2}{r} \cos \alpha - mg \sin \alpha.$$

For the car not to skid, $F \leqslant \mu N$, so

$$\frac{mV^2}{r} \cos \alpha - mg \sin \alpha \leqslant \mu \left(\frac{mV^2}{r} \sin \alpha + mg \cos \alpha \right).$$

It is convenient to divide through the equation by $\cos \alpha$, and to use $\dfrac{\sin \alpha}{\cos \alpha} = \tan \alpha$. Rearranging the inequality and dividing by m,

$$\frac{V^2}{r} (1 - \mu \tan \alpha) \leqslant g (\tan \alpha + \mu).$$

There are now two possibilities. If the road is so rough that $\mu \tan \alpha$ is greater than 1, the left side is negative and the right side is positive. In that case the inequality holds however large V is, so the car can round the bend at any speed.

Otherwise you can multiply the inequality by the positive quantity $\dfrac{r}{1 - \mu \tan \alpha}$ to get

$$V^2 \leqslant \frac{rg (\tan \alpha + \mu)}{1 - \mu \tan \alpha}.$$

The greatest speed at which a car can go round the curve is $\sqrt{\dfrac{rg (\tan \alpha + \mu)}{1 - \mu \tan \alpha}}$.

Method 2   Instead of resolving parallel and perpendicular to the acceleration with the forces at an angle to these directions, you can resolve perpendicular to each unknown force in turn with the acceleration at an angle.

$\mathcal{R}(\parallel$ to the slope) $F + mg \sin \alpha = m \dfrac{V^2}{r} \cos \alpha,$

$\mathcal{R}(\perp$ to the slope) $N - mg \cos \alpha = m \dfrac{V^2}{r} \sin \alpha.$

These equations give

$$F = \frac{mV^2}{r} \cos \alpha - mg \sin \alpha, \qquad N = \frac{mV^2}{r} \sin \alpha + mg \cos \alpha,$$

as obtained by solving the simultaneous equations in Method 1. This method gets the expressions for F and N directly, and you can now complete the solution just as in Method 1.

Method 3   This method uses the angle of friction λ, where $\tan \lambda = \mu$.

Fig. 11.12 is derived from Fig. 11.11 by combining N and F into a total contact force C, which makes an angle θ with the normal to the slope. If the car is not to skid, then $\theta \leqslant \lambda$.

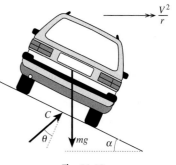

The effect of this is to reduce the number of forces on the car to two, so that C is the force which both supports the weight and provides the acceleration. You can now see that Fig. 11.12 is essentially the same as Fig. 11.9, with two differences: the speed v is replaced by V, and the force makes an angle $\alpha + \theta$, rather than α, with the vertical.

Fig. 11.12

So the result of part (a) can be adapted to give the equation

$$V^2 = rg \tan(\alpha + \theta).$$

Now $\tan(\alpha + \theta) \leqslant \tan(\alpha + \lambda) = \dfrac{\tan \alpha + \tan \lambda}{1 - \tan \alpha \tan \lambda} = \dfrac{\tan \alpha + \mu}{1 - \mu \tan \alpha}.$

It follows that, for the car not to skid,

$$V^2 \leqslant \frac{rg\,(\tan \alpha + \mu)}{1 - \mu \tan \alpha}.$$

Exercise 11B

Try to find the most efficient method to solve the problems in this exercise.

1 A batsman B strikes a cricket ball, and it hits the pavilion clock C 14 metres above the level of the pitch at a horizontal distance of 48 metres. The initial direction of the trajectory makes an angle of $\tan^{-1} \frac{4}{3}$ with the horizontal. What is the angle between the initial direction and the line BC? Find

   (a) how long the ball is in the air before it hits the clock,

   (b) the speed with which the ball was struck,

   (c) the greatest height above the pitch reached by the ball.

2 On a golf course players have to drive the ball across a lake. The far side of the lake is a distance a horizontally and $a \tan \alpha$ vertically below the tee. If a player strikes the ball with initial speed u at an angle θ to the horizontal, show that u has to satisfy the inequality

$$u^2 > \frac{ag \cos \alpha}{\sin(2\theta + \alpha) + \sin \alpha}.$$

The far side of the lake is 150 metres horizontally from the tee and 20 metres below it.

(a) What value of θ will enable the player to clear the lake with the smallest possible initial speed?

(b) If the ball may leave the tee at any angle with the horizontal between 20° and 60°, with what speed must the player hit it to be sure of clearing the lake?

3 A hollow cone has base radius 4 metres and height 3 metres. It is mounted with its axis vertical and vertex pointing downwards, and a small pebble is placed on the inside surface of the cone at a distance of 2 metres from the vertex. In this position the pebble is in limiting equilibrium, about to slip down the cone towards the vertex. The cone is now set rotating about its axis. What is the greatest angular speed for which the pebble will remain in the same position on the surface of the cone?

4 A track for aspiring young racing drivers consists of a hollow in the shape of part of a sphere of radius 80 metres. A child and her car have a total mass of 200 kg. At low speeds she drives round the track in horizontal circles banked at an angle θ to the horizontal; as the speed increases, θ increases. Find the speed when $\theta = 40°$ if there is no sideways frictional force on the wheels.

As a safety procedure, a cord is attached to the side of the car and to an anchor at the lowest point of the hollow. When θ reaches the value 40° this cord becomes taut, so that the angle cannot get any bigger. Find the tension in the cord when the child is driving at $25 \, \mathrm{m \, s^{-1}}$.

5 The figure shows, in diagrammatic form, a governor for controlling the speed of an engine. This consists of a framework set in a vertical plane which rotates with the vertical shaft driven by the engine. A is a fixed point on the rotating shaft. Heavy spheres, each of mass m, are attached to the framework at B and D. C is a sleeve, of mass M, which can move up and down the shaft without friction. AB, BC, CD and DA are rods of equal length l and negligible mass, hinged at A, B, C and D so that the rhombus $ABCD$ can change its shape. When the shaft rotates with angular speed Ω, each rod is at an angle θ to the vertical. Find an expression for the tension in one of the lower rods in terms of m, l, Ω, θ and g, and deduce that $(M + m)g = ml\Omega^2 \cos \theta$.

11.3 Energy and momentum

Many problems about moving objects are in several stages, and you need a strategy to decide how to put the various stages together.

One of the most important decisions is whether to use Newton's second law to find the acceleration produced by the forces, or whether to bypass this by using equations involving energy and work. You should bear the following points in mind.

- Energy equations can be very effective for finding the speed in different positions, but they are of no use if you want to find the time to get from one position to another.

- Energy equations can't be used for stages in which objects collide (unless $e = 1$, when the objects are perfectly elastic).

- If there are no collisions, an energy equation can sometimes be used for more than one stage at a time.

Example 11.3.1

Fig. 11.13 shows the roof of a building. A lump of ice initially at rest at A starts to slide down the roof, and falls to the ground 8 metres below B. Find where it hits the ground, and its velocity when it does so. Frictional force and air resistance can be neglected.

Method using energy The motion is in two stages, the slide down the roof and then the projectile motion. But the transition from one stage to the next occurs smoothly without any collision, so that energy is conserved from the beginning of the motion at A until the ice hits the ground.

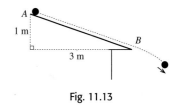

Fig. 11.13

Let the mass of the lump of ice be m kg. At A it is 9 metres above the ground, so it has potential energy $9.8m \times 9$ J. If it hits the ground with a speed of V m s^{-1},

$$9.8m \times 9 = \tfrac{1}{2}mV^2,$$

so $V = \sqrt{2 \times 9.8 \times 9} = 13.3$, correct to 3 significant figures,

To find where it hits the ground you need the equation for the path of a projectile, so you have to begin by finding how fast the ice is moving at B. This can again be done by energy. The loss of potential energy as it falls from A to B is $9.8m \times 1$ J, so the speed at B is $\sqrt{2 \times 9.8 \times 1}$ m s^{-1}, which is $\sqrt{19.6}$ m s^{-1}.

It was shown in Section 1.3 that, in the standard notation, the trajectory of a projectile has equation

$$y = x \tan \theta - \frac{gx^2 \sec^2 \theta}{2u^2}.$$

As the ice leaves the roof its velocity is directed along the line of the slope, so $\tan\theta = -\frac{1}{3}$. From this you can calculate $\sec^2\theta = 1 + \tan^2\theta = \frac{10}{9}$. Also $g = 9.8$ and $u = \sqrt{19.6}$, so

$$y = -\tfrac{1}{3}x - \frac{9.8 \times \frac{10}{9}}{2 \times 19.6}x^2,$$

which can be simplified to

$$y = -\tfrac{1}{3}x - \tfrac{5}{18}x^2.$$

You want to find x when the ice hits the ground, which is when $y = -8$. So x satisfies the quadratic equation

$$-8 = -\tfrac{1}{3}x - \tfrac{5}{18}x^2,$$

which is $5x^2 + 6x - 144 = 0$, or $(5x - 24)(x + 6) = 0$.
Since x is obviously positive, $5x - 24 = 0$, giving $x = 4.8$.

The last thing to find is the direction in which the ice is moving when it hits the ground. Differentiating the equation of the path gives $\dfrac{dy}{dx} = -\frac{1}{3} - \frac{5}{9}x$, and when $x = 4.8$ this has the value $-\frac{1}{3} - \frac{8}{3}$, which is -3. So the ice is moving at an angle to the horizontal of $\tan^{-1} 3$, which is $71.6°$ to the nearest tenth of a degree.

The lump of ice hits the ground 4.8 metres horizontally beyond B, with a speed of about $13.3\,\mathrm{m\,s}^{-1}$ at an angle to the horizontal of $71.6°$.

Alternative method   Instead of using energy to find the speed at B, you could find the acceleration of the ice by resolving parallel to the roof. You can calculate that the length of AB is $\sqrt{10}$ metres so, denoting the angle of the roof with the horizontal by α, $\sin\alpha = \dfrac{1}{\sqrt{10}}$. The acceleration in $\mathrm{m\,s}^{-2}$ is then $g\sin\alpha = \dfrac{g}{\sqrt{10}}$. The speed at B is given by the constant acceleration formula $v^2 = u^2 + 2as$ with $u = 0$, $a = \dfrac{9.8}{\sqrt{10}}$ and $s = \sqrt{10}$, so $v = \sqrt{19.6}$.

You could then find x by the previous method, but this would not give the speed when the ice hits the ground. To find this, you need to split the velocity at B into vertical and horizontal components $v\sin\alpha$ and $v\cos\alpha$, which are

$$\frac{\sqrt{19.6}}{\sqrt{10}}\,\mathrm{m\,s}^{-1} = 1.4\,\mathrm{m\,s}^{-1} \text{ and } \frac{\sqrt{19.6} \times 3}{\sqrt{10}}\,\mathrm{m\,s}^{-1} = 4.2\,\mathrm{m\,s}^{-1}.$$

The vertical speed when the ice hits the ground can now be found by applying $v^2 = u^2 + 2as$ again, this time with $u = 1.4$, $a = 9.8$ and $s = 8$, which gives $v = \sqrt{158.76} = 12.6$.

This has to be combined with the constant horizontal velocity of $4.2\,\mathrm{m\,s}^{-1}$ to give a resultant velocity in $\mathrm{m\,s}^{-1}$ of magnitude $\sqrt{158.76 + 4.2^2} = \sqrt{176.4} = 13.3$, at an angle of $\tan^{-1}\dfrac{12.6}{4.2} \approx 71.6°$ to the horizontal.

In Example 11.3.1 the method using energy is quicker, but this depends on what you are trying to find. If you wanted to know how long the ice takes to reach the ground, then you would have to adopt a different strategy. On the other hand, if you only wanted to know the velocity but not the place where the ice hits the ground, it would not be necessary to find the equation of the trajectory. Instead, you could simply combine the energy method with the constancy of the horizontal component of velocity to show that the angle on hitting the ground is

$$\cos^{-1}\left(\frac{v_B \cos \alpha}{V}\right) = \cos^{-1}\left(\frac{\sqrt{2 \times 9.8 \times 1} \times \frac{3}{\sqrt{10}}}{\sqrt{2 \times 9.8 \times 9}}\right)$$

$$= \cos^{-1}\left(\frac{1}{\sqrt{10}}\right) = 71.6°.$$

Example 11.3.2

Fig. 11.14 shows a board fixed at an angle to the horizontal. A smooth groove is cut in the board in the shape of an ellipse with one of its axes AB along a line of greatest slope. The height of B above A is h. Two balls, of mass m and $2m$, are placed in the groove at A and B respectively. The ball at B is then slightly displaced, so that it runs round the groove and collides with the ball at A. After the collision the lighter ball runs round the groove from A to B, and comes to rest at B. Find the coefficient of restitution, and describe the motion of the heavier ball after the collision.

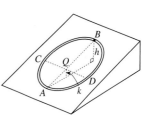

Fig. 11.14

The sequence of events can be split into three stages.

Stage 1   The heavier ball moves round the groove from B to A.

Stage 2   The balls collide.

Stage 3a   The lighter ball moves round the groove from A to B.

Stage 3b   The heavier ball moves in the groove.

In Stages 1 and 3 the only method available to you is to use the conservation of energy principle, since you don't know how to write equations for objects moving in an elliptical path. But energy is not conserved at Stage 2.

Before collision

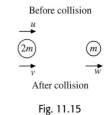

After collision

Fig. 11.15

Suppose that when the heavier ball reaches A it is moving with speed u, and that after the collision the heavier ball has speed v and the lighter ball has speed w (see Fig. 11.15).

Stage 1   When it is at B the heavier ball has potential energy $(2m)gh$. There is no gain or loss of total energy as it descends; the only other force comes from the groove, and since that is smooth the force is always perpendicular to the direction of motion and does no work. By the time it reaches B, the ball has kinetic energy $\frac{1}{2} \times (2m)u^2$. So

$$2mgh = mu^2, \quad \text{which gives } u^2 = 2gh.$$

Stage 3a The pattern of Stage 1 is now reversed for the lighter ball. Kinetic energy of $\frac{1}{2}mw^2$ is converted into potential energy of mgh, so

$$\tfrac{1}{2}mw^2 = mgh, \quad \text{which gives } w^2 = 2gh.$$

Stage 2 When the collision occurs momentum is conserved, so

$$2mu = 2mv + mw, \quad \text{which gives } 2u = 2v + w.$$

Since $u = w = \sqrt{2gh}$, $v = \frac{1}{2}u = \frac{1}{2}\sqrt{2gh}$.

The approach speed is u and the separation speed is $w - v = u - \frac{1}{2}u = \frac{1}{2}u$, so the coefficient of restitution is $\frac{1}{2}$.

Stage 3b Suppose that the heavier ball rises to a height k after the collision. Then kinetic energy of $\frac{1}{2}(2m)\left(\frac{1}{2}\sqrt{2gh}\right)^2 = \frac{1}{2}mgh$ is converted into potential energy of $(2m)gk$. It follows that $k = \frac{1}{4}h$.

In Fig. 11.14, Q is the point one-quarter of the way from A to B, and C and D are points of the groove such that the line CQD is horizontal. After the collision the heavier bead continues to move along the groove until it comes to rest at C. It can't remain there, so it then returns along the groove through A until it reaches D, where it comes to rest again. It then returns to C, and continues to oscillate between C and D. The total amount of energy stays constant, taking the form of kinetic energy at A and potential energy at C and D.

Example 11.3.3

A framework has the shape of a right-angled triangle ABC with angle $CAB = 30°$. It is fixed with AB horizontal and C above B, and a smooth track runs up the hypotenuse AC. A light pulley is fixed to the framework at C, and a light rope runs over the pulley (see Fig. 11.16). At one end of the rope is a particle P of mass m which runs on the track; at the other end is a particle Q of mass $2m$ which hangs vertically. Initially the particles are at rest and the hanging particle is at a height h above an inelastic floor. Investigate the subsequent motion of the system.

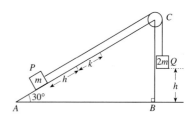

Fig. 11.16

The motion can be analysed in five stages.

Stage 1 Q descends and P runs up the track for a distance h.

Stage 2 Q hits the floor and stops, P continues up the track.

Stage 3 P runs up the track, comes to rest and then runs back.

Stage 4 The rope becomes taut again and Q is jerked into motion.

Stage 5 Q rises and P continues down the track until both come to rest.

How far can you get by considering energy alone?

Stage 1 As Q descends a distance h, P rises by $h \sin 30° = \frac{1}{2}h$. So Q loses potential energy $2mgh$, and P gains $\frac{1}{2}mgh$, a net loss of $\frac{3}{2}mgh$. If the particles are then moving with speed U, they have combined kinetic energy of $\frac{1}{2}(m + 2m)U^2$. So

$$\tfrac{3}{2}mgh = \tfrac{3}{2}mU^2, \quad \text{which gives } U^2 = gh.$$

Stage 2 Q strikes the floor and comes to rest, since the floor is inelastic. The rope becomes slack, and P continues up the track with speed U.

Stage 3 If P goes a further distance k up the track, it gains further potential energy of $mg\left(\frac{1}{2}k\right)$ and loses kinetic energy of $\frac{1}{2}mU^2$, which is $\frac{1}{2}mgh$. So $k = h$; that is, P goes a further distance h up the track.

P then returns, and the potential energy gained on the upward journey is converted back into kinetic energy. By the time the rope becomes taut, the kinetic energy is the same as at the beginning of this stage, so P is again moving with speed U.

Stage 4 As the rope becomes taut, there is a sudden large tension which jerks Q into motion. This is the equivalent of a collision (compare with Example 7.2.2), so energy will be lost at this stage and you have to use ideas of impulse and momentum. Denote the impulse of this tension by I, and suppose that after the jerk P and Q are both moving with speed V (see Fig. 11.17).

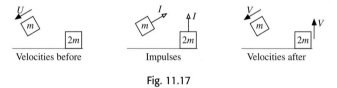

Velocities before   Impulses   Velocities after

Fig. 11.17

The impulse–momentum equations for P and Q are

$$-I = mV - mU \quad \text{and} \quad I = 2mV - 0,$$

so $-2mV = mV - mU$, which gives $V = \frac{1}{3}U$.

Notice that the weights of P and Q don't come into this equation. The jerk occurs in such a short time that it is reasonable to neglect the impulse of the weights.

Stage 5 This is like Stage 1 in reverse, with kinetic energy being converted into potential energy. Since the speeds are now only one-third of what they were, the kinetic energy is only one-ninth, so the potential energy gained as P and Q come to rest is one-ninth of the potential energy lost in Stage 1. This means that Q rises to a height $\frac{1}{9}h$ above the floor.

The particles are now in the same state as they were originally, but with Q at only one-ninth of the height. The stages will therefore go through a second cycle, but with h replaced by $\frac{1}{9}h$. After that there will be a third, fourth, fifth, …, cycle.

You now have a complete description of the motion, except that you do not know how long it takes. You could investigate this by finding the accelerations at each stage, but it is more interesting to find the time from a graph of the motion.

Fig. 11.18 is a (t, v) graph for the motion of P.

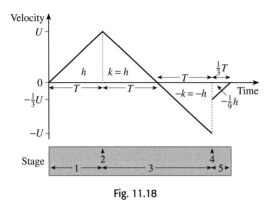

Fig. 11.18

You will see that it is made up of four triangles, of which the first three have the same area, since you know that P goes a distance h in Stage 1 and then a further distance h up the plane in the first half of Stage 3. Notice the discontinuity at Stage 4, when the rope becomes taut. The area of the last triangle is one-ninth of the area of the other three triangles.

The graph shows that, if Stage 1 takes time T, then the total time for a cycle is $\frac{10}{3}T$, and also that $h = \frac{1}{2}TU$. Since $U^2 = gh$, this means that the total time for a cycle is

$$C = \frac{20}{3}\sqrt{\frac{h}{g}}.$$

For each successive cycle the height of Q is divided by 9, so the time is divided by 3. Motion will therefore continue altogether for a time

$$C\left(1 + \tfrac{1}{3} + \left(\tfrac{1}{3}\right)^2 + \left(\tfrac{1}{3}\right)^3 + \cdots\right),$$

an infinite geometric progression with sum

$$\frac{C}{1 - \frac{1}{3}} = \tfrac{3}{2}C = 10\sqrt{\frac{h}{g}}.$$

Exercise 11C

1 A ramp of length 10.5 metres and inclination θ is fixed on horizontal ground. A ball is projected with speed $32\,\mathrm{m\,s^{-1}}$ from the bottom of the ramp and moves up a line of greatest slope. It reaches the top of the ramp with speed $30\,\mathrm{m\,s^{-1}}$. The ramp may be modelled as smooth, the ball may be modelled as a particle, and air resistance may be ignored. Show that θ is approximately $37°$.

The ball leaves the ramp and moves freely under gravity. The highest point reached by the ball in the motion is C. Find

(a) the speed of the ball at C,

(b) the height of C above the ground.   (OCR)

2 Two blocks, of mass 4 kg and 3 kg, are joined by a string which passes over a smooth rail. The blocks are held steady, with the string vertical on either side of the rail, and with the base of each 0.7 metres above the floor. Collisions between the blocks and the floor are inelastic. Find

(a) the speed with which the 4 kg block hits the floor,

(b) how high the 3 kg block rises above the floor,

(c) the speed with which the 4 kg block is jerked into motion again,

(d) the height to which the 4 kg block rises before it comes to rest,

(e) the time between the two instants when both blocks are at rest.

3 Two spheres, A and B, are suspended side-by-side by long parallel strings of equal length. A is pulled aside to a height h above the point of contact, and then released. After the first impact with B, A comes to rest and B rises to a height $\frac{1}{4}h$. Find the ratio of the mass of A to the mass of B, and the coefficient of restitution.

Given that all subsequent impacts take place at the lowest part of the swings, find the heights to which A and B rise

(a) after the second impact,   (b) after the third impact,

(c) after the sixth impact,   (d) after the seventh impact.

4 In a situation similar to that in Question 3, suppose that the spheres A and B have mass m and km respectively, that before the first impact B is stationary and A collides with it at a speed u, and that the coefficient of restitution is e. Find the speeds of the spheres after the nth impact

(a) if n is even,   (b) if n is odd.

Miscellaneous exercise 11

1 A uniform beam of length 6 metres and mass 20 kg is hinged to a wall at one end O. A load of 10 kg is placed at the far end of the beam. The beam is supported at 60° to the upward vertical by the tension, T newtons, in a cable whose other end is fixed to the wall at A, 4 metres above the hinge. Where should the cable be attached to the beam for the magnitude of the force from the hinge to be as small as possible?

2 A uniform cylindrical drum, of base radius 0.5 metres and height 1 metre, can rest in equilibrium with its circular base in contact with a rough ramp inclined at 30° to the horizontal. Find the least possible value of the coefficient of friction between the base of the drum and the ramp.

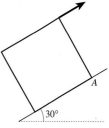

The coefficient of friction is, in fact, 0.6. An attempt is made to drag the drum up the ramp by attaching a rope to the topmost point of the drum and pulling in a direction parallel to a line of greatest slope of the ramp. Show that the drum will turn about the point A shown in the diagram. Would this still be the case if the coefficient of friction were greater than 0.6?   (OCR)

3 A projectile is launched from a point O with initial speed u at an angle θ to the horizontal. Its subsequent path is observed from O. At a certain instant it is seen at an angle of elevation α, and at time t later it is seen to land at the same level as O. Show that
$$t = \frac{2u}{g}\cos\theta\tan\alpha.$$

A cannonball was fired across a level plain. After 10 seconds it was seen at an angle of elevation of 20°, and 5 seconds later it landed. Find the initial velocity of the cannonball.

4 Two particles P and Q, of equal mass m, are attached to the ends of a light inextensible string. The string passes through a small smooth hole at the vertex of a cone fixed with its axis vertical. The cone has semi-vertical angle α, where $\alpha = \tan^{-1}\frac{4}{3}$. The particle P hangs inside the cone and the particle Q is free to move on the smooth surface of the cone (see diagram). Particle Q is projected so that it moves in a horizontal circle of radius 0.5 metres on the surface of the cone with constant angular speed ω rad s^{-1}. Particle P remains at rest. Find, in either order,

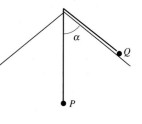

(a) the magnitude of the force exerted on Q by the cone, in terms of m and g,

(b) the value of ω, giving your answer correct to 3 significant figures.   (OCR)

5 A hemispherical bowl, of radius r, is fixed with its rim horizontal. A uniform rod of length l is in equilibrium at an angle α to the horizontal, resting against the rim of the bowl and with its lower end on the inside surface of the bowl. Prove that, if both contacts are smooth, then $l\cos\alpha = 4r\cos 2\alpha$.

6 A surface of revolution is formed by rotating a curve with equation $y = f(x)$, for $x > 0$, about the y-axis. The surface is modelled in a thin layer of smooth metal. A particle is placed on the surface at the point of the curve with coordinate x, at which $f'(x) > 0$, and set in motion round the surface in a horizontal circle with constant angular speed Ω. Prove that
$$\Omega^2 = \frac{gf'(x)}{x}.$$

(a) Obtain the equation of the curve $y = f(x)$ if the time T to complete one revolution is the same wherever the particle is placed.

(b) Obtain the equation of the curve if the speed V of the particle is the same wherever it is placed.

(c) The surface is used to demonstrate how the planets go round the sun. Kepler's third law states that, if x is the radius of an orbit (approximated as circular), then $\Omega^2 = \frac{c}{x^3}$, where c is constant. Obtain the equation of the curve needed to simulate this motion.

7 Particles P and Q, each of mass M kg, are connected by a light inextensible string and are arranged to lie in contact with the smooth faces of a triangular wedge ABC, which is fixed to a horizontal plane along BC. The triangle ABC is right-angled at A, and the string joining P and Q passes over a small smooth pulley at A. The length of AB is 1.5 metres and the height of A above BC is 1.2 metres. Show that the length of AC is 2 metres.

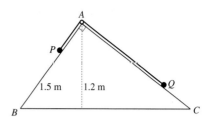

Initially the string is taut, with $AP = 0.5$ metres and $AQ = 1.5$ metres.

(a) The particles are released from rest. Show that the acceleration of P is $0.98 \, \text{m s}^{-2}$ and find the tension in the string in terms of M. Show that the speed of P as it reaches B is $1.4 \, \text{m s}^{-1}$.

(b) On hitting the horizontal plane, P is immediately brought to rest, while Q continues to travel up AC. Find the location at which Q comes instantaneously to rest.

(c) Find the speed with which P is next jerked into motion.

Without doing any more calculation, describe the subsequent motion of the particles.

(OCR)

Revision exercise 2

1 Two smooth spheres A and B, of equal radius and of masses 0.3 kg and 0.2 kg respectively, are free to move on a smooth horizontal table. A is moving with speed $5\,\mathrm{m\,s^{-1}}$ when it collides directly with B, which is stationary. As a result of the collision B starts to move with speed $4.5\,\mathrm{m\,s^{-1}}$.

   (a) Find the coefficient of restitution between the spheres.

   (b) The sphere B subsequently strikes a fixed barrier at right angles. The barrier exerts an impulse of magnitude 1.7 N s on B. Find the speed with which B rebounds from the barrier.

   (c) Find also the speed with which B moves towards the barrier following its second collision with A. (OCR)

2 The diagram shows a vertical cross-section through the centre of a circular cycle track. The track is banked at 27° to the horizontal. A cyclist moves at constant speed on the track, in a horizontal circular path of radius 40 m.

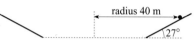

   The mass of the cyclist and his machine is 85 kg. Using a model in which the cyclist and his machine are considered as a single particle and in which the track is smooth, find

   (a) the magnitude of the acceleration of the cyclist,

   (b) the time taken for the cyclist to complete one lap of the track (OCR)

3 (a) A uniform lamina $ABCD$ has the shape of a trapezium which is right-angled at A and D, and $AB = 1.5$ m, $AD = 1.2$ m and $CD = 0.5$ m, as shown in the diagram. Show that the distance of the centre of mass of the lamina from AB is 0.5 m.

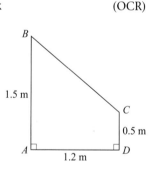

   (b) A cupboard door, of weight 165 N, is modelled by the uniform lamina $ABCD$. The door has smooth hinges at the points P and Q of the edge AB, which is vertical. $AP = BQ = 0.2$ m. The door is open and is in equilibrium. Find the magnitude and direction of the horizontal component of the force on the door at each of P and Q.

   (c) A wedge is now placed between the door and the floor at D, exerting a vertically upward force on the door of magnitude F newtons. The horizontal components of the forces on the door at P and Q are now both zero and the door is in equilibrium. Calculate F, and state the magnitude of the resultant force on the door due to the hinges. (OCR)

4 Two uniform smooth spheres, A and B, have the same radius. The mass of A is 0.24 kg and the mass of B is m kg. Sphere A is travelling in a straight line on a horizontal table, with speed $8\,\mathrm{m\,s^{-1}}$, when it collides directly with sphere B, which is at rest. As a result of the collision, sphere A continues in the same direction with a speed of $6\,\mathrm{m\,s^{-1}}$.

(a) Find the magnitude of the impulse exerted by A on B.

(b) Show that $m \leqslant 0.08$.

It is given that $m = 0.06$.

(c) Find the coefficient of restitution between A and B.

On another occasion A and B are travelling towards each other, each with speed $4\,\mathrm{m\,s^{-1}}$, when they collide directly.

(d) Find the speeds of A and B immediately after the collision.   (OCR)

5 A ball of mass $0.08\,\mathrm{kg}$ is attached by two strings to a fixed vertical post. The strings have lengths $2.5\,\mathrm{m}$ and $2.4\,\mathrm{m}$, as shown in the diagram. The ball moves in a horizontal circle, of radius $2.4\,\mathrm{m}$, with constant speed $v\,\mathrm{m\,s^{-1}}$. Each string is taut and the lower string is horizontal. The modelling assumptions made are that both strings are light and inextensible, and that there is no air resistance.

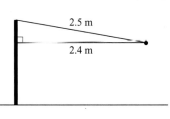

(a) Find the tension in each string when $v = 10.5$.

(b) Find the least value of v for which the lower string is taut.   (OCR)

6 A uniform right-angled triangular lamina ABC with sides $6\,\mathrm{cm}$, $8\,\mathrm{cm}$ and $10\,\mathrm{cm}$ and of weight $30\,\mathrm{N}$ is freely suspended from a hinge at its vertex A (see diagram).

(a) Calculate the angle that the side AB makes with the vertical.

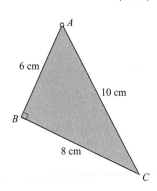

The lamina is now held in a position such that BC is horizontal with B below A. This is achieved by means of a wire which is attached to C and to a fixed point $10\,\mathrm{cm}$ directly above the hinge at A.

(b) Calculate the tension in the wire.

(c) Find the magnitude of the force on the lamina at A.   (OCR)

7 A small sphere lies at rest at the edge of a smooth horizontal shelf which is fixed to a vertical wall. The shelf is $2\,\mathrm{m}$ above the floor (see diagram). The sphere has mass $0.2\,\mathrm{kg}$ and is given an impulse of $3\,\mathrm{N\,s}$ towards the wall. It strikes the wall at right angles and rebounds towards the edge of the shelf. The coefficient of restitution between the sphere and the wall is 0.6. Air resistance is to be ignored.

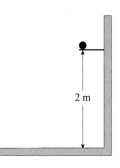

(a) Calculate the speed at which the sphere returns to the edge of the shelf.

(b) Find the horizontal distance from the edge of the shelf to the point where the sphere strikes the floor.   (OCR)

8 A light inextensible string passes through a small hole in a fixed smooth horizontal plane. One end of the string is attached to a particle of mass 0.7 kg which hangs in equilibrium below the plane. The other end of the string is attached to a particle of mass 0.4 kg which rotates with constant angular speed in a circle of radius 0.3 m on the surface of the plane (see diagram). Calculate

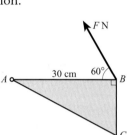

(a) the tension in the string,

(b) the angular speed of the particle on the plane.

The string breaks.

(c) Find the speed of the particle on the plane, and describe its motion.

9 A uniform triangular lamina ABC of weight 200 newtons is right-angled at B and has $AB = 30$ cm. It is smoothly pivoted at A to a fixed point, and maintained in equilibrium with AB horizontal by a force of magnitude F newtons, which acts at 60° to the horizontal, as shown in the diagram. Find the value of F, and the magnitude and direction of the force exerted on the triangle by the pivot.

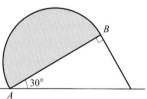

10 On a fairground there is a cylindrical chamber of radius 2 metres which can rotate about a vertical axis. Customers stand inside the chamber with their backs to the side wall. The coefficient of friction between their clothes and the wall of the chamber is 0.4. The chamber is then set rotating. When it is rotating fast enough, the floor of the chamber is suddenly removed, and the customers stay in position supported by friction. What angular speed is necessary for this to happen?

11 The acceleration that an electric car of mass 1200 kg can produce is limited by two factors: the frictional force between the driving wheels and the road cannot exceed 6000 newtons, and the maximum power output of the engine is 30 kW. What is the shortest time in which it could reach a speed of $20 \, \mathrm{m \, s^{-1}}$ from a standing start?

12 A uniform ornamental stone has the form of half a circular cylinder, and weighs 150 newtons. The diagram shows the cross-section containing the centre of mass. The stone is in equilibrium with this cross-section in a vertical plane, with one end A of the diameter in contact with horizontal ground. The other end B of the diameter is supported by a prop, which is in the same vertical plane as the cross-section and at right angles to AB. The diameter AB makes an angle of 30° with the horizontal. Find

(a) the magnitude of the force exerted by the prop on the stone,

(b) the magnitude and direction of the force exerted by the ground on the stone.

13

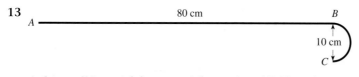

A thin walking stick has a straight section AB 80 cm long, and a semicircular handle BC with diameter 10 cm. Locate the point X of AB about which the stick will balance with the straight section horizontal.

The stick is now hung over a shelf with the end C resting on the shelf. What angle will AB then make with the vertical?

14 A fireman wishes to estimate the speed V of the water emerging from the nozzle of his hosepipe. He holds the nozzle at ground level, and gradually increases θ, the angle which the nozzle makes with the horizontal, until, when $\theta = \theta_1$, the jet just passes over a vertical wall, 4 metres high and 5 metres away from him on level ground. Air resistance is to be neglected, and the water jet treated as a stream of particles.

(a) Show that $\dfrac{V^2}{g} = \dfrac{25(1 + \tan^2 \theta_1)}{2(5 \tan \theta_1 - 4)}$ metres.

(b) Explain why $\theta_1 > \tan^{-1} 0.8$.

(c) The jet hits the ground at a point c metres beyond the wall. Show that $c = \dfrac{20}{5 \tan \theta_1 - 4}$.

(d) Given that c is measured to be 20, find $\tan \theta_1$ and show that $\dfrac{V^2}{g} = 25$ metres.

(e) Without changing V, the fireman increases θ to θ_2 so that the jet just clears the wall, but this time on its way down. Find the value of $\tan \theta_2$ and the new value of c.   (OCR)

15 A simple lift-bridge (commonly used on canals) can stay open without the use of any restraining forces. A mathematical model of the structure is shown in the figure. The bridge is represented by two thin rods AO and OB, rigidly joined and freely pivoted at a fixed point O. The rod AO has length 2.5 metres, mass 400 kg and centre of mass 1.8 metres from O. The rod 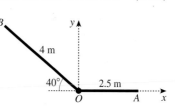 OB has length 4 metres, mass 350 kg and centre of mass 2 metres from O. In the closed position AO is horizontal and OB is inclined at an angle of 40° with the horizontal. In the open position OB is horizontal.

(a) Calculate the position of the centre of mass of the bridge in the closed position, referred to the coordinate axes indicated in the figure, correct to 3 significant figures. Draw a sketch showing the position of the centre of mass.

(b) Describe how the position of the centre of mass of the bridge changes as the bridge is opened.

(c) Establish that this bridge will stay open or closed once moved to that position.

(d) When closed, the bridge is opened by pulling on a chain attached to the point B. The chain is pulled perpendicular to OB. What is the tension in the chain when the bridge just begins to turn?   (MEI)

16 A golfer drives the ball from the tee with a speed of $40\,\mathrm{m\,s^{-1}}$ at $20°$ to the horizontal. Find how far from the tee it will land

(a) if the ground is horizontal,

(b) if the ground slopes down from the tee at $5°$ to the horizontal.

What forces might act on the ball which would cast doubt on the accuracy of answers obtained by using the simple gravity model?

17 The figure shows the forces acting on a car of mass m travelling round a bend of radius $200\,\mathrm{m}$ on a track banked at $20°$ to the horizontal. The car does not slip sideways, provided the speed is not too large. Given that at the greatest possible speed $F = 0.95R$, find this speed.   (OCR)

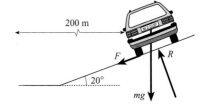

18 A cyclist and her machine have total mass $80\,\mathrm{kg}$. The resistance to her motion is $(4 + kv^2)$ newtons (where v is her speed in $\mathrm{m\,s^{-1}}$ and k is a constant). Initially she is free-wheeling at a steady speed of $9\,\mathrm{m\,s^{-1}}$ down a slope of inclination $\sin^{-1}\frac{5}{196}$ to the horizontal. Show that $k = \frac{16}{81}$.

Find the power she would have to exert to maintain a steady speed of $6\,\mathrm{m\,s^{-1}}$ on a level road.

Continuing on the level road, she brakes to avoid an obstacle, thus reducing her speed to $4\,\mathrm{m\,s^{-1}}$. If she exerts the same power as before, what is her acceleration the instant after she has finished braking?   (OCR, adapted)

19 An ancient civilisation constructed monuments in the shape of circular cones. Some of these have fallen over, and are lying on their sides on level ground. An archaeologist wants to move these, and the first step is to place small rollers underneath them. To do this, a rope is attached to the highest point of the rim, and this is pulled horizontally by a team of student volunteers so as to lift either

(a) the vertex,   or   (b) the rim

of the monument off the ground. If in the fallen position the base of the monument is at an angle α to the horizontal, find in terms of α how to decide which of (a) or (b) will require less effort.

20 Since 1686 the 'Corbière cannon' has stood on a cliff on the north coast of Brittany. An inscription at the site reads:
'From its position thirty-six metres above the sea, with a ten degree barrel elevation, it was capable of throwing an $11\frac{3}{4}\,\mathrm{kg}$ ball two thousand metres.'

(a) Calculate the muzzle velocity of the cannonball.

(b) Assuming that the energy of projection was unchanged, how far could the cannon have thrown a $10\,\mathrm{kg}$ ball at the same angle of elevation?

(c) Assume that the effect of the impact of the cannonball is measured by the magnitude of its momentum when it hits the target. Which of the two cannonballs would have the greater effect on a target at a height of $6\,\mathrm{m}$ above sea level (and at the appropriate distance for the ball, projected at an angle of $10°$, to have fallen to this height)? (OCR)

21 A hollow cone is fixed with its vertex O downwards and its axis vertical. A particle of mass m on the smooth inner surface of the cone moves round it in a horizontal circle whose centre is at a height h above O. Prove that it has kinetic energy $\frac{1}{2}mgh$.

22 The figure shows a soap dispenser for use in a washroom. It consists of a hemisphere of radius 3 cm joined at its rim to a cone of height 4 cm. It is made of thin metal of uniform thickness, and it can pivot about a horizontal axis which passes through its centre of mass. Find how far this axis is below the level of the rim of the hemisphere.

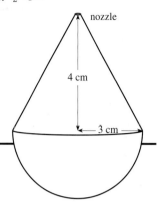

The dispenser is now filled with liquid soap up to the level of the nozzle at the vertex of the cone. (Users tilt the dispenser upside-down so that soap comes out of the nozzle.) Show that the centre of mass of the dispenser and its contents is below the axis.

23 A roofer is replacing the slates on a roof inclined at 40° to the horizontal. An old broken slate of mass 0.4 kg, which may be treated as a particle, is placed on the roof and slides from rest. It slides 5 metres down the roof and then falls a further vertical distance of 6 metres to the ground, as shown in the figure. While the slate is sliding down the roof the resistance to its motion is a constant 2 newtons; when the slate reaches the edge of the roof it falls freely and air resistance can be neglected. Calculate the gravitational potential energy lost by the slate in moving from the point of release to the ground. Calculate also the speed with which the slate hits the ground.

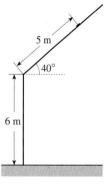

A crate of new slates of total mass 12 kg is pulled up from the ground by the roofer using a light rope. This crate is lifted 6 metres vertically from the ground and then slides 5 metres up the sloping roof before coming to rest. When the crate is being raised vertically there is negligible resistance to motion. When the crate is sliding up the roof the coefficient of friction between the crate and the roof is 0.6 and the rope is parallel to the roof.

(a) Calculate the normal reaction of the roof on the crate.

(b) It takes the roofer 25 seconds to pull up the crate of slates. Calculate the average power he must develop to achieve this.

(c) Show that, if the crate is not secured when the rope is removed, it will slide back down the roof. What would be the least value of the coefficient of friction between the crate and the roof for this not to happen? (MEI)

24 A bird-lover suspends a half-coconut of mass $\frac{1}{2}$ kg from a tree by a string attached to a point of the rim. Modelling the half-coconut as a hemispherical shell of radius r, find the angle which the plane of the rim makes with the vertical.

A bird now perches on the lowest point of the rim, and as a result the angle is reduced to 20°. Find the mass of the bird.

25 A uniform lamina is in the shape of an equilateral triangle
    ABC, and rests in equilibrium inside a vertical circular hoop
    with B and C in contact with the hoop, and A at the centre of
    the circle, as shown in the diagram. Contact is smooth at C
    but rough at B, where the coefficient of friction is μ. The
    lamina is in limiting equilibrium with B lower than C, and
    the axis of symmetry through A makes an angle θ with the
    vertical. By first taking moments about A, show that

    $$\tan\theta = \frac{\mu\sqrt{3}}{\sqrt{3} - 2\mu}.$$

    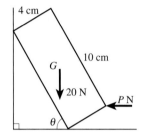

    The lamina ABC is placed so that $\theta = 0$, and the hoop is slowly rotated about its centre in
    a vertical plane so that θ increases. Find the value, θ_0, of θ beyond which the lamina will
    topple about B, if it has not slid already. Also find the least value of μ for which θ will
    reach the value θ_0 without the lamina sliding.   (OCR)

26 A book is resting in equilibrium on a horizontal shelf and
    against a vertical wall, and makes an angle θ with the
    horizontal. A horizontal force of magnitude P newtons is
    applied at an edge, as shown in the diagram. The force P
    acts in a vertical plane which passes through the centre
    of mass G of the book, and is perpendicular to the wall.

    The book is modelled by a uniform rectangular block of
    height 10 cm and width 4 cm, and of weight 20 N. The
    coefficients of friction between the book and the shelf, and
    between the book and the wall, are each 0.4.

    (a) Show that the least value of P needed to move the book is given by

    $$P = \frac{84\cos\theta + 33.6\sin\theta}{10\sin\theta - 8.64\cos\theta}.$$

    (b) Find the interval in which the value of θ must lie, giving the end points correct to the
        nearest 0.1°.   (OCR)

27 A hollow circular cone is fixed with its axis vertical and its vertex
    V downwards. A particle P, of mass m, is attached to a fixed
    point A on the axis of the cone by means of a light inextensible
    string of length equal to AV. The particle moves with constant
    speed v in a horizontal circle on the smooth inner surface of the
    cone, with the string taut. The radius of the circle is r, and angles
    APV and AVP are each 30° (see diagram).

    (a) Find an expression, in terms of m, g, v and r, for the tension in the string.

    (b) Deduce that $\dfrac{v^2}{gr} > \sqrt{3}$.   (OCR)

28 The diagram shows the cross-section of a banked circular cycle racing track, in a vertical plane through its centre O. A cyclist C moves at a constant speed on the steepest part of the track in a horizontal circular path of radius 20 metres. The mass of the cyclist and his machine is 80 kg and the angle between the steepest part of the track and the horizontal is 50°. By using a model in which the cyclist and his machine are considered as a single particle and in which the track is smooth,

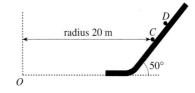

radius 20 m

50°

(a) calculate the normal component of the contact force on the machine due to the track,

(b) show that the magnitude of the acceleration of C is $11.7 \, \mathrm{m \, s^{-2}}$, correct to 3 significant figures,

(c) calculate the speed of C.

Another cyclist D moves at constant speed on the steepest part of the track in a higher horizontal circular path. Determine which of the cyclists C and D completes one circuit of the track in the shorter time.   (OCR)

29 The figure shows a cyclist on a banked track. He is moving at constant speed v in a horizontal circle of radius r at a point of the track where the angle of bank is ϕ.

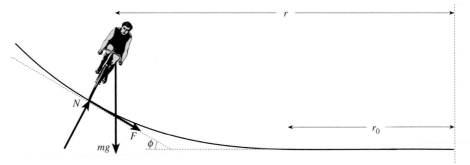

The normal force N and the frictional force F, exerted on the cycle by the track, act in the vertical plane normal to the direction of motion. Show that $N = \dfrac{mg}{\cos\phi - k\sin\phi}$, where m is the mass of the cyclist and cycle, and $k = \dfrac{F}{N}$. By considering the acceleration of the cyclist, obtain an expression for v^2 as a function of r, g, ϕ and k.

During a race the maximum speed of the cyclist (without slipping across the track) corresponds to a value of k equal to 1. The designer of the track has chosen the variation of the bank angle ϕ with r in such a way that the maximum angular speed of the cyclist round the track is independent of the radius r of the circle which is being followed. Show that the profile of the banking should be given by $r = r_0 \tan\left(\phi + \frac{1}{4}\pi\right)$, where the inner edge of the banking corresponds to $r = r_0$.   (OCR)

30 A bird is flying in a horizontal straight line AB, h metres above level ground. It flies over a point O on the ground, where there is a hunter with a shotgun. The hunter fires directly at the bird when it is at A, where OA makes an angle $\tan^{-1}\frac{4}{3}$ with the horizontal, as shown in the diagram. Ox and Oy are horizontal and vertical axes respectively, and the units of x and y are metres. The shot leaves the gun at a speed of $80\,\mathrm{m\,s^{-1}}$, and air resistance on the shot is to be neglected.

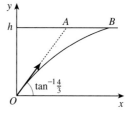

(a) Neglecting the height of the gun above the ground, express x and y in terms of the time, t seconds, after the shot leaves the gun, and hence obtain the equation of the path of the shot in the form $y = \frac{4}{3}x - 4.9\left(\dfrac{x}{48}\right)^2$.

(b) The bird is flying at a constant speed of $10\,\mathrm{m\,s^{-1}}$ and the shot hits it at $B(x_1, h)$. Show that $h = \frac{19}{18}x_1$.

(c) Use the equations in parts (a) and (b) to find the numerical value of h.

(d) After being shot, the bird falls and hits the ground T seconds later. Show that $T > 5.3$.

(OCR)

Practice examination 1

Time 1 hour 30 minutes

Answer all the questions.

Graphic calculators are permitted.

1 A station escalator raises passengers a height of 15 m, moving at $4 \, \text{m s}^{-1}$ up the slope.

   (i) A passenger of mass 75 kg steps on the escalator (with zero velocity). How much energy does the escalator mechanism expend in taking her to the top and delivering her at a speed of $4 \, \text{m s}^{-1}$? [4]

   (ii) In the rush hour 200 passengers per minute, of average mass 75 kg, use the escalator. At what power must the motor work to cope with this demand? [2]

2 A car of mass 700 kg is travelling along a straight road which is inclined at an angle α to the horizontal. The car is going up the hill, and resistances to its motion are negligible. At an instant when the power of the car's engine is 15 kW, the speed is $20 \, \text{m s}^{-1}$ and the deceleration is $0.25 \, \text{m s}^{-2}$. Find α. [6]

3 A ball of mass 50 grams is batted vertically downwards with a speed of $2.1 \, \text{m s}^{-1}$ from a point at a height of 0.4 m above the floor. It bounces from the floor, and just rises to the point from which it was hit. Find

   (i) the coefficient of restitution between the ball and the floor, [4]

   (ii) the magnitude of the impulse which the ball receives from the floor. [3]

4 A uniform solid has cross-section *ABCDEF* in the shape of a rectangle measuring 10 cm by 2 cm joined to a semicircle of radius r cm, as shown in the diagram.

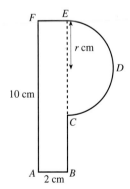

The centre of mass of the solid is a distance x cm from *AF*.

   (i) Show that $x = \dfrac{20 + \pi r^2 + \frac{2}{3} r^3}{20 + \frac{1}{2} \pi r^2}$. [5]

   (ii) The solid is placed with *AB* on horizontal ground, and remains in equilibrium. Find the greatest possible value of *r*. [3]

5 A smooth wire in the shape of a circular arc *ABC* is fixed in a vertical plane. *B* is the lowest point of the wire, and *A* is 1.6 m higher than *B*.

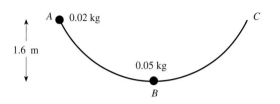

Two beads are threaded on the wire; one bead of mass 0.05 kg is at rest at *B*, the other bead of mass 0.02 kg is held at *A*. When it is released, the bead at *A* slides down the wire and collides with the bead at *B*. The coefficient of restitution between the beads is $\frac{1}{2}$.

   (i) Find the speed of the 0.02 kg bead just before the collision.   [3]

   (ii) Find the velocities of the two beads just after the collision.   [5]

   (iii) Calculate the amount of energy lost as the result of the collision.   [2]

6 The diagram shows a carousel at a fairground. Children are strapped into chairs at the end of poles 4 m long. The poles are hinged at the top to a horizontal drum of radius 3 m, which rotates about a vertical axis. When the carousel is rotating at full speed, the poles swing out at 20° to the vertical, in vertical planes through the axis of rotation. The mass of the poles is small, and can be neglected.

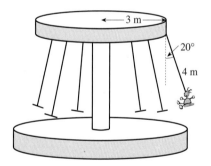

   (i) Calculate the time that the carousel takes to make one complete revolution at full speed.   [9]

   (ii) State one modelling assumption (other than that concerning the negligible mass of the poles) that is needed in the solution in part (i).   [1]

7 A uniform beam AB has length $4l$ and weight W. It rests in equilibrium in contact with a small fixed peg P, where $AP = 3l$, and with the end A on horizontal ground. The beam makes an angle α with the ground (see diagram).

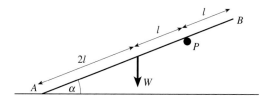

(i) Suppose that the contact at A is smooth and the contact at P is rough.
   (a) Find the normal reaction acting on the beam at P. [2]
   (b) The coefficient of friction at P is μ_P. Show that $\mu_P \leqslant \tan \alpha$. [2]

(ii) Suppose instead that the contact at A is rough, with coefficient of friction μ_A, and the contact at P is smooth. Show that $\mu_A \leqslant \dfrac{2 \sin \alpha \cos \alpha}{3 - 2 \cos^2 \alpha}$. [7]

8 A projectile is launched from ground level with initial velocity V at an angle θ to the horizontal.

(i) Write down equations for the horizontal and vertical displacements of the projectile from its launch point after time t, assuming that air resistance can be neglected. Hence obtain the cartesian equation of the trajectory in the form

$$y = x \tan \theta - \frac{gx^2}{2V^2}(1 + \tan^2 \theta).$$ [4]

An anti-aircraft gun fires shells with an initial speed of $350\,\mathrm{m\,s^{-1}}$ at an angle θ above the horizontal, and shells may be assumed to move freely under gravity. The target is a pilotless aircraft which flies at a steady speed of $100\,\mathrm{m\,s^{-1}}$ directly towards the gun at a constant height of $5250\,\mathrm{m}$. A shell fired from the gun hits the aircraft when it is at a horizontal distance of x m from the gun.

(ii) Show that $T = \tan \theta$ satisfies the quadratic equation
$$x^2 T^2 - (2.5 \times 10^4)xT + (x^2 + (1.3125 \times 10^8)) = 0.$$ [2]

(iii) Find the greatest value of x for which the equation in part (ii) has a real root for T. [2]

(iv) For a hit at the greatest possible value of x, find
   (a) the angle to the horizontal at which the shell should be fired, [2]
   (b) the angle of elevation of the aircraft from the gun at the instant when the shell is fired. [4]

Practice examination 2

Time 1 hour 30 minutes

Answer all the questions.

Graphic calculators are permitted.

1 The sloping part of a 'slide' in a children's playground is 8 m long and slopes at 35° to the horizontal. A child of mass 20 kg slides down, starting at rest at the top and reaching a speed of 6 m s⁻¹ at the bottom.

   (i) Calculate the total change in energy of the child during this motion, stating whether it is an increase or a decrease. [4]

   (ii) The child's motion is resisted by a force of constant magnitude F N. Find F. [2]

2 A uniform solid cone has vertical angle 45°, slant height 10 cm and weight 250 N. The cone is suspended by two vertical strings, as shown in the diagram. One string is attached to the vertex A and the other string is attached to a point B on the circumference of the base of the cone. The cone hangs in equilibrium with AB horizontal.

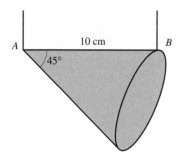

   (i) Find the distance of the centre of mass of the cone from A [2]

   (ii) Find the tensions in the two strings. [4]

3 The diagram shows a uniform lamina $ABCD$ in which $AB = 2$ m, $AC = CD = 1$ m and angles BAC and ACD are right angles. The centre of mass of the lamina is at the point G.

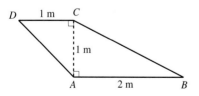

   (i) Show that the distance of G from AC is $\frac{1}{3}$ m, and find its distance from AB. [6]

   (ii) The lamina is freely suspended from B, and hangs in equilibrium. Find the angle that AB makes with the vertical. [2]

4 Fig. 1 shows part of a fairground ride in which a car is moving on rails horizontally with a speed of $15\,\text{m s}^{-1}$, and rounding a bend of radius $20\,\text{m}$. The mass of the car with its passengers is $800\,\text{kg}$. The car is kept on the rails by means of flanges on the wheels, as shown. The two rails are at the same level.

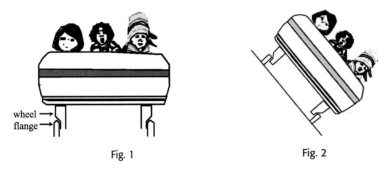

Fig. 1   Fig. 2

(i) As the car rounds the bend, one of the rails exerts a sideways force on the flanges on the wheels on that side of the car. State whether this is the inside or the outside rail, and find the magnitude of the total force on these wheels. [3]

(ii) A disadvantage of this design is the friction it causes between the rail and the flanges. To avoid this, the ride is redesigned by tilting the track as shown in Fig. 2, so that the car can round the bend with no sideways force between the rail and the flanges. Find the angle to the horizontal that the track should make in order to achieve this. [5]

5 The total mass of a cyclist and her bicycle is $120\,\text{kg}$. While pedalling she generates power of $640\,\text{W}$. Her motion is opposed by road resistance of magnitude $16\,\text{N}$, and by air resistance of magnitude $8v\,\text{N}$, where $v\,\text{m s}^{-1}$ is her speed.

(i) Find the cyclist's acceleration when she is riding along a level road at $5\,\text{m s}^{-1}$. [3]

(ii) Find the greatest speed that she can maintain on a level road. [3]

(iii) When cycling down a hill she finds that she can maintain a speed of $10\,\text{m s}^{-1}$. Find the angle of inclination of the hill to the horizontal, giving your answer to the nearest tenth of a degree. [3]

6 Two small spheres P and Q can move without resistance along a straight line which is perpendicular to a vertical wall. P has mass 30 grams and Q has mass 70 grams, and Q is between P and the wall, as shown in the diagram. Initially Q is at rest, and P is moving towards it at a speed of $12\,\text{m s}^{-1}$.

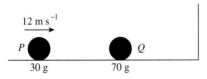

(i) The coefficient of restitution between P and Q is $\frac{2}{3}$ and the coefficient of restitution between Q and the wall is $\frac{5}{6}$. Find the speeds at which the spheres are moving after all possible collisions have occurred. [6]

(ii) Calculate, in joules, the total amount of energy lost as a result of the collisions. [3]

(iii) Explain why the total momentum of the two spheres after all the collisions is different from the total momentum before the collisions. [1]

7 A uniform girder AB of length 10 m and weight 20 000 N rests with its end A on the rough horizontal floor of a factory and with its other end B supported by a cable. In the position shown in the diagram, the girder makes an angle α with the floor, and the cable is inclined at an angle β to the horizontal. The girder is in limiting equilibrium, and the coefficient of friction between the girder and the floor is μ.

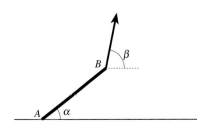

(i) By resolving horizontally and vertically, show that $\tan \beta = \dfrac{20\,000 - R}{\mu R}$, where R N is the magnitude of the normal force acting on the girder at A. [4]

(ii) Given that $\tan \alpha = \frac{3}{4}$ and $\tan \beta = 5$,
   (a) show that $\mu = \frac{2}{7}$, [4]
   (b) find the tension in the cable. [2]

8 A fire-fighter directs a jet of water so that it passes horizontally through the window of a block of flats 11 m above ground level. The jet is delivered from a hose with a speed of $25\,\mathrm{m\,s^{-1}}$ at a height of 1 m above the ground.

   (i) Find the angle above the horizontal at which the jet is directed. [4]

   (ii) Find the horizontal distance of the fire-fighter from the foot of the building. [3]

The fire-fighter now moves to a position which is a horizontal distance of 25 m from the foot of the building and adjusts the direction of the jet so that it still passes through the same window.

   (iii) Find the smaller of the two possible angles above the horizontal at which the jet can be directed. [5]

   (iv) For this angle of projection, determine the vertical component of the water's velocity as it passes through the window. [3]

Answers

Most non-exact numerical answers are given correct to 3 significant figures.

1 The motion of projectiles

Exercise 1A (page 4)

1 48 m, 2.5 s

2 3.5 m

3 1.3 s

4 40 m at 30° below horizontal
   24 m s^{-1} at 62° below horizontal

5 (b) 1.3 s, 2.8 s

Exercise 1B (page 11)

1 13 m s^{-1}, 19.6 m s^{-1} downwards

2 75 m, 30.6 m

4 $\begin{pmatrix} 30 \\ -19.6 \end{pmatrix}$ m

5 80.4 m, 23.4 m; 26.8 m s^{-1},
   6.90 m s^{-1} downwards

6 (a) 5.71 s   (b) 56 m s^{-1} (c) 400 m

7 0.59 s, 6.9 m s^{-1}

8 485 m

9 (a) 0.429 s   (b) 4.2 m s^{-1}
   (c) 15.7 m s^{-1} (d) 6.72 m

10 45.7 m s^{-1}

11 47.3°

12 20.8 m s^{-1} at 70.3°; 28 m

13 (a) 20 m s^{-1} (b) 14.7 m s^{-1}
    24.8 m s^{-1} at 36.3° above horizontal

14 35.6°

15 28 m s^{-1}, 24.2 m s^{-1}

16 19.4 m s^{-1}

17 1.44 s

18 14.5 m

19 24.4 m s^{-1} at 53.5° above horizontal

20 3.55 s, 74.2 m

Exercise 1C (page 17)

1 17.4°, 72.6°

2 112 m s^{-1}

3 2.62 s; 40.2 m

4 11.4 m s^{-1}

5 78.5°

6 7.98 m s^{-2}

7 383 m; 20.3 m, 333 m

8 36.5 m s^{-1}

9 74.3° or 23.7°

10 17.5 m s^{-1}

11 35.9°

12 30.8 m s^{-1}

13 21.8°

Miscellaneous exercise 1 (page 19)

1 10 m s^{-1}, 2.28 m s^{-1} downwards

2 41.3°, 22.5 m s^{-1}

3 24.3 m s^{-1}, 28° below horizontal

4 (a) (i) 42.4 m s^{-1} at 23.2° below horizontal
       (ii) 25.8 m
    (b) no air resistance

5 53.1°, 37.5; air resistance

6 (b) 12 m   (c) size of ball ignored

7 (c) $\dfrac{4\sqrt{3}k^2}{9g}$

8 (a) 13.6 m s^{-1} (b) 1.39 s   (c) 3.59 m s^{-1}
    air resistance

9 (a) For example, there is no air resistance.
    (b) 150 m s^{-1}, 15.6° above horizontal; 8.25 s

10 (a) 22.1 m s^{-1}
    (b) (i) 1.32 s   (ii) 6.07° descending
    (c) ball is particle, no air resistance

11 10.1t cos α, 10.1t sin α − 4.9t^2
    (b) 20.8 sin α cos α   (c) 1.03 sin α
    (d) $y = x \tan α − 0.048x^2 \sec^2 α$
    9.11 m

12 15 − 4.9t^2; 13.3; 16.7, 36.9°

13 (a) 2.2t, 8.8t − 4.9t^2 (b) 4 m

2   Work, energy and power

Exercise 2A (page 26)

1 (a) 1620 J   (b) 300 kJ
   (c) 8.68×10^6 J   (d) 1600 J
   (e) 6.4×10^8 J

2 700 J; 0 J; 0 J; 700 J

3 4 N

4 50 N

5 240 J, 8 N

6 1008 kJ

7 1130 J

8 5330 J

9 4800 J

10 22 N

11 102 N

12 (a) 280 kJ   (b) 423 kJ   (c) 208 kJ
    Anyone so irresponsible as to attempt to
    drive down such a steep gradient would need
    to apply the brakes to restrict the final speed
    to $30 \, \mathrm{m \, s^{-1}}$.

13 684 kJ

14 807 kJ

Exercise 2B (page 30)

1 32.7 kW

2 110 W

3 157 W

4 110 kW

5 600 N

6 16 kW

7 880 W

8 $2.5 \, \mathrm{m \, s^{-2}}$

9 30.7°

10 7.8 kW

11 $0.2 \, \mathrm{m \, s^{-2}}$, $2.55 \, \mathrm{m \, s^{-1}}$

12 2.43 s

13 $0.433 \, \mathrm{m \, s^{-2}}$

14 145 kW

16 3.10 kW, 6.20 kW

17 7.2 s; 96 kJ, 505 N

18 31.4 kW

Miscellaneous exercise 2 (page 31)

1 433 J

2 500 N

3 56.4 J

4 16.8 kW, friction forwards at driving wheels

5 $1.5 \, \mathrm{m \, s^{-2}}$

6 13.0 kW

7 173 kJ

8 200 kW; $0.049 \, \mathrm{m \, s^{-2}}$

9 100 kJ; 2.51 s

10 85.1 kJ; 2.04 kW, 5.11 kW, 3.89 kW

11 4.01°; $0.8 \, \mathrm{m \, s^{-2}}$

12 5.38 s; 133 kJ, 744 N; 22.7 s

13 $40 \, \mathrm{m \, s^{-1}}$. No, a single person could not push
    easily with a force of 750 N. $28.8 \, \mathrm{m \, s^{-1}}$

14 54.9 kW, mass must not exceed 1950 kg

15 $180 \, \mathrm{m \, s^{-1}}$; 6.64°

3   Potential energy

Exercise 3A (page 41)

1 392 J

2 40 J, 5.10 m

3 1.33×10^6 J, 66.6 kW; the kinetic energy of the
   rotor

4 $12.1 \, \mathrm{m \, s^{-1}}$

5 2.04×10^6 J

6 16.7°

7 10 m

8 8.93 m

9 $1.67 \, \mathrm{m \, s^{-1}}$; $1.53 \, \mathrm{m \, s^{-1}}$

10 26.3°

11 (a) $2.42 \, \mathrm{m \, s^{-1}}$ (b) $4.2 \, \mathrm{m \, s^{-1}}$

12 $u = 2\sqrt{ag}$

13 1.49 m

14 $40.3 \, \mathrm{m \, s^{-1}}$, $30.0 \, \mathrm{m \, s^{-1}}$

Exercise 3B (page 45)

1 $2.52 \, \mathrm{m \, s^{-1}}$

2 0.204 m; 1.84 m

3 0.332 m

4 (a) 1.25 m   (b) $3.80 \, \mathrm{m \, s^{-1}}$

5 (a) $1.46\,\mathrm{m\,s^{-1}}$ (b) $2.11\,\mathrm{m}$

6 $1.98\,\mathrm{m\,s^{-1}}$; $0.784\,\mathrm{J}$, $1.31\,\mathrm{N}$

7 $2.5\,\mathrm{m}$; $44.55\,\mathrm{J}$, $17.8\,\mathrm{N}$

8 $4.43\times10^9\,\mathrm{J}$

9 $14.1\,\mathrm{m\,s^{-1}}$

10 $76.7\,\mathrm{N}$; $129\,\mathrm{N}$

Miscellaneous exercise 3 (page 46)

1 $\sqrt{2ag(1-\cos\theta)}$

2 $14.7\,\mathrm{m\,s^{-1}}$

3 (a) $18\,800\,\mathrm{J}$ (b) $23.7\,\mathrm{m\,s^{-1}}$
   $230\,\mathrm{N}$

4 $1.4\,\mathrm{m\,s^{-1}}$, $2.45\,\mathrm{m\,s^{-2}}$

5 $1.98\,\mathrm{m\,s^{-1}}$; air resistance

6 $1.4\,\mathrm{m\,s^{-1}}$, falling

7 (a) $325\,\mathrm{kJ}$ (b) $222\,\mathrm{kJ}$
   $257\,\mathrm{N}$, $9.01\,\mathrm{kW}$; $0.707\,\mathrm{m\,s^{-2}}$

8 (a) $7.20\,\mathrm{m\,s^{-1}}$ (b) $(5.9, 5.1)$
   The bead retraces its motion back to A, with the same speed as before at each point of the wire.

9 (b) $\dfrac{m(Mg+F)}{M+m}$ (c) $\dfrac{M(mg-F)h}{M+m}$

10 (b) (i) $\sqrt{\frac{7}{5}gr}$ (ii) $\sqrt{\frac{3}{5}gr}$
   (d) The resolved force of gravity at C exceeds the resistance, so the condition is satisfied.

4 Moments

Exercise 4A (page 56)

1 $16\,\mathrm{N}$

2 $5.04\,\mathrm{m}$

3 $28\,\mathrm{kg}$, $32\,\mathrm{kg}$; $58.8\,\mathrm{N}$

4 $46\,\mathrm{cm}$

5 (a) 48 (b) 4 (c) 360

6 (a) no   (b) yes

7 $58.8\,\mathrm{N}$

Exercise 4B (page 60)

1 (a) $X=4.8, Y=7.2$ (b) $X=6, y=24$
   (c) $X=55, Y=45$ (d) $x=34, Y=50$

2 $80\,\mathrm{N}$, $120\,\mathrm{N}$

3 $2.5\,\mathrm{m}$

4 $2.5\,\mathrm{m}$

5 The force from the smooth ice is vertical, and so is the weight. $25\,\mathrm{N}$

6 (a) $253\,\mathrm{N}$ (b) $668\,\mathrm{N}$

7 $8080\,\mathrm{N}$, $12\,300\,\mathrm{N}$

8 $13.1\,\mathrm{N}$, $1140\,\mathrm{N}$; $2\,\mathrm{kg}$

9 $9\,\mathrm{m}$

10 $55.5\,\mathrm{N}$, $71.9\,\mathrm{N}$; assuming the weight acts in a line midway across the curtain's 'spread', $0.8\,\mathrm{m}$

11 $125\,\mathrm{N}$, $125\,\mathrm{N}$; $112.2\,\mathrm{N}$, $117.8\,\mathrm{N}$

12 (a) $617\,\mathrm{N}$ (b) $278\,\mathrm{N}$ (c) $3.09\,\mathrm{m\,s^{-2}}$

Exercise 4C (page 66)

1 (a) $360\,\mathrm{N\,m}$ anticlockwise
   (b) $384\,\mathrm{N\,m}$ anticlockwise
   (c) $385\,\mathrm{N\,m}$ anticlockwise
   (d) $170\,\mathrm{N\,m}$ anticlockwise

2 (a) $210\,\mathrm{N\,m}$ clockwise
   (b) $280\,\mathrm{N\,m}$ anticlockwise
   (c) $200\,\mathrm{N\,m}$ anticlockwise
   (d) $900\,\mathrm{N\,m}$ clockwise

3 (a) $326\,\mathrm{N\,m}$ anticlockwise
   (b) $247\,\mathrm{N\,m}$ anticlockwise
   (c) $333\,\mathrm{N\,m}$ anticlockwise
   (d) $126\,\mathrm{N\,m}$ anticlockwise

4 (a) 10 (b) 12 (c) 8

5 (a) $30.0°$ (b) $165.5°$ (c) $9.6°$ (d) $172.8°$

6 $10\,800\,\mathrm{N}$

7 $78.4\,\mathrm{N}$

8 $23.8\,\mathrm{N}$

9 (a) $\frac{1}{2}WN$ (b) $\frac{1}{2}\sqrt{2}WN$

10 $14.0\,\mathrm{N}$

11 $7.28\,\mathrm{N}$

12 49.9

13 $708\,\mathrm{N}$

15 (a) $58.8\,\mathrm{N}$ (b) $126\,\mathrm{N}$ (c) $53.3\,\mathrm{N}$

16 $34.7\,\mathrm{N}$
   (a) $25\,\mathrm{N}$ (b) $4.41\,\mathrm{N}$ (c) $4.34\,\mathrm{N}$

Miscellaneous exercise 4 (page 69)

1 490; 1015, 700

2 $94\,\mathrm{N}$

3 (a) $12.3\,\mathrm{N}$, $14.2\,\mathrm{N}$ (b) 70

4 $10.9\,\mathrm{N}$, $15.5\,\mathrm{N}$

5 $0.48\,\mathrm{m}$

6 50 N into the door, 50 N away from the door; 100

7 8.38

8 18.4°

9 371 N

10 3750 N, 1250 N; 200; 11.8 N

5 Centre of mass

Exercise 5A (page 77)

1 40 cm

2 0.47 m

3 4610 km

4 13.0 cm

5 33.1 cm

6 106.5 cm

7 16.0 cm

8 0.83 m

9 (1.4 cm, 2.3 cm)

10 (a) 5 cm   (b) 7.5 cm

11 19.2 cm

12 0.934

13 (a) 8 cm   (b) 6.4 cm

14 39.5 cm, 28.6 cm

15 2.1, 5.55

16 6.86 cm, 3.74 cm

Exercise 5B (page 85)

2 (a) vertical, with A above B
  (b) vertical, with B above A
  (c) at any angle

3 (a) 0, 9.8 N   (b) 6.53 N, 3.27 N

5 $53.1° < \alpha < 126.9°$

6 H: 33.7° L: 10.8° N: 33.7° T: 42.0° V: 15.3°

7 42.4 cm

8 36.9°

9 (a) 56.3°   (b) 25.5°   (c) 38.0°   (d) 57.4°

10 (a) 51.0°   (b) 5.7°   (c) 59.3°   (d) 27.4°

11 21.2°

12 (a) 23.0°   (b) 2.0°

Miscellaneous exercise 5 (page 88)

1 (a) 5.58 cm   (b) 2.08 cm

2 39.2 cm

3 11.8 cm

4 0.6 m

5 $\frac{1}{3}H$

6 24.4°

7 (a) 37.625 (b) 13.625

8 (a) P   (b) S   (c) R   (d) Q

9 63.4°

11 topples; not the same (that is, it does not topple)

6 Rigid objects in equilibrium

Exercise 6A (page 97)

1 (a) $P = 25, Q = 50, R = 50$
  (b) $P = 20, Q = 16, x = 5$
  (c) $P = 50, Q = 40, x = 7$
  (d) $P = 160, Q = 90, R = 200$
  (e) $P = 30\sqrt{3}, Q = 30, x = 4$
  (f) $P = 30, Q = 35\sqrt{2}, R = 5\sqrt{2}$

2 (a) 100 N, 400 N, 100 N
  (b) 97.5 N, 475 N, 62.7 N

3 (a) $600x$ N   (b) 0.588

4 237; 0.297

5 (a) 672 N   (b) 955 N

6 0.275; 31.4 N, 104 N; 54.1 N, 73.2°

7 71.0 N, 37.6 N, 0.530

8 $\frac{24}{25}, \frac{7}{25} W$; 2.2

Exercise 6B (page 107)

1 1 m

2 90.9 N, tilts

3 113 N

4 (a) 20°   (b) 21.8°
  by toppling

5 between 0.2 and 0.3

6 more than 0.165 m from the back of the sledge

7 (a) 25 N
  (b) greater than 0.174

8 $\tan \alpha > 2 - \dfrac{1}{\mu}$

10 100, 6

11 (a) 13
 (b) 67.4°
 (c) $8\frac{2}{3}$ m

12 75 N, 25 N; $3y = x + L$

13 (a) $\begin{pmatrix} -2 \\ -4 \end{pmatrix}$, $y = 2x$

 (b) $\begin{pmatrix} -4 \\ -1 \end{pmatrix}$, $y = \frac{1}{4}x + 4$

 (c) $\begin{pmatrix} 0 \\ 2 \end{pmatrix}$, $x = 3$

 (d) given forces are already in equilibrium
 (e) impossible to achieve equilibrium with a single force

14 24.5 cm

15 (a) $G + R = W$, $S = F$, $W + 4F = 2R$,
  $4S + 2G = W$
 (b) $4S + W = 2R$, no
 (c) (i) no   (ii) yes
 (d) $\sqrt{5} - 2$

Miscellaneous exercise 6 (page 110)

1 $y = 2x - 20$

2 (a) 11.0
 (b) 11.0 N into the wall, 31.4 N upwards

3 (a) 5.53 N
 (b) 1.89 N, 6.57 N

4 60.1 N, 80.2 N; 0.577

5 (b) $(100 \cot \theta - 25)$ N
 (c) 49.6°

6 (a) slides down plane
 (b) topples

7 (a) topples
 (b) remains in equilibrium

8 (a) horizontal, 152 N
 (b) 152 N, 588 N
 less, less, equal

11 it falls first

12 (b) W (c) 0.248

13 (a) $\sqrt{3}kW$, $(2k + 1)W$
 (b) $k(\sqrt{3} \tan \theta - 1)$

14 (a) $\frac{1}{5}\sqrt{3}W$, $\frac{1}{20}\sqrt{3}W$, $\frac{7}{10}W$, $\frac{9}{20}W$

15 (c) $\sqrt{3}\mu^2 - 8\mu + \sqrt{3} = 0$, 0.228

Revision exercise 1 (page 115)

1 22.5 W

2 (a) 6000 N
 (b) 30 000 N, 45 000 N

3 35.5 m

4 $l > 45$ cm

5 (a) 38.7°
 (b) Yes, it will slide when the angle reaches 36.9°, and 36.9 < 38.7.

6 50 m s^{-1}; 0.305 m s^{-2}; 3.82°

7 19.1 N, 13.9 N

8 (a) 1000 J, 3136 J
 (b) 55.2 m
 (c) 0.925 m s^{-2}

9 (a) 2.5 N
 (b) 12.3 N at 79.1° to the horizontal

10 (a) 2.92
 (b) 1.13

11 (a) 8.81 m s^{-1}
 (b) 12.5 m s^{-1}
 (c) 52.4° to the horizontal

12 (a) $-\frac{1}{4}mgl$ (b) $-\frac{1}{2}mgl$
  $\sqrt{\frac{1}{2}gl}$

13 (b) 4.02
 (c) 6.09° above the horizontal
 larger, since the ball needs additional energy to overcome the resistance

14 (a) 8.10 m s^{-1}
 (b) 5.07 m s^{-1}

15 (a) 7 cm
 (b) 8.2 cm

16 The left finger slips when the force is 0.375 N; the force gradually increases to 0.5 N, when the left finger reaches the 20 cm mark. Then both fingers move symmetrically, with no further increase in force, until they meet at the 50 cm mark.
 Up to the 69.2 cm mark.

17 800; 373 N

18 (b) 55.8°, 33.3°; 2.87 s

19 (a) It can be up to 1.6 m above the ground, at up to 0.3 m from the axis.
 (b) (i) 36.9° (ii) 23.6°

20 (a) 4.9
 (b) 53.1°

21 The tension increases from $\frac{1}{2}\sqrt{2}W$ when $\theta = 0°$ up to about $0.79W$ when $\theta \approx 28°$, then decreases to $\frac{1}{2}W$ when $\theta = 90°$.

7 Impulse and restitution

Exercise 7A (page 124)

1 1.8 N s

2 0.025 N s

3 $1\frac{2}{3}$ N s; $1\frac{5}{6}$ N s

4 14 N s vertically upwards

5 980 N s

6 (a) 6.5 m s^{-1}, 900 N s
 (b) 6 m s^{-1}, front truck, 1200 N s

7 (a) 1.25 m s^{-1}
 (b) 2.25 m s^{-1}

8 (a) $2mu$
 (b) mu

9 (a) 2 m s^{-1} in the opposite direction
 (b) 0.8 kg
 (c) 4.5 m s^{-1}

10 (a) 14 m s^{-1}
 (b) 600 N s
 (c) 6 m s^{-1}

Exercise 7B (page 132)

1 $Q, \frac{1}{2}$

2 $Q, \frac{1}{6}$

3 0.9, 0.3

4 0.75
 (a) 4 N s
 (b) 7 N s

5 0.927

6 $9.8t$ m s^{-1}, $9.8(T-t)$ m s^{-1}, $\frac{T}{t} - 1$

7 0.6 m s^{-1}, $\frac{1}{3}$; 0.6 m s^{-1}, 1 m s^{-1}

8 0.4 m s^{-1}, 0.6

9 (a) 0.8 m s^{-1} changed, 2.8 m s^{-1} changed
 (b) 0, 2 m s^{-1} changed
 (c) 0.8 m s^{-1}, 1.2 m s^{-1} changed

10 (a) 0.12 m s^{-1} changed, 1.78 m s^{-1}
 (b) 0, 1.75 m s^{-1}
 (c) 0.12 m s^{-1}, 1.72 m s^{-1}

11 $\frac{1}{3}$

12 3 m s^{-1}, 2.6 m s^{-1}

13 0.2 m s^{-1}, 2.2 m s^{-1}

15 (a) Separation speed would exceed approach speed.
 (b) Speed of A would exceed speed of B.
 between 4.8 m s^{-1} and 6.6 m s^{-1}

16 400 kg

17 (a) 1.6 m s^{-1}
 (b) 0.32 N s, 0.28 N s
 $\frac{7}{8}$

18 $\frac{21}{32}$ N s, $\frac{39}{160}$ N s, $\frac{13}{35}$

19 $\frac{2}{3}$ m s^{-1}, $1\frac{1}{3}$ N s; $\frac{4}{15}$ N s, 0.2 or $1\frac{1}{15}$ N s, 0.8

20 1 m s^{-1}, 2 m s^{-1}; 0.6 N s, 0.5

21 $\frac{1}{2}(1-e)u$, $\frac{1}{2}(1+e)u$; $\dfrac{2e^2 d}{1+e^2}$

Exercise 7C (page 138)

1 1800 J, 288 J, 648 J

2 (a) 0.5 m s^{-1}
 (b) 19 500 J

3 (a) 0.1 m s^{-1}
 (b) 0.0006 J

4 4.98 J loss, 2.84 J gain; 1.42 J loss, 1.96 J gain

Miscellaneous exercise 7 (page 138)

1 0.69 N s

2 0.748

3 15 m s^{-1}; ball is a particle, no other impulses act

4 1.9 m s^{-1}, 1.1 m s^{-1}

5 4.5 m s^{-1}, 0.5

6 0 (a) 4.4 m s^{-1} (b) 0.12 N s

7 (a) 8 m s^{-1}
 (b) 4 N s

8 (a) 1 m s^{-1}
 (b) $m_P : m_Q = 8 : 1$

9 2.5 m s^{-1}; 1.39 m s^{-1}

10 (a) 7 m s^{-1}
 (b) 0.714 s
 (c) 5.6 m s^{-1}, 3.78 N s
 (d) 1.6 m
 greater, less, greater, same

11 $6mU$, $2mU$; $v_A = \frac{1}{5}U$, $v_B = \frac{6}{5}U$

12 $2u$, $1.5u$, both directions reversed

13 $\frac{1}{2}u(1-e)$, $\frac{1}{2}u(1+e)$; $\frac{5}{9}u$, $\frac{4}{9}u$

8   Motion round a circle

Exercise 8A (page 143)

1 $1.5\,\text{rad}\,\text{s}^{-1}$

2 $0.449\,\text{rad}\,\text{s}^{-1}$

3 $1.70\,\text{rad}\,\text{s}^{-1}$, $0.849\,\text{m}\,\text{s}^{-1}$

4 $463\,\text{m}\,\text{s}^{-1}$

5 $2\,\text{m}$

6 $0.262\,\text{rad}\,\text{s}^{-1}$, $26.7\,\text{m}$

7 $0.654\,\text{rad}\,\text{s}^{-1}$, $0.916\,\text{rad}\,\text{s}^{-1}$

8 $8.17\,\text{rad}\,\text{s}^{-1}$, $1.23\,\text{m}\,\text{s}^{-1}$

9 $\frac{1}{12}\,\text{rad}\,\text{s}^{-1}$

10 $2.12\,\text{cm}$

11 1.61

Exercise 8B (page 147)

1 (b) $0.346\,\text{m}\,\text{s}^{-1}$
   (c) $1.19\,\text{m}\,\text{s}^{-2}$ towards axis

2 $8\,\text{N}$; $7.75\,\text{m}\,\text{s}^{-1}$, $12.9\,\text{rad}\,\text{s}^{-1}$

3 $0.24\,\text{m}$

4 1.11

5 $0.781\,\text{kg}$

6 0.383

7 $7 \times 10^{4}\,\text{N}$

8 $27\,\text{N}$

9 11. For example the railway engine is a particle. $9900\,\text{N}$

10 The tension in the rod is $MR\omega^{2}$ and
    $m(a - R)\omega^{2} . \dfrac{ma}{M + m}$

11 $35\,900\,\text{km}$

12 $0.0338\,\text{m}\,\text{s}^{-2}$; objects at the north pole, by $0.0338\,\text{m}\,\text{s}^{-2}$

Exercise 8C (page 151)

1 $4.28\,\text{m}\,\text{s}^{-1}$

2 $57.0°$

3 (a) $11.5\,\text{N}$, $6.91\,\text{rad}\,\text{s}^{-1}$
   (b) $7.84\,\text{N}$, 5.72
   (c) $0.96\,\text{N}$, $3.44\,\text{N}$

4 $\dfrac{mga}{h}\,\text{N}$

5 $18.8°$

6 $1.06\,\text{N}$, $0.21\,\text{N}$

7 (a) $16.0\,\text{N}$
   (b) $4.72\,\text{m}\,\text{s}^{-1}$

8 $37.4°$, $24\,700\,\text{N}$; $67.7°$, $51\,700\,\text{N}$

9 $25\,\text{N}$, 11.9

Miscellaneous exercise 8 (page 152)

1 (a) $17\,400\,\text{m}\,\text{s}^{-1}$
   (b) $0.714\,\text{m}\,\text{s}^{-2}$

2 2.21

3 $7.07 \times 10^{6}\,\text{m}$

4 13; $3040\,\text{N}$, friction

5 7.83

6 (b) $1.8\,\text{m}\,\text{s}^{-2}$ towards O
   (c) 0.184

7 $4.52\,\text{rad}\,\text{s}^{-1}$

8 1.56

9 $40.0°$

10 $2.98°$, $51.5\,\text{km}\,\text{h}^{-1}$

11 (a) $mg \sec\theta$
    $\sqrt{\dfrac{2g}{a}}$; $\sqrt{0.3}v_P$

12 (b) $\sqrt{\dfrac{\sqrt{3}g}{l}}$ The tension has to be positive.

13 (a) $14.7\,\text{N}$
    (b) $8.32\,\text{m}\,\text{s}^{-1}$

14 mg; $\frac{4}{3}ma\Omega^{2}$

9   Geometrical methods

Exercise 9A (page 158)

1 (a) 1640, $72°$, $5.5\,\text{m}$
   (b) 1810, $96°$, $6.1\,\text{m}$
   (c) 1220, $125°$, $4.8\,\text{m}$

2 (a) 1400, $14.6°$, $10\,\text{m}$
   (b) 1970, $40°$, $3.95\,\text{m}$
   (c) 1800, $58.7°$, $5.88\,\text{m}$
   (d) 2750, $66.2°$, $6.09\,\text{m}$

3 $2.08\,\text{m}$

4 $100\,\text{N}$ along the diameter AB

Exercise 9B (page 161)

1 $40.8\,\text{N}$ at $16.1°$ to the upward vertical, $11.3\,\text{N}$

2 $480\,\text{N}$ at $38.7°$ to the horizontal

3 $1.71\,\text{m}$

4 (a) $16.1\,\text{N}$ at $13.2°$ to the upward vertical
   (b) $16.1\,\text{N}$ at $13.2°$ to the upward vertical in the opposite sense to part (a)

5 9 m, 373 N, 236 N

6 50°; 61.3 N, 51.4 N

7 50°

8 37.9°

Exercise 9C (page 165)

1 0.289; 0.520

2 0.346

3 0.940

4 237; 0.297

5 more than 0.165 m from the back of the sledge

6 (a) 25 N
   (b) greater than 0.174

Miscellaneous exercise 9 (page 166)

1 5° to the vertical, 99.6 N, 8.72 N

2 16.3 N, 22.0°; 0.375 m

3 33.7°, 13.9 N, 8.3 N

4 0.979 m

5 on AD 2 m from A, 100 N at 36.9° to DA

6 7.31 m from the centre of mass, 40°

7 36.9°

8 0.335

9 49.6°

12 0.228

10 Centres of mass of special shapes

Exercise 10A (page 173)

1 (a) $\frac{4}{3}$ m   (b) 196 N, 392 N

2 10 N, 20 N; 14.0°

3 1.99 cm

4 36.9°

5 0.1 m

6 (5.56, 5.08)

8 0.866

9 0.453 m

10 (a) P   (b) R   (c) Q

11 10.4°

12 $2kr\alpha$, $2kr(\pi - \alpha)$; $\dfrac{r\sin\alpha}{\alpha}$, $\dfrac{r\sin\alpha}{\pi - \alpha}$

13 4.24 cm

Exercise 10B (page 179)

1 58.1 cm

2 38.7°

3 6.9 cm

4 3.08 cm

5 (a) cylindrical part in contact
   (b) hemispherical part in contact

6 10.25 cm, 10.29 cm from the two sides; no

7 66.3°

8 2.46 cm, 4.95 cm

9 $0.316\,l$

10 11.2°

11 3.85°

Miscellaneous exercise 10 (page 181)

1 $10\sqrt{3} \approx 17.3$

2 (b) 25.5°

4 a (b) 2

9 $1.09W$ at 23.0° to the vertical

11 The vase topples without first overflowing.

12 7.75 cm

13 1.60 cm

14 18.45

11 Strategies for solving problems

Exercise 11A (page 189)

1 (a) 52.0 N at 30° to the vertical
   (b) 39.7 N at 19.1° to the vertical
   (c) 30 N vertical

2 (a) 679 N   (b) 392 N at 60° to the vertical

3 24.8 N, 0.978

4 0.372

6 $0.4W$, 0.421

Exercise 11B (page 195)

1 $\tan^{-1}\frac{3}{4}$
   (a) 3.19 s   (b) 25.0 m s^{-1} (c) 20.5 m

2 (a) 41.2°
   (b) 40.9 m s^{-1}

3 4.58 rad s^{-1}

4 20.5 m s^{-1}; 641 N

5 $\frac{1}{2}ml\Omega^2 - \frac{1}{2}mg\sec\theta$

Exercise 11C (page 202)

1 (a) $23.9\,\mathrm{m\,s^{-1}}$ (b) $23.0\,\mathrm{m}$

2 (a) $1.4\,\mathrm{m\,s^{-1}}$ (b) $1.5\,\mathrm{m}$ (c) $0.6\,\mathrm{m\,s^{-1}}$
 (d) $\frac{9}{70}\,\mathrm{m}$ (e) $1\frac{5}{7}\,\mathrm{s}$

3 $m_A : m_B = 1 : 2,\ e = \frac{1}{2}$
 (a) $\frac{1}{4}h,\ \frac{1}{16}h$ (b) $\frac{1}{16}h,\ \frac{9}{64}h$
 (c) $\frac{121}{1024}h,\ \frac{441}{4096}h$ (d) $\frac{441}{4096}h,\ \frac{1849}{16\,384}h$

4 (a) $\dfrac{1+ke^n}{1+k}u,\ \dfrac{1-e^n}{1+k}u$ (b) $\dfrac{1-ke^n}{1+k}u,\ \dfrac{1+e^n}{1+k}u$

Miscellaneous exercise 11 (page 203)

1 $2\frac{2}{3}$ m from O

2 0.577; yes

3 $99.7\,\mathrm{m\,s^{-1}}$ at $47.5°$ to the horizontal

4 (a) $\frac{1}{2}mg$ (b) 3.13

6 (a) $y = \dfrac{2\pi^2}{gT^2}x^2 + k$

 (b) $y = \dfrac{V^2}{g}\ln x + k$

 (c) $y = -\dfrac{c}{gx} + k$

7 (a) $T = 6.86M$ N
 (b) $\frac{1}{3}$ m from A
 (c) $0.7\,\mathrm{m\,s^{-1}}$
 Succession of impacts between P and the plane and jerks into motion, but smaller and smaller amplitude; eventually P comes to rest at B.

Revision exercise 2 (page 206)

1 (a) $\frac{1}{2}$
 (b) $4\,\mathrm{m\,s^{-1}}$
 (c) $1.4\,\mathrm{m\,s^{-1}}$

2 (a) $4.99\,\mathrm{m\,s^{-2}}$
 (b) $17.8\,\mathrm{s}$

3 (b) 75 N outwards, 75 N inwards
 (c) 68.75 N, 96.25 N

4 (a) $0.48\,\mathrm{N\,s}$
 (c) $\frac{1}{4}$
 (d) $2\,\mathrm{m\,s^{-1}},\ 4\,\mathrm{m\,s^{-1}}$

5 (a) 2.8 N, 0.987 N   (b) $8.98\,\mathrm{m\,s^{-1}}$

6 (a) $33.7°$
 (b) 17.9 N
 (c) 16.1 N at $29.7°$ to the vertical

7 (a) $9\,\mathrm{m\,s^{-1}}$
 (b) 5.75 m

8 (a) 6.86 N
 (b) $7.56\,\mathrm{rad\,s^{-1}}$
 (c) $2.27\,\mathrm{m\,s^{-1}}$ in a straight line

9 154, 102 N at $40.9°$ to the horizontal

10 $3.5\,\mathrm{rad\,s^{-1}}$

11 $8.5\,\mathrm{s}$

12 (a) 49.0 N
 (b) 110 N at $77.2°$ to the horizontal

13 32.9 cm from B; $15.6°$

14 (b) The right side of the equation in part (a) must be positive.
 (d) 1   (e) 9, $\frac{20}{41}$

15 (a) $(0.245\,\mathrm{m}, 0.600\,\mathrm{m})$
 (b) It rotates about O through $40°$.
 (c) The centre of mass crosses the y-axis between the two states.
 (d) 450 N

16 (a) 105 m   (b) 131 m
 air resistance and aerodynamic lift

17 $62.7\,\mathrm{m\,s^{-1}}$

18 66.7 W; $0.119\,\mathrm{m\,s^{-2}}$

19 (a) if $\alpha > 54.7°$
 (b) if $\alpha < 54.7°$

20 (a) $228\,\mathrm{m\,s^{-1}}$
 (b) 2320 m
 (c) the heavier one

22 $\frac{7}{33}$ cm

23 36.1 J, $11.4\,\mathrm{m\,s^{-1}}$
 (a) 90.1 N
 (b) 54 W
 (c) 0.839

24 $26.6°$; 93.4 grams

25 $60°,\ \frac{1}{3}\sqrt{3}$

26 (b) $40.8° < \theta < 68.2°$

27 (a) $m\left(\dfrac{v^2}{\sqrt{3}\,r} - g\right)$

28 (a) 1220 N   (c) $15.3\,\mathrm{m\,s^{-1}}$
 C

29 $gr\,\dfrac{\sin\phi + k\cos\phi}{\cos\phi - k\sin\phi}$

30 (a) $x = 48t,\ y = 64t - 4.9t^2$ (c) 138

Practice examinations

Practice examination 1 (page 215)

1 (i) $11\,625$ J   (ii) 38.75 kW

2 $7.75°$

3 (i) 0.8 (ii) 0.315 N s

4 (ii) $\sqrt[3]{30} \approx 3.11$

5 (i) $5.6\,\mathrm{m\,s^{-1}}$
   (ii) $0.4\,\mathrm{m\,s^{-1}}$ towards A,
        $2.4\,\mathrm{m\,s^{-1}}$ towards C
   (iii) $0.168\,\mathrm{J}$

6 (i) $6.95\,\mathrm{s}$
   (ii) Model the children (and chairs) as
        particles.

7 (i) (a) $\frac{2}{3}W\cos\alpha$

8 (iii) 5000
   (iv) (a) $68.2°$ (b) $30.7°$

Practice examination 2 (page 219)

1 (i) decrease of $539\,\mathrm{J}$ (ii) 67.4

2 (i) $6.93\,\mathrm{cm}$ (ii) $90.0\,\mathrm{N},\ 160\,\mathrm{N}$

3 (i) $\frac{4}{9}\,\mathrm{m}$ (ii) $14.9°$

4 (i) outside, $9000\,\mathrm{N}$ (ii) $48.9°$

5 (i) $0.6\,\mathrm{m\,s^{-2}}$ (ii) $8\,\mathrm{m\,s^{-1}}$ (iii) $1.6°$

6 (i) $5.5\,\mathrm{m\,s^{-1}},\ 3.5\,\mathrm{m\,s^{-1}}$
   (ii) $1.2775\,\mathrm{J}$
   (iii) An external impulse (from the wall) acts
         during the second collision.

7 (ii) (b) $12\,000\,\mathrm{N}$

8 (i) $34.1°$ (ii) $29.6\,\mathrm{m}$
   (iii) $34.6°$ (iv) $2.28\,\mathrm{m\,s^{-1}}$ (upwards)

Index

The page numbers refer to the first mention of each term, or the blue box if there is one.